1,000,000 Books

are available to read at

Forgotten Books

www.ForgottenBooks.com

Read online
Download PDF
Purchase in print

ISBN 978-1-333-51512-6
PIBN 10514115

This book is a reproduction of an important historical work. Forgotten Books uses state-of-the-art technology to digitally reconstruct the work, preserving the original format whilst repairing imperfections present in the aged copy. In rare cases, an imperfection in the original, such as a blemish or missing page, may be replicated in our edition. We do, however, repair the vast majority of imperfections successfully; any imperfections that remain are intentionally left to preserve the state of such historical works.

Forgotten Books is a registered trademark of FB &c Ltd.
Copyright © 2018 FB &c Ltd.
FB &c Ltd, Dalton House, 60 Windsor Avenue, London, SW19 2RR.
Company number 08720141. Registered in England and Wales.

For support please visit www.forgottenbooks.com

1 MONTH OF FREE READING

at
www.ForgottenBooks.com

By purchasing this book you are eligible for one month membership to ForgottenBooks.com, giving you unlimited access to our entire collection of over 1,000,000 titles via our web site and mobile apps.

To claim your free month visit:

www.forgottenbooks.com/free514115

* Offer is valid for 45 days from date of purchase. Terms and conditions apply.

English
Français
Deutsche
Italiano
Español
Português

www.forgottenbooks.com

Mythology Photography **Fiction** Fishing Christianity **Art** Cooking Essays Buddhism Freemasonry Medicine **Biology** Music **Ancient Egypt** Evolution Carpentry Physics Dance Geology **Mathematics** Fitness Shakespeare **Folklore** Yoga Marketing **Confidence** Immortality Biographies Poetry **Psychology** Witchcraft Electronics Chemistry History **Law** Accounting **Philosophy** Anthropology Alchemy Drama Quantum Mechanics Atheism Sexual Health **Ancient History Entrepreneurship** Languages Sport Paleontology Needlework Islam **Metaphysics** Investment Archaeology Parenting Statistics Criminology **Motivational**

DAVID LAING, LL.D.

A Memoir of His Life and Literary Work

BY

GILBERT GOUDIE, F.S.A.Scot.

AUTHOR OF
'THE CELTIC AND SCANDINAVIAN ANTIQUITIES OF SHETLAND'
EDITOR OF MILL'S 'DIARY,' ETC. ETC.

WITH INTRODUCTION BY
LORD GUTHRIE

EDINBURGH
PRINTED FOR PRIVATE CIRCULATION
BY T. AND A. CONSTABLE
1913

A.283160
250 Copies printed

PREFACE

It has been said that to write a Life as it should be written it should be done 'while the memory of the man himself is still vivid in the mind of his biographer and of others.' In the present instance more than thirty years had passed between Laing's demise and the time when I was asked to undertake his memoir. I could yet, however, claim to have had the privilege of his acquaintance and to have retained a vivid impression of his personality. The request was therefore complied with, though not without hesitation, because the undertaking was obviously attended with difficulties due to the lapse of time and the uncertainty as to the adequacy of any biographic materials that might be available. These difficulties were, however, gradually surmounted as the work proceeded.

My aim has been to present the man, his life and character, not from any preconceived idea of my own, but as he is portrayed by himself in the occasional biographic scraps he has left, by the tone and tenor of his works, and by the independent testimony of men of light and leading, contemporaries of his own, in this country and abroad, who knew him well, who were entitled to speak, and did speak, with no uncertain voice both during his lifetime and after his decease. It is not claimed for Laing in these pages that he was an Admirable Crichton in universal knowledge or a Mezzofanti in languages, but his learning and his labours were of a more solid, useful and enduring type than theirs. He was the recognised guide and reserve force of the literary clubs of his day, and by his own numerous issues and reprints he to a large extent anticipated the work of the Scottish Text Society, the Scottish History Society, and of others who have followed in his steps in recent years, sometimes with scant acknowledgment of indebtedness to him. He was, in short, the unique and unrivalled authority on the ancient literature, the Church history and the antiquities of Scotland, especially of his dearly loved native city of Edinburgh.

Lord Guthrie and Mr. James Macdonald, W.S., Depute Keeper of the Great Seal for Scotland, personal friends of Dr. Laing, have been friendly referees in all questions during the progress of the work; and I am indebted to his Lordship for

PREFACE

supplying an Introduction, summarising special aspects of Laing's work and character, as brought out in the biography, a contribution which adds very materially to its interest and value. My thanks are also due to Dr. Hay Fleming and Dr. George Neilson for the Notes which appear at the end of Lord Guthrie's Introduction.

Mr. Archibald Constable, LL.D., and Mr. Cecil White, F.S.A.Scot., have been good enough to go over the manuscript, favouring me with valuable suggestions and improvements; and I have to express my obligation to the officials of the libraries here and in London for their uniform kindness and courtesy in aiding my efforts towards accuracy in dealing with Laing's numerous, and often rare, publications.

To the Council of the Society of Antiquaries of Scotland I am indebted for the engraving of the picture of Laing in his private study, by Sir William Fettes Douglas, *P.R.S.A.*, which forms the frontispiece, and to Mr. James L. Caw, Director of the National Galleries of Scotland, for permission to reproduce the somewhat similar picture by Robert Herdman, R.S.A., which is preserved in the National Portrait Gallery.

GILBERT GOUDIE.

31 GREAT KING STREET,
EDINBURGH, *November* 1913.

CONTENTS

INTRODUCTION xv

I

ANCESTRY

David Laing's grandfather—His father, William Laing, bookseller—Marriage and family of William Laing—His business tours abroad—Publications of ancient classics—Removal from Canongate to South Bridge—Death in 1832 1

II

PERSONAL HISTORY

Birth of David Laing, 1793—His own narrative of his early days—School and college—Assistant to his father—Business visits, to London, 1809, Dublin, 1810, again to London for Roxburghe sale, 1812—Visits to the Continent, 1816 and 1819—Forgathers with John Gibson Lockhart—Lockhart's description of the Laings—David's first publication—Applies for librarianship of the Advocates' Library, 1819—Youthful attempts at poetry and the drama—Appointed secretary of the Bannatyne Club, 1823—Fellow of Society of Antiquaries, 1824—His reprints of Scottish early poetry—Appointed chief librarian of the Signet Library, 1837—Testimonials—In France, Switzerland and Germany in 1838—In Italy · Rome, Florence, Bologna, Venice. also Germany and Belgium in 1840—Visited by Carlyle in 1843—His tour in Orkney, Shetland, and the north of Scotland in 1845—The old family residence, Ramsay Lodge, Lauriston, sold—Removal to Portobello—His historical researches and literary labours incessant—Visits to scholars and book collections in Britain and abroad—Again in Holland in 1856, when he discovered a missing Cottonian MS.—In Denmark, Sweden and Norway in 1858, and in Belgium and France in 1860—Elected Professor of Ancient History to Royal Scottish Academy in 1861—Dissolution of Bannatyne Club, for which thirty-nine volumes edited by him—Presentation of plate by the club—His portrait by Sir William Fettes Douglas, 1863—Honorary degree of LL.D. of University of Edinburgh, 1864—His portrait by Robert Herdman, R.S.A., presented by the Society of Antiquaries after fifty years of labour in its service—His last tour in England in 1875—'A weary Night's travel in Roxburghshire'—Three important works issued this year—His care for and restoration of Edinburgh sepulchral monuments—In London for the last time in 1876—Four papers submitted to Society of Antiquaries in 1877—Two important works issued by him in 1878 Failing health—Death on 18th October in his 86th year —Funeral—Pulpit references—Obituary notices . . 14

III

TESTAMENTARY BEQUESTS

To the University of Edinburgh—To the Society of Antiquaries of Scotland—The National Gallery of Scotland —The Royal Scottish Academy—Private papers to Sir Arthur Mitchell for preparation of a biography—Amount of personal estate 126

IV

THE LIBRARY

Directions by will for sale in London—Catalogues—The sale —Amount realised—Some details of prices . . 138

V

LITERARY WORK

His literary labours generally—Chronological list of books edited and miscellaneous treatises issued, 1815 to 1878 . 148

CONTENTS

VI

CORRESPONDENTS

	PAGE
Letters and draft replies, nearly eight thousand : from Peers, Lords of Session, and miscellaneous correspondents—Special excerpts and copies of letters—Selection of names of correspondents at home and abroad	238

VII

FAMILY CONNECTIONS

William Laing *primus*—William Laing *secundus* : his family (including David) and descendants—Family sepulchre in New Calton Burying-Ground 296

INDEX 305

ILLUSTRATIONS

LAING IN HIS STUDY. By Sir W. Fettes Douglas, P.R.S.A. . . . . . . *Frontispiece*

WILLIAM LAING AND MRS. WILLIAM LAING . PAGE 12

FACSIMILE OF PAGES OF LAING'S SKETCH OF HIS EARLY LIFE 16

LAING IN HIS STUDY. By Robert Herdman, R.S.A. . 100

LAING'S DWELLING-HOUSE IN PORTOBELLO . . 125

INTRODUCTION

BY

LORD GUTHRIE

Member of the Royal Commission on Ancient and Historical Monuments in Scotland; President of the Scottish Text Society; Vice-President of the Society of Antiquaries of Scotland.

DAVID LAING was born in 1793, one hundred and twenty years ago, twenty-two years later than his friend and patron Sir Walter Scott; and thirty-five years have passed since his death in 1878. Thus interest in the man, as distinguished from the literary expert, can now be expected only among few. The late Mr. T. G. Stevenson issued in 1878 for private circulation a useful but imperfect list of Dr. Laing's works, with sundry documents bearing on his career; but his friends had hoped that an authorised and complete record of his long and laborious life, so fruitful in benefit to Scottish literature and literary men, would have appeared within reasonable time after his death; and that the book would have been written by the late Sir Arthur Mitchell, K.C.B. Unfortunately Sir Arthur, whose co-operation with Laing in the work of the Society of Antiquaries of Scotland gave him a special knowledge both of the man and of the littérateur, was unable to carry through the pious duty, in which he had made considerable progress, by careful arrangement of the papers, and which, for a time, he expected to accomplish. But no one, among the younger generation who knew Dr. Laing, could have brought more loyal enthusiasm to the task than Mr. Goudie, or a more thorough appreciation of Dr. Laing's special lines of service to literature and to men of letters. The biography, prepared by him at the request of the trustees of Miss Euphemia Laing, Dr. Laing's sister, is a model of exhaustive research, notwithstanding great difficulties caused by the vast mass of material, including nearly eight thousand letters, the death of Dr. Laing's most intimate friends, his fondness for writing anonymously, and the fact that many documents in his hand, written on old envelopes and scraps of waste paper, were almost impossible to decipher. Mr. Goudie is to be specially congratulated on his remarkable success in tracing so large a number of Dr. Laing's writings.

But, if the personal interest in David Laing has largely passed away, there are ample reasons of a permanent kind, in the interests of literature, to justify the preparation of this biography.

In 1862, when David Laing respectfully declined the degree of LL.D. offered him by the University of St. Andrews, his reasons were characteristically said to be: 'My insuperable aversion to being called Doctor, and to all public appearances.' A bachelor (notwithstanding youthful verses, possibly academic, addressed to 'Marian dear') living happily in household with his maiden sister; a sociable man, who could both give and take a joke, but who was almost never found in so-called 'society'; devout, destined originally for the Church, interested but never engrossed in the Church politics of his own time; an enthusiastic Scotsman, taking, however, no part in public life, except indeed on a certain occasion in Paris fit for comic opera (see pp. 39-40), to which he never liked any reference, when he fisticuffed a cohort of the French National Guard in supposed vindication of his country's outraged honour; a shrewd business man, yet labouring neither for the fame nor the money that perish,—the world knew him, or rather knew about him, in two ways only. These were *first*, through his very numerous publications, during a period of more than sixty years, in Scottish literature, history and archæology, and *second*, because of his immense personal services as guide, philosopher and friend to two generations of literary men. These services extended over his forty-two years in office as librarian at Edinburgh to 'The Society of Writers to His [afterwards Her] Majesty's Signet in Scotland,' in succession to Professor Macvey Napier, the editor of the *Edinburgh Review*. The Writers to the Signet Library, although belonging to a private body, has been treated by its owners, and by its librarians, with great public spirit, as a national institution. To scholars, its somewhat peculiar title will always recall the name of David Laing, as well as the fascinating personality, and the career, so full of contrasts, of the profound scholar who succeeded him, the beloved Thomas Graves Law.

Laing was a man of an original and independent mind, reluctant to form any opinion until the whole evidence was before him, a cautious and unprejudiced seeker after truth. But none of his many publications, more than two hundred in number, would be ordinarily classed as original works. He spent his long life in the comparatively prosaic, but most useful and truly patriotic work of rescuing his country's earlier literature from oblivion, and rendering it accessible in an accurate and convenient form, made intelligible and educative by introductions, memoirs, notes, glossaries and indexes prepared by him, or by others under his direct supervision. So far as his publishers would allow, his own personality was always kept out of sight. As Mr. Goudie brings out in Chapter v., headed 'Literary Work,' David Laing's name is not to be found in several of the books there rightly credited to him, or only his initials were given.

INTRODUCTION xix

He contributed many articles to reviews, magazines and encyclopædias, which cannot now be traced; and he read more than a hundred papers, rectifying and adding to previous knowledge, on all kinds of antiquarian subjects, directly or indirectly connected, within the period of history—he took little interest in the prehistoric—with his beloved Scotland. These papers were read to the Society of Antiquaries of Scotland, in which, as we shall presently see, he began his career by being blackballed !

Sometimes he discoursed on general subjects, such as 'The Origin and Progress of Dramatic Exhibitions in Scotland,' 'The State of the Fine Arts in Scotland during the 15th, 16th and 17th Centuries,' 'Early Historical Writers of Scotland'; or he described a 'Calendar of Scottish Saints.' In other papers he treated these and similar subjects concretely, as, for example, in the matter of dramatic exhibitions, by a paper on 'A Visit of English Comedians to the Court of James VI. in 1599,' and again, 'Ben Jonson in Edinburgh in 1618.' John Knox, not Mary of Scots, nor yet Prince Charlie, was his historical Scottish hero. To his labours, with those of Dr. Thomas M'Crie, Thomas Carlyle and Professor Hume Brown, is due the place which the Scottish Reformer now rightly holds in his country's history and in the history of the world. But an examination of his papers, in the *Proceedings* of the Society of Antiquaries, shows that he was equally thorough and equally fair, when throwing fresh light on the death of the Roman Catholic archbishop Blackader in 1508, during a pilgrimage to the Holy Land, and on the careers of the Episcopalian archbishops Leighton and Sharp, as when dealing with the man whom he considered Scotland's greatest churchman and greatest statesman. An account from Rome of the birth of 'The Young Pretender' was as good grist to his mill as 'An Inventar of Popish trinkets gotten in my Lord Traquair's house, anno 1688, all solemnly burnt at the Cross of Peebles.'

In his communications to the Antiquarian Society he sometimes indulged the taste for the gruesome, which, I suppose, all archæologists possess. Thus, in 1850, he made a communication on 'An obligation by John Campbell, then prisoner under sentence of death, to undertake the office of Executioner in the Stewartry of Strathearn in 1675,' and he read more than one paper on the hotly debated question as to the identity of two unnamed corpses, in royal cerements, dug up by the North British Railway Company, when constructing part of the Waverley Station in Edinburgh, on the site of the Pre-Reformation Trinity College Church. One lady was in an oak, and the other in a lead coffin.

INTRODUCTION xxi

The first found was identified as Mary of Gueldres, wife of James II. of Scotland, and was transferred with much ceremony to the Royal Vault in Holyrood Abbey. When the second equally royal coffin was subsequently exhumed near the same spot, Scottish antiquarians were sharply divided into hostile camps; and David Laing took his full share in the attempt and the failure to settle the knotty question of identification. He acquiesced finally in the wise resolution to leave the first-placed coffin, inscribed as Queen of Scotland and encased in new crimson velvet, to repose in the Royal Vault, on the shelf, where I have seen it, and to bury the other immediately outside.

In book form, justifying the quaint statement of Dr. Jamieson, the Scottish lexicographer, that 'Laing instinctively viewed the papyrus as his natural aliment,' he was the sole or the main agent in the production of more than a hundred works, ranging from the stately and costly issues of literary societies to cheaper and more popular products. Some fifty were issued by himself, or by private arrangement, and the same number by the Bannatyne and Abbotsford Clubs of Edinburgh, the Hunterian and Maitland Clubs of Glasgow, the Spalding Club of Aberdeen, the Wodrow Society of Edinburgh, and the Shakespeare Society of London. Several of the club and the society publications included a number of

volumes; and some were miscellanies, embraci[ng]
in one volume as many as thirty entirely separ[ate]
subjects. The first volume of the Bannatyne Cl[ub]
Miscellany was 'printed under the joint superi[n]-
tendence of the President [Sir Walter Scott] a[nd]
Secretary [David Laing].'

He gave the same conscientious labour [to]
the adequate presentation of comparatively u[n]-
important publications, like *Poems by Alexan[der]
Scott*, 1568, prefaced and annotated by him at t[he]
beginning of his career in 1821, and *The Poeti[cal]
Works of Patrick Hannay*, 1622, published by h[im]
in 1878, the year he died, as he did to the works [of]
more famous authors. But his name will alwa[ys]
be associated with such 'Scotch classics,' to [use]
another phrase of Dr. Jamieson's, as *The Poems [of]
William Dunbar* (who may well be called 'T[he]
Scottish Chaucer,' even by those who think [it]
grotesque to dub George Jamesone 'The Vandy[ke]
of Scotland,' an epithet said to have been coin[ed]
by Horace Walpole), two volumes, issued in 18[34];
Principal Baillie's *Letters and Journals*, and Jo[hn]
Row's *Historie of the Kirk of Scotland*, [in 18[42];
Daniel Defoe's *Memoirs of the Church of Scotla[nd]*
in 1844 (a 'Scotch classic,' although Defoe m[ay]
have had the misfortune to be an Englishma[n];
John Knox's *Works*, 'now first collected a[nd]
edited with Bibliographical Notices, Notes a[nd]
Illustrative Papers,' six volumes, in 1846 and s[ix]

sequent years; Lord Fountainhall's *Historical Notices*, in 1848; Calderwood's *History of the Kirk of Scotland*, vol. viii., in 1849; *The Poems and Fables of Robert Henryson*, in 1865; *The Gude and Godlie Ballates, changeit out of prophane sangis in[to] godlie sangis, for avoyding of sin and harlatrie*, in 1868; *Poetical Works of Sir David Lyndsay, Lyon-King-at-Arms*, in 1871; and Wyntoun's *Orygynale Cronykil of Scotland*, two volumes, in 1872. 'These editions,' the *Athenæum* said, ' exhibit almost the perfection of accurate and deep-knowledged editing.'

I doubt if any literary man in Scotland or out of it, except perhaps in Germany, has equalled the quantity and variety of Laing's literary output, maintained throughout, year after year, at such a steady and high level of thoroughness; certainly no one has done so much literary work of so much value and received for it so little pecuniary reward. He himself would have modestly attributed the amount, if not the quality, of this output in some measure at least to his splendid health, which was so robust that, throughout his whole working career, he never had occasion to seek medical advice till within a few weeks of his death.

The quality of his work was in striking contrast with that of some of his predecessors and contemporaries in Scotland. The standard both of literary and artistic accuracy, or, as it perhaps ought to be called, honesty, needed raising. In the work of the Royal Commission on Ancient and Historical Monuments in Scotland, we find that the old draughtsmen did not hesitate to insert imaginary windows and represent non-existent towers in the historical buildings which it was their duty to depict, and which it is our business to catalogue and describe and classify. In archæology, we know from Sir Walter Scott something of the credulity of the old type of Scottish antiquary; and literary men of eminence have not been unknown in Scotland as elsewhere, who thought it no sin to quote from memory, without verification from the original, or, if they quoted verbatim, to omit intervening and qualifying passages without intimation of the omission; and these men's political and ecclesiastical opinions, and inherited or acquired personal likes and dislikes, consciously or unconsciously, prevented them from giving a fair gloss of their authors' facts and arguments.

No one ever accused David Laing of being slipshod or inaccurate or unfair. Some years ago, when preparing a popular abbreviated edition of John Knox's *History of the Reformation in Scotland,* I had occasion to examine, sentence by sentence, his reprint of that History, contained in the six-volume edition of Knox's *Works,* prepared by him for the Bannatyne Club and the Wodrow Society. It was impossible not to be impressed throughout by the anxious care with which the readings in varying MSS., fourteen in number, and in several previous printed editions, had been weighed, and the knowledge and shrewdness displayed in the text preferred, the rejected variations of any moment (sometimes, I presumptuously thought, of none) being printed in the Notes, so that the reader might form his own judgment. What Thomas Carlyle wrote in the *Westminster Review* about Laing's edition of Principal Baillie's *Letters and Journals*, applied to everything he had a hand in :—'Laing has exhibited his usual industry, sagacity and correctness, with notes brief, illuminative, ever in the right place, not over plenteous, nor more than needed.'

It is not suggested that, had Dr. Laing lived now, his work would not have been better than it was. Even the Carnegie Research Scholar, although a mere tyro in comparison, works with linguistic and other tools which David Laing did not possess; the standard of editing is still rising; new manuscripts have come to light and have been made readily available; and material for notes and memoirs and introductions, coming from the archives of all European countries (the Vatican archives included) and from the labours of recent scholars, European and American, has enormously increased. Confining attention to Scotland, neither the Scottish History Society nor the

Scottish Text Society existed at Laing's death. His knowledge of contemporary European literature, in the time of William Drummond, might not have enabled him to discover that many of the Laird of Hawthornden's supposed original poems, when not mere translations, more or less literal (the technical word, I believe, is 'loans'), draw their inspiration from French and Italian poets, as Dr. Kastner of Manchester, following out the earlier researches of Ward, has recently proved. And Laing would probably have been astonished to find the Scottish Text Society publishing in 1911 an entirely new edition of *The King's Quair*, edited by the late Professor Skeat, the society having published the same royal (?) book so recently as 1884, edited by the same distinguished scholar!

Dr. Laing's interesting narrative, 1793-1823, printed by Mr. Goudie (pages 16 to 27), shows that he received a very scrappy education, in the Canongate Grammar School and in Professor Dalzel's Greek class in the University of Edinburgh, of which he writes: 'I came away with, if possible, a less knowledge of Greek than when I entered.' But he possessed special qualifications for his life-work of editor and literary adviser, which enabled him to do what no mere scholar could have done. Before he became librarian to the Signet Library, he spent some thirty years of boyhood, youth and manhood, as assistant and as partner, in the shop of a bookseller and publisher, which was daily haunted by the *literati* of a period distinguished for a great outburst of literary activity in Edinburgh; and the shop, for part of the time, was in the historic surroundings of Chessels Court in the Canongate of Edinburgh, and later in immediate proximity to the University. His shop and office life, in which, as he tells us, he went through 'a course of reading of the most indiscriminating kind,' was varied and enlarged by frequent book-buying and library-visiting journeys to London, beginning in 1809, when Laing was only sixteen, with the sale of the books of that erudite and inebriate Grecian, Richard Porson. Again, in 1812, he was in London, buying at the great Roxburghe sale, at which the copy of Caxton's *Recueyl of the Warrs of Troye*, sold by his father to the Duke twenty years before for £50, fetched £1050. He made also occasional raids on Paris, returning laden with spoils—books and prints—from the great libraries confiscated during the Revolution, which he picked up in bookshops and in the bookstalls on the Quais. On his first visit to Holland, young as he was, he set himself to break up a trade ring or corner, devised by Dutch booksellers to buy up all books at auction under their value, in order to re-sell at exorbitant profits. And there were other journeys to France and Holland, and to Germany, Flanders, Sweden and Denmark.

On one of these, in 1816, he was accompanied by two professional brethren, Adam Black and William Blackwood (the latter then full of plans for starting *Blackwood's Edinburgh Magazine*), whose names are still worthily commemorated in great publishing houses. In these visits abroad, as we see by his Journal, the paramount claims of literature did not prevent the pleasures of congenial companionship, or obscure the charms of Art and Music and the Drama, or the vivid interests of Waterloo, which he visited thirteen months after the battle, and of Copenhagen, with its libraries ruined by Nelson's bombardment.

But we must not think of his father's shop in the Canongate, or of the shop of W. and D. Laing, after he became a partner with his father in 1821, in the South Bridge (both of them, as John Gibson Lockhart put it, ' quite out of the way of all the fashionable promenades and lounges '), as if either resembled a modern bookstore. You might have been bewildered by their serried tomes, classical, theological, historical, archæological and scientific; you would have looked in vain for ordinary fiction, or for picture postcards, or for Christmas illustrated booklets; newspapers were not sold either on the streets or in shops: they were supplied direct by newspaper proprietors and only to subscribers. There were no trains to catch; so nobody rushed in for a Bradshaw or a Murray.

A woman seldom crossed the doorstep; there was nothing for the women *of that period* to see or to buy. Such a shop was a regular 'howff' for literary men, and the shopkeeper was their personal friend. (See *Peter's Letters to his Kinsfolk*, published in 1819, where John Gibson Lockhart, writing of himself as 'Wastle,' and speaking of David Laing, then a very young man, as Wastle's 'young friend,' tells us that 'Wastle commonly spends one or two hours every week he is in Edinburgh turning over, in company with his young friend, all the Aldines, the Elzevirs, the Wynkyn de Wordes and Caxtons in the collection; nor does he often leave the shop without being tempted to take some little specimen of its treasures home with him.') In an unsuccessful application he made in 1819 for the librarianship of the Advocates' Library, Laing refers to his 'profession of a bookseller.' In some hands, bookselling is a trade; in others, it was then and is still (the names of such Edinburgh veterans as David Douglas of Castle Street and Andrew Elliot of Princes Street will occur to many) a learned profession.

After David Laing abandoned bookselling and publishing to become librarian of the Writers to the Signet Library, he was entirely free to establish the other claim to remembrance to which I have already alluded, namely, personal service as an adviser on any bibliographical question or archæological puzzle or doubtful point of Scottish ecclesiastical or literary history; and it must be remembered those were the days when cyclopædias and other works of reference were few and incomplete, and subject indexes were unknown. From 1837, when he was appointed librarian (his backers including Wordsworth, Southey, John Gibson Lockhart, Sir William Hamilton, Patrick Fraser Tytler and Allan Cunningham), to 1878, when he died, that is to say for forty-two years, day by day, at personal interviews and by correspondence, home and foreign, he was, 'with simple and unostentatious liberality' (as Dr. Hibbert-Ware put it), gratuitously advising all sorts and conditions engaged in literary, historical and archæological research with a view to publication. In Chapter VI. Mr. Goudie shows the number and variety of his correspondents, regular and occasional, and the wide area of subjects on which they consulted him, most of them wishing information or advice. Lord Lindsay thanked him for corrections on *The Lives of the Lindsays*, and Mrs. Thomas Slidell, Newport, U.S.A., requested Laing to provide her 'with an unbroken chain,' proving her direct descent from John Knox! Unfortunately there are not many men now alive who can recall the patience with honest ignorance, the readiness to communicate, even with regard to

INTRODUCTION   xxxi

matters he was himself investigating, the extraordinary range of information, as rich as it was accurate, including subjects only remotely connected with Scottish literature or history, which he lavished on all *bona fide* inquirers—the poor Highland student equally with Sir Walter Scott, John Gibson Lockhart, Lord Jeffrey or Thomas Carlyle. In 1864, when presenting him for laureation by the University of Edinburgh, the learned Cosmo Innes, Professor of Constitutional History, who had edited several important works in the Bannatyne Club series, said: 'No wise man will undertake any literary work in Scotland without taking counsel with Mr. Laing.' Mr. Goudie, at page 248 of this book, does not exaggerate when he asserts, 'Laing was the historical referee of his day more than any man in Scotland.'

David Laing received many honours and rewards in the course of his long life of eighty-five years, and he had his share of failures and disappointments.

In 1823 Sir Walter Scott, the founder and first president of the Bannatyne Club, and chairman at its dinners from 1823 till the year before his death, selected him for the honorary secretaryship of the club, an appointment which lasted for thirty-eight years, and was a determining factor in his whole career. John Gibson Lockhart had met Laing some years before, and in *Peter's*

Letters, quoted by Mr. Goudie at page 45 *et seq.*, he has paid him an imperishable tribute, justifying the 'prodigious liking' which he says he took to him when they met casually at Rotterdam and travelled together through Holland.

In 1837, on the motion of Sir James Gibson-Craig of Riccarton, seconded by James Tytler of Woodhouselee, the Writers to the Signet elected him their librarian. In 1854 the Royal Scottish Academy appointed him Honorary Professor of Antiquities, and, some years later, of Ancient History. In 1865 Thomas Carlyle nominated him his representative as Lord Rector's Assessor in the University of Edinburgh, which, the year before, had made Laing a Doctor of Laws, a degree which he received with courtesy but declined to use, or to let others use, socially. He was also an honorary member of English, Danish and American learned societies. In 1809 Archibald Constable's partner, jesting about a Scottish expedition to be fitted out against the English booksellers, proposed that David Laing, then only sixteen, should be appointed 'Deputy Adjutant General.' Laing lived to earn a much higher title, for Professor Masson called him 'the Prince of the Scottish literary antiquaries of the century.'

On the other hand, he had his disappointments and his failures. In youth he had two cherished ambitions; the one was the Fellowship of the

Royal Society of Edinburgh, the other the Fellowship of the Society of Antiquaries of Scotland; and *both learned bodies blackballed him!* A mere erudite and travelled bookseller (albeit also a publisher), the son of a mere erudite and travelled bookseller and publisher (albeit also a director of the Commercial Bank) was not thought fit company by some, whose only claim to consideration, perhaps, was their right to sign F.R.S.E. or F.S.A.Scot. after their names! Verily Laing had his reward and his revenge. Much to their credit, the Society of Antiquaries elected him, in 1824, without his knowledge; and, at a subsequent crisis in its history, by most generous expenditure both of time and money, he lived to save the society's collection of Scottish antiquities, which was in imminent risk of being sold for debt; he lived also to become and to continue, during more than fifty years, the largest, most varied, and most important contributor to its literary, historical and archæological work. The Royal Society did its best to make amends. He was asked to renew his application, with assurances that he would be welcomed; but he declined.

Then, on two occasions, in 1819, at the age of twenty-five, when his application was supported by Sir Walter Scott, and again, in 1848, he was, for reasons which are now, at least on the second occasion, absolutely inscrutable, an unsuccessful candidate for the librarianship of the Advocates' Library.

I cannot close this Introduction to Dr. Laing's Life without referring to the man as I knew him. As his counsel, a very junior one, I advised him, not long before his death, about a right-of-way case in which he was interested. His manner, as I recollect it, was very genial and kindly, but occasionally a little peppery and slightly impatient. He was clear that he was in the right; but, at the same time, he was very desirous that nothing should be done to interfere with what might be a substantial advantage to the public, whether they were legally entitled to it or not. Then after his death, in advising his trustees, I came across an instance of his shrewdness and business ability. By his will he left his very valuable collection of more than five thousand manuscript documents (many of which, as Mr. Goudie brings out at page 130, came to Laing from the most unlikely quarters) to the University of Edinburgh. His books, on the other hand, were thus dealt with: 'The whole of my printed books shall be sent to London for sale by public auction in two separate divisions, where such books are more highly appreciated and more carefully catalogued than in this place.' Mr. J. T. Gibson-Craig, who knew a great deal about bookbuying and bookselling, thought that Laing's books, being of most interest to Scottish people, might fetch as much as £6000 to £8000 if sold in Edinburgh, but would go for an old song in the event of the testator's orders for a London sale being carried out. He was much disappointed when I advised the trustees that they were bound to carry out Dr. Laing's perfectly reasonable and possibly sound instructions. I always wondered what were Mr. Gibson-Craig's reflections when, as Mr. Goudie brings out on page 140, the London sale of these books by Sotheby's firm, in 11,743 lots, realised £16,536 l

David Laing's career, dealt with in detail by Mr. Goudie, was well summed up by two men, who were considering him from different points of view. In *Blackwood's Edinburgh Magazine* for July 1818, his early friend, John Gibson Lockhart, thus described the young bookseller of twenty-five:

> ' David, the most sagacious and the best,
>   As all Old Reekie's erudites opine,
> Of Scottish Bibliopoles, who knows the zest
>   And cream of every title-page *Aldine*;
> A famous Bibliomaniac, and a shrewd,
> Who turns his madness to no little good.'

In 1874, fifty-six years after, Sir Arthur Mitchell, the friend of later years, presenting Dr. Laing's portrait to the Society of Antiquaries of Scotland, on the completion of fifty years of membership and service in the society's various honorary offices, sketched the man of whom all of Scotland born, who are deeply interested in their country's history, literature and archæology, will ever think with gratitude, respect and affection: 'Mr. Herdman's portrait gives expression to the feelings of personal regard and affection which we entertain towards a high-minded and kind-hearted gentleman. We honour Dr. Laing as a man of learning; but he is endeared to us by his pleasant, helpful, loyal, unselfish and unostentatious ways.'

CHARLES J. GUTHRIE.

SWANSTON COTTAGE, COLINTON,
November 1913.

NOTE by D. HAY FLEMING, LL.D., Author of '*Mary Queen of Scots,*' '*The Reformation in Scotland,*' etc. etc.

It is more than thirty years since I began to use David Laing's editions of works relating to Scottish history and literature. Familiarity with these works has increased my respect for him and my confidence in his reliability. I have checked considerable portions of his edition of Knox's *History* with the MS. which he followed, and have found it to be very accurate. At the present moment I only remember one error in the text. In the notes there are a few slips, but these are not serious. In printing Knox's letters from the MS. volume which belonged to Dr. M'Crie, he accepted the year-dates as correct, although several of them can be proved to be wrong, and this led him to contradict one of his own earlier statements which was quite right, and also misled several subsequent writers.

Laing's impartiality was manifested by his drawing attention to the fact that, in the *Treasurer's Accounts*, then unprinted, reference is made to a child of Patrick Hamilton's, although he supposed that it was illegitimate and therefore a stain on the memory of the proto-martyr of the Scottish Reformation, for whom he had a profound admiration. Happily for Hamilton's reputation, Dr. Lorimer soon afterwards discovered satisfactory proof that Hamilton had been married. Laing was thoroughly honest in other ways. A bookseller notified him that he had bought Dr. M'Crie's library, and offered him the first choice of its treasures. He duly called and looked over them. Holding one out, he asked—'What do you want for this?' 'A pound,' was the reply. 'I won't take it for a pound,' Laing said; 'it is worth more. I will not take it for less than five pounds.'

Considering the width of his range, the minuteness of his knowledge was amazing. And although he had done nothing else than amass the huge collection of MSS. which he bequeathed to Edinburgh University Library, he would have deserved the gratitude of all workers in Scottish history. Many of these MSS. he saved from impending destruction. Some forty years ago or more there was a man in Edinburgh (I think his name was Adcock) who advertised for documents of all kinds which he undertook to destroy. Fortunately for us he allowed Laing to run through them before they were sent off. These were not the only ones he saved. One day, in passing through Parliament Square, he noticed a great pile of papers, which had been thrown out of a government office in order to be carted away as rubbish. Naturally he looked over them, and picked out a few things which he thought worth saving; but, before proceeding very far in his search, he found several documents which he deemed much too valuable to be appropriated even from a rubbish heap. Putting them to one side, he went to the government office and told what he had done. On going out again into the Square, he found that some one less scrupulous had carried them off!

D. HAY FLEMING.

4 CHAMBERLAIN ROAD,
EDINBURGH, *November* 1913.

NOTE by GEORGE NEILSON, LL.D., Author of 'John Barbour, Poet and Translator,' 'Huchown of the Awle Ryale, the Alliterative Poet,' etc. etc.

David Laing's name stands high and maintains itself in the estimation of Scottish antiquaries for the value and variety of his contributions. His range was practically as wide as the subject of Scottish antiquity itself, and his intimate knowledge of bibliography, reinforced by an extensive study of manuscript, helps to explain the powerful influence he exerted over the literary and historical clubs of Scotland. From the very outset of that movement which reflects so favourable a light on the culture of the age of Walter Scott and Thomas Thomson, it is clear that Laing was not merely an auxiliary but was also somewhat of an inspiration. If comparisons were needful, it might be said that his own work had its chief value in its service to Scottish literary antiquity. He still ranks as our greatest literary antiquarian editor, and the criticisms of half a century, while they have often corrected his facts and improved upon his editorial method, make but small deduction from his merits or from the gratitude due to him by workers in history who have to follow where he led. How profound his labours were was recently brought graphically home to me when there came into my possession the original manuscript of his notes to Knox's *History*—a pile of 'copy' for the press written for the most part on the vacant spaces of printed quarto sheets cut in two. It is needless to characterise the notes: Lord Guthrie and Dr. Hay Fleming have well attested their extraordinary erudition, their minute attention to every detail of collation, and their prevalent fidelity. But the sheets on which they are written have also a particular interest as exhibiting the industrious antiquary in his club atmosphere as well as his own share in the activities which the Bannatyne Club under his guidance so successfully pursued. One sheet is a paper in which Sir Walter Scott nominates Dawson Turner for membership. Other sheets utilised include the top half of Laing's lithographed application in 1837 for appointment as Signet librarian, and a print of Patrick Fraser Tytler's testimonial in his favour. Over and over again used were papers of the Bannatyne Club such as lists of candidates (including a vote paper with its mark supporting Fraser Tytler's admission), lists of members, circulars to meetings and the like. Repeatedly used also were fragments of title-pages, including those of several of the Club's *Garlands*, Douglas's *Palice of Honour* (1827), Bannatyne *Miscellany* (1827), Spald-

INTRODUCTION   xli

ing's *Troubles* (1828), Bannatyne's *Memorials* (1829), Melville's *Memoirs* (1837), and *Assembly Proceedings* (1845). Similar use was made of pieces of works of Dunbar, Sir William Alexander, Walter Kennedy and William Mercer, and of fugitive verses 'On the Miseries of the Tyme' (Bannatyne MS. No. 105), as well as of *disjecta membra* of a circular announcing proposals of the *Origines Parochiales* (1845). A frequently recurring piece is a reminiscence of Laing's treasurership of the Society of Antiquaries of Scotland: it is an intimation to dilatory members in which occasion is taken 'to remark how much the prosperity of the Society depends on regular payment by members of their annual subscriptions.' Some of them are signed—a token that these reminders were ready in advance against a steady percentage of defaulters!

A more systematic account would show how round about the year 1844 Laing gathered into these scraps his immense body of annotations of Knox as historian—a collection representing, whatever more it may be, a wonderful persistency in taking pains and collecting exactly the material required. A collation of many of the notes with the printed work published in 1846-48, reveals only those minor alterations to be expected when so large a book was passing through the press. It is pleasant to see the actual form in

d

which all that erudition assembled itself by the industry of a keenly interested and inexhaustible editor, and to see his own manuscript title-page —bearing a date a year earlier than the eventual imprint—for 'The Works of John Knox . . . Volume First. Edinburgh, 1845. Printed for the Wodrow Society.' Indeed the notes are themselves no inconsiderable monument of David Laing.

GEO. NEILSON.

GLASGOW, *November* 1913.

MEMOIR OF DAVID LAING

MEMOIR OF DAVID LAING

I.

ANCESTRY

DAVID LAING was born in 1793 and died in 1878. In tracing his ancestry I have not been able to get beyond the two preceding generations; and, indeed, Laing's own definite information did not carry him further back.

His grandfather was William Laing, designed at the time 'Merchant Taylor' in the Canongate, then perhaps the most important business and residential quarter in the city. He died in February 1795, at the age of sixty. His wife was —— Straiton, the daughter of William Straiton, whose name appears in Peter Williamson's Directory of 1773-74 as a smith in the Pleasance. His nephew William, a smith at the same address, died in Edinburgh early in the nineteenth century.

David understood that his grandfather, William Laing, was the son of a small farmer in the parish of Alves, near Elgin; and in 1854 he instituted inquiries in the district with results which, though interesting, threw no definite light upon the origin or local connections of the family. It was thought that this William, probably a younger son, came in early life to Edinburgh. David relates in a note that his grandfather during his apprenticeship was sent one Sunday in great haste to the meeting-house, in Nicolson Street, of Adam Gib,[1] with an intimation to request the prayers of the congregation for his master's wife, who was dangerously ill. On the way he sprained his leg, which, being neglected at the time, made amputation necessary. Of William Laing nothing further is known; but there is among the Laing papers a burgess ticket of the burgh of Canongate, dated 26th March 1772, in favour of 'William Laing,' without designation, but which can only have reference to him, and which clearly indicates his having then been a person of substance and reputation. He had a half-brother, James Laing, who also came to Edinburgh and carried on business as a 'Merchant' in the Luckenbooths, High Street.

[1] Adam Gib of the 'meeting-house' was a prominent Nonconformist minister of the time, described on the family tombstone on the west wall of Greyfriars Churchyard as 'Minister of the Associate Congregation, Edinburgh' (the original of the Nicolson Street United Free Church, formerly 'U.P.,' of the present day), who was born in 1714 and died in 1778. His grandsons, Adam Gib Ellis and Robert Ellis, both Writers to the Signet, were well-known professional men in Edinburgh until their deaths in 1865 and 1868 respectively.

WILLIAM LAING (David's father), son of the preceding, was born on 20th July 1764. After being educated at the Grammar School of the Canongate he is next heard of as entering apprentice for six years to Campbell Denovan, printer in Edinburgh. By the indenture he becomes bound ' to be a faithful, diligent, and obedient servant to his said master,' and ' is not to absent himself from his business at any time during his apprenticeship, week day or holy-day, without first liberty asked and obtained, and if he does on the contrary he shall perform two days' service for each day's absence after the expiry' of the six years. He is not to ' discover or reveal any of his master's secrets of business,' and if he hears, sees, knows, or is partaker in any ' skaith or damage ' of his master he is ' to advise him timeously thereof and stop the same to the utmost of his powers,' paying twopence for each penny of loss sustained by his fault and negligence. On his part Denovan binds himself to ' teach and instruct the said William Laing in his art and trade of Printing, and to conceal no part thereof from him.' William is to be paid the sum of two shillings sterling per week for the first two years, two shillings and sixpence weekly for the third and fourth years, and three shillings and sixpence weekly for the fifth and sixth years. The indenture is dated 13th April 1778, and William Laing senior, the father, is taken bound as cautioner for the fulfilment of the stipulations on the part of the apprentice.

By the discharge of the indenture on 16th July 1784 on the expiry of the six years, William is declared to be 'entitled to work in any printing office that may have occasion for a compositor.' But he would appear to have had aspirations beyond the printing press or the compositor's frame, though the experience there gained could not but have been materially helpful towards the development of the literary taste and the knowledge of books which was displayed in his later life. The delicacy of his eyesight has also been named as a contributing cause to his relinquishing the printer's calling; but whatever the predominating cause may have been, the fact is, as recorded in a note by David, that he began business as a bookseller in 1784, the year when his apprenticeship expired, at the head of the Canongate, on the north side, a few doors beyond Leith Wynd—(now demolished, but which proceeded northward, opposite to the opening of St. Mary's 'Wynd,' now 'Street'). This he quitted some time after for a shop lower down on the opposite side of the Canongate, at the left-hand side of the entrance to Chessels' Court. The dwelling-house, formerly for a time

ANCESTRY

in St. David Street, New Town, then a rising quarter after the opening of the North Bridge, was also removed to Chessels' Court, on the second or third flat above the shop.

In 1786 he was admitted a burgess of the Canongate, with the designation of bookseller and stationer there. The burgess ticket is dated 13th March, and bears that a sum of forty pounds Scots had been paid by him.

In 1794 he takes as an indentured apprentice Hendrie Young, lawful son of Hendrie Young, vintner in the Canongate, for four years, for his ' trade and Profession of Bookseller.' The deed is dated 1st May.

The business in the Canongate gradually developed into a well-known and important book emporium, and its financial success had been so well assured that in 1798 William Laing removed his family to a larger house in St. John Street, west side, belonging to the Earl of Wemyss; thereafter to a house at the foot of Chalmers' Close, Netherbow; and, some time later, to the corner house at the north-west side of Argyle Square, entering from the close beyond. This place last named wholly disappeared with the opening of Chambers Street and the erection of the Royal Scottish Museum there.

In 1802 he became a member of the Society

in Scotland for Propagating Christian Knowledge, etc., for which he was proposed and elected by ballot at a quarterly meeting on 3rd June. At the time the Society must have desired to be regarded as a select and exclusive body, issuing a formal diploma, or certificate of election, signed and sealed.

In 1803 (31st October) he was served heir to his father, William Laing, merchant; and in the same year he removed his business premises from the Canongate to the South Bridge (at first to No. 44, and afterwards to No. 49), in the vicinity of the University, where the business continued to be conducted until it was disposed of by David, his son and successor, on his receiving the appointment of Librarian of the Signet Library in 1837. A further important incident in his history in this year, 1803, was the removal of the family to a large house, within its own grounds of two acres or thereby —Ramsay Lodge, at the west end of Lauriston Place—which was occupied by them for forty years until sold to the Corporation of the city, in 1843, as a site for the Sheep and Cattle Markets.

The date of William Laing's marriage I have not ascertained. His wife was Helen, only daughter of David Kirk, 'Smith and Box Master in Calton,' then a separate municipality from Edinburgh, by his wife Elizabeth Melville, of a

Fife family. There is among the papers a postnuptial contract between Laing and his wife, by which he provides an annuity to her of £40 sterling—a not unreasonable sum at the time —to be restricted to £30 in the event of a second marriage. The deed is dated at Canongate, 9th December 1788.

They had a large family, some of whom died in infancy. Of those who attained maturity the sons were:

> William, minister of Crieff.
> David, the subject of this memoir.
> Gilbert, a minister of the Free Church of Scotland after the Disruption of 1843.
> James, Deputy Postmaster, Ceylon.

The daughters were Mary, Jessie Miller, Agnes, Margaret, and Euphemia.

In 1804 William Laing executed a deed of nomination of tutors, curators, and guardians for his wife and children, appointing

> Thomas Thomson, Esq., advocate, Edinburgh;
> Rev. Walter Buchanan, minister of the Canongate;
> Gilbert Laing, Esq., merchant, Edinburgh;
> Mr. Archibald Constable, bookseller, Edinburgh;

William Beveridge, Writer to the Signet, Edinburgh;

and by a codicil in 1818, Andrew Steele, W.S., in place of W. Beveridge, deceased.

Both for professional knowledge and general business ability William Laing possessed a high reputation. His acquaintance with the editions of the works of famous authors, ancient and modern, was unsurpassed, and he was resorted to by all who were in quest of rarities or treasures of literature in any form. The value of books published abroad became equally the object of his keen observation; and for the purpose of familiarising himself with this, and at the same time enlarging his holding of such literature, he went once and again to the Continent. His first expedition of the kind was to Paris, in the midst of the revolutionary crisis of 1793. He was in Denmark in 1799 when he learned that the king proposed to sell the duplicates in the Royal Library in Copenhagen; and the correspondence preserved shows, following upon that visit, a large extent of purchases by him, and also sales, apparently more or less by way of exchange, carried through with Dr. Moldenhawer, the king's librarian.

In 1802 a passport in French was issued to William Laing, ' négociant, Anglais,' native of Edinburgh, going to Paris by Dover; age thirty-eight, hair and eyebrows brown, forehead high, eyes blue, chin round, etc. The document bears to be issued at Rotterdam by the Sub-Commissioner for Commercial Relations in the —— year of the French Republic, '*une et indivisible.*' No details regarding this journey are preserved.

At an early period in his business career William Laing had become impressed with the idea that Edinburgh ought to be not only a centre in Scotland for the study of the classics, but for their production from the press as well. Accordingly, in 1804, he issued an edition of the works of *Thucydides* in the original Greek, with a Latin translation, in six volumes, 12mo. The Rev. Peter Elmsley, a Greek scholar of note, was the responsible editor, and it is a beautiful piece of work. *Herodotus*, in seven volumes, followed in 1806, and *Xenophon*, in ten volumes, in 1811.[1]

---

[1] In connection with William Laing's interest in the Greek tragedians it may not be out of place to print here a letter from him to Archibald Constable, on the occasion of the latter's first visit to London :

'Edinr. 5 March 1795.

'DEAR SIR,—I shall thank you to deliver the two letters as directed. Would you have the goodness to buy for me *Euripidis Phœnissæ* Gr. Lat. Valkner 4°. Payne has one, it is some 12 or 15/. I shall pay it with thanks to Mr. Willison, and do as much for you again. I wanted also *Euripides, Ammonius* 4° by Valkner, but this I suppose cannot be got.

'Wishing you success in every enterprise,—I remain, Dr Sir, Your mo. obed. Servt., WILLM. LAING.'

For the use of this letter I am indebted to Mr. Archibald Constable, LL.D., to whose grandfather the letter was addressed.

But prior to these he had issued, in 1795, Androw of Wyntoun's *Orygynale Chronykil of Scotlande* in two volumes 8vo, and it is strange to note that on the reissue of this *Chronykil* his son David was intently engaged when death put an end to his career in 1878. In 1815 he issued a catalogue (prepared by his son David) of the library of William Drummond of Hawthornden in the University of Edinburgh. The 'new' edition of Pinkerton's *Enquiry into the History of Scotland*, issued in 1814, has also been quoted as one of his publications, but it would appear to have been a joint adventure, the imprint bearing that it was printed by James Ballantyne & Co. for Bell & Bradfute, William Laing, William Blackwood, and others.

Regular catalogues of books on hand for sale were issued by Laing from 1786 onwards. Among the foreign correspondents from whom he drew supplies was L. Bennet, bookseller, Rotterdam, to whom, on 5th April 1793, he addressed an order for twenty-five different volumes; and, at the same time, for one thousand Dutch *quills*; and it may be mentioned, as a further indication of the quality of his customers and of those generally who frequented his premises, that so early as 22nd August 1796 he agreed, in a letter to Andrew Foulis, printer, Glasgow, to take from him three hundred copies of the *Tragedies of Euripides*—the price 2s. 6d. per volume. We should now, in the twentieth century, scarcely look for such an order being issued by a bookseller in the Canongate, or indeed, perhaps, in any other quarter of Edinburgh.

In 1842 the remainders on hand of Laing's classical publications, *Thucydides*, *Herodotus*, and *Xenophon*, 860 volumes in all, were purchased from David Laing by Henry G. Bohn, London, at the rate of ' Fivepence per volume, to be delivered free of all expense on Shipboard, at twelve month's Credit.'

We have seen that in 1802 William Laing was on the Continent for business purposes, but as his son David grew to experience as his assistant such expeditions were usually entrusted to him. William's last visit abroad of which we have any knowledge was in 1823. In the passport in French issued at the Embassy in London, to 'Mr. William Laing, natif d'Angleterre, Marchand,' going from London to Dieppe, he is described as fifty-eight years of age, height five feet eight inches, and wearing a wig.

William Laing in his later years was a man of acknowledged wealth, interested in financial affairs, and a director of the Commercial Bank of Scotland, of which he was one of the promoters, and a director from 1825. He died in his house, Ramsay Lodge, Lauriston, on 10th April 1832. Laudatory notices in the newspapers of the day show that he was esteemed and regretted by a wide circle. He was interred in the family burying-place in the New Calton Burying Ground.

The movable effects in the house were valued, in the inventory, at £389, including thirteen paintings, estimated at £70, an eight-day clock, £2, 10s., two pairs silver candlesticks, £15, 15s., two silver trays, £7, 5s., teapot, etc., £8, 15s. 6d., etc., etc. A quantity of Madeira wine was valued at 3s. per bottle, port at 2s. 6d., champagne at 4s. 6d., and fourteen and a half gallons whisky at 8s. per gallon, prices deserving to be noted in comparison with those now current, eighty years later.

The books in the house were fifty-seven volumes, value 15s., from which it is clear that the rare and costly literary possessions were stored in the business premises, and not admitted into the family dwelling. Likenesses of Mr. and Mrs. William Laing have been preserved, and are here reproduced.

With these notices we pass from a good and

WILLIAM LAING

MRS WILLIAM LAING

MRS. WILLIAM KING.

honoured citizen, and turn to his more distinguished, but not more worthy, son David, the subject of this memorial. Mrs. Laing, David's mother, survived till 20th January 1837.

II

PERSONAL HISTORY

1793-1823

It is perhaps scarcely necessary to say that David Laing was a native and denizen of Edinburgh, for, as is well known, his life's work and interests centred there, and his love of Edinburgh and of everything connected with Edinburgh was a leading inspiration throughout his whole career. He was born in April 1793 (there is some uncertainty as to the day), and his baptism on 8th May following is recorded in the register of St. Andrew's parish. The place of birth was in St. David Street, where his parents resided at the time, but the number in the street was not known to Laing himself.

While he was thus a child of the ' New Town ' Laing's earliest memories were of the Canongate and the old town, where his early years were spent, and where the memorials of Scottish history and the faded remains of the rank and dignity of other times were encountered by him at every step. Several representatives of the old nobility and gentry still lingered in the neighbourhood; and the cumulative influence of all this appealed powerfully, from his early days, to his natural inquisitiveness and taste for history.

Though intended by his parents for a professional career, his tastes and the force of circumstances led to his being attached to his father's business from the completion of his school and college education. With such training and environment he could not fail to prove an assistant of a high order; and of this we have evidence in the fact of his having been sent to London in 1809, at the age of sixteen, to attend a book sale; to Dublin for the same purpose in 1810; and again to London, in 1812, for the great Roxburghe sale. He was in Holland in 1816 at the age of twenty-three, and again on the Continent in 1819, on business expeditions on his father's account. He thus obtained at an early age a wide knowledge of books, formed acquaintances with book buyers and men of letters, and came to be recognised as an authority on bibliography.

In beginning this sketch of Laing's life it seems right to give the place of honour to a short account prepared by himself in 1866, when he was seventy-three years of age, under circumstances which he explains; for we can readily understand that his innate modesty would not have allowed him to frame such a notice of his own motion, for the express purpose of present or posthumous publication. The account unfortunately breaks off abruptly in the year 1823, at the foundation of the Bannatyne Club, an early but important point in his history. Though it thus covers only his first thirty years we may be grateful that it is in existence; and it will be our effort to amplify the narrative, and to continue it through his later years as best we may, by the aid of such material as we may be able to gather from other sources.

LAING'S OWN NARRATIVE

1866

' Some time ago I was asked to correct a brief notice of myself for a Biographical Dictionary then in progress. Whether it ever appeared I do not know—but this led me to mark down some points, not indeed of much importance, connected with the past course of my life, for the purpose of recording a few dates, although only interesting to myself.

' While examining the Edinburgh Register of Births and Baptisms to obtain an official [extract] for a friend in England, I met with the following

David Laing) 466.

Sometime ago I was asked to correct a brief notice of myself for a Biographical Dictionary, then in progress. Whether it ever appeared I do not know — but this led me to mark down some points, not indeed of much importance, connected with the past course of my life, for the purpose of recording a few dates, although interesting to myself.

While examining the Edinburgh Register of Births & Baptisms, to obtain an official for a friend in England, I met with the following entry — which I had formerly expected to have found in the Canongate Register.

"8th May 1793.

"William Laing Bookseller and Helena Kirk his Spouse, St Andrews Kirk parish, a son born the 20th April last, named DAVID. Bapt'd in Church."

(Edin'. Register of B. & B. Vol. 22.)

The house in which I was born was in N. St Davids' Street, which accounts for the above entry, (the No. I do not know,); but I remember my Mother telling me the day in the Register had been mistaken — by antedating it 2 or 3 days. — (See some notes in this book respecting my Father & Mother, & their family.) My earliest recollections however are connected with these moments, my Father then carrying on business as a Bookseller in the shop at

entry—which I had formerly expected to have found in the Canongate Register:

> "8th May 1793, William Laing, Bookseller, and Helena Kirk, his spouse, St. Andrew's Kirk parish, a son born the 20 April last, named DAVID, Baptized in Church." (Vol. 22.)

The house in which I was born was in N[orth] St. David Street, which accounts for the above entry (the No. I do not know): but I remember my mother telling me the day in the Register had been mistaken—by antedating it two or three days. (See some notes in this book respecting my Father and Mother, and their family.) My earliest recollections, however, are connected with the Canongate, my Father then carrying on business as a Bookseller in the shop at the left hand of the entrance to Chessells' Court—and his house the second or third story above. He afterwards moved to a larger house in St. John Street, built by Richard Cooper the Engraver, which became the property of the Earl of Wemyss. In my Father's book is this entry:

> "1798 Novr. 12. By Earl of Wemyss for house in St. John's Street, per Mr. Anderson, £400, 0s. 0d."

It was on the west side—and had, as it seemed to me, a charming garden, enclosed with a high wall, while the interior of the house was ornamented with landscapes by Norie or some of his scholars. It has for many years been a most ungainly building when converted into a hat manufactory.

'I remember, without knowing the date, that one year we lived up a stair in the court at the foot of Chalmers' Close, Netherbow—and another year in the corner house at the north-west of Argyll Square, the entrance door being at the head of —— Close.

'It is singular what vivid impressions remain on the mind from the time of childhood. I was probably not four years old when I was taken a voyage, in a small vessel or fishing-boat, across the Firth, and was boarded during the summer with one of my Mother's relations (probably William Goodsir, a farmer), but the name of the place I cannot remember—but I amused myself looking at the pigs or poultry, and running about the fields, or getting on the top of a small hill or rising ground and whistling, " O'er the hills and far awa." Also the long dreary voyage back, and getting to the Canongate on a cold dark winter night.

'I was then sent to learn to read—at a school with a large number of boys and girls kept by one Williamson. In the old Edinburgh Directories between 1793-180- his name appears as

"Williamson (Charles), teacher, opposite Linen Hall, Canongate." Moray House was so called in its being occupied by the British Linen Bank before moving up the street to the Netherbow [in Tweeddale Court, the mansion of the Earls of Tweeddale, in the entrance to which Begbie, the Bank's porter, was murdered in 1808]. The precise date I can ascertain by an alarming fire which happened one day, and the reflexion of the flames upon the windows gave us all a holiday.

' 1800. On the 8th of January the Edinburgh Sugar House in the Canongate was completely burnt down, and most of the materials and utencils were destroyed. From recollection it was a most alarming sight seen from the S. back of the Canongate.

'When little more than seven years old (in or about 1800) I was put to the Grammar School, Canongate, to learn Latin—but the rector said I had much better go back to the English school to learn both to read and spell!—Certain it is, neither at the one or other did I ever acquire a proper knowledge of grammar—although my Father wished that I should become a famous classical scholar, and talked of the learned Printers of former times, he having commenced publishing a series of the Greek Writers—but which only included the three great Historians [Thucydides, Xenophon, and Herodotus].

'The Canongate School was then in a tolerably flourishing condition. The course extended over five years—but the first and second classes sitting together in one room under the charge of an assistant teacher—and the other three classes in the rector's room, it so happened that we sat half the day idle, unless when engaged with slate and pencil on lessons in Arithmetic. After that came the study of Geography—with Greek in the fourth and fifth years. In the fifth year the class to which I belonged had dwindled down from upwards of thirty scholars to five! The dux was Alexander Kyle, the second William Drummond,[1] and I stood third—and on our last examination day we stood up to declaim Virgil's *Bucolick*. The school was at length closed in 182–, and the rector, Mr. James Cumming, originally educated for the Church, but never ordained, continued to reside at 30 Lothian Street, as a teacher of Latin and Greek, till his death in 1833 or 4.

'Mr. Cumming's assistant was a rough old fellow of the name of Johnstone—and was succeeded by Thomas Smith, who soon after went to teach an Academy in the neighbourhood of London—but came back to Scotland many years later on being appointed Rector of the Grammar School of Lanark.

[1] This was doubtless the father of James Drummond, R.S.A.

'On leaving the Canongate School I was enrolled in the Greek class under Professor Dalziel in October 1805, but this most excellent man was unable to come even one day to the class-room—but once or twice he had us in his own house—the class being taught by George Dunbar,[1] appointed, through the influence of Sir William Fettes, assistant and successor. I came away with, if possible, a less knowledge of Greek than when I entered; and instead either of carrying out my Father's intention—or complying with my Mother's wish that I should study for the Church, I continued in my Father's shop (then 49 South Bridge) to assist in his business, and was left to my own discretion, in a course of reading of the most indiscriminating kind, when not engaged in writing catalogues and attending book sales, acquiring a taste for buying rather than selling. My practice was to begin with the books as they stood in the shelves—reading or glancing over them—whether Voyages and Travels, Romances, Poetry, Biography, or whatever they chanced to be, standing in alphabetical order. However unprofitable such a course of reading proved necessarily to be, it aided, along with the skill required in attending sales, to give me a love and knowledge of books which had its

---

[1] This was the Greek Professor well remembered by schoolboys for his *Lexicon*.

advantage—and obtained for me the favourable notice of several eminent bibliographers in England and Scotland. It also furnished opportunities for frequent excursions. The first was a voyage to London, in one of the old Leith and Berwick smacks. This was in June 1809, when I attended the sale of Porson's Library, and also bought a few books at Alexr. Dalrymple's. On arriving in the Thames old William Martin, who undertook to look after me, set off and left me to shift for myself—and I started to find out Robert Ogle's in Holborn—but, on enquiry [found that I] had crossed London Bridge—but at length found my way, and he got me a room near hand in ——

'My next journey was to Dublin to attend the sale of the Honb^{le.} Denis Conyngham's Library. This occupied from May to July 1810, and I was most hospitably entertained by an excellent and worthy man, Mr. Gilbart, originally from Scotland, of the well-known firm of Gilbart & Hodges in Dame Street.

'The notable sale of the Roxburghe Library in 1812 led to a second visit to London from May to July. The sale commenced on the 18th of May, and I attended every day—seeing of course Boccaccio [the first edition of the *Decameron*] sold for the enormous sum of £2260 [to the Marquess of Blandford, afterwards Duke of

Marlborough], and the *Caxton's Recueyl of the Warrs of Troye* [printed in 1471] for £10— [£1050], which my father had sold to the Duke for £50 some twenty years previously. At this time I lodged with Kenneth Treasurer, the tailor in Sherrard Street, Golden Square. I then made acquaintance with my old friend George Chalmers, author of *Caledonia* (although his nephew and coadjutor had a year or two before spent some months in examining the records in the General Register House) [in Edinburgh]—and in all my subsequent visits to London I never failed in spending many agreeable hours in his house No. 3 James's Street, Buckingham Gate. Both in going and returning, I went by one of the Leith smacks, the voyage varying from about three or four days to eight or ten.

'Two years later I was twice in London—one time from May to July 1814, attending the first Townsley [1] sale, and the larger sale of George Nicol's books; the other in —— [there appears to be no record of this visit or of its date] for the purchase of Joe Foulder's stock. Such visits, and the success attending those from Scotland who settled in London to push their fortunes, might have suggested a similar course to myself— but never setting my heart on the mere accumula-

---

[1] Charles Townley or Townsley, an important collector of classical antiquities.

tion of wealth, I greatly preferred remaining free and following my own inclinations to an exclusive or slavish attendance on business.

'In 1816 the Continent being opened up [I went abroad] in the month of August, accompanied by Mr. James Wilson and Adam Black, with David Brown [who] also joined us in this excursion. We sailed from Leith to Rotterdam — visited the chief towns of Holland and Flanders in our route to Paris, returning by London—James Wilson extending his tour to Switzerland, he only of the party not being engaged in business. From London I returned by land, along with Wm. Blackwood, stopping on the way at Leeds, etc. (he having some person to visit); but all the way down he was full of the idea of starting a new magazine, which he thought would do wonders. The scheme did not seem to me so feasible—but there can be no doubt that it was not suggested by some [one] else, as I have seen it asserted, but wholly his own conception, which led to the appearance of the *Edinburgh Magazine*, and, after the dispute with Cleghorn and Pringle, whom he considered incompetent, to the well-known *Blackwood's Edinburgh Magazine*, to which he sacrificed all his energies, and his ordinary business. I was so intimate with him at the time that I knew everything that occurred.

'Another Continental tour was in 1819. I had

again as a travelling companion Mr. James Wilson — brother of *the* Professor. My object was to arrange some long outstanding accounts with Dr. Moldenhawer of the Royal Library, Copenhagen. We sailed from Leith in a vessel named the *Oscar* (Captn. Hardy), to Elsineur—and after two or three weeks' residence in Copenhagen, crossed to Sweden, but the lateness of the season prevented our getting so far as Stockholm—we returned to Copenhagen—were eight days in reaching Keill, then to Hamburgh—Wilson crossing to Leith, while I visited London and returned by the mail in ——

'Hitherto I had devoted a good deal of time to collecting and studying the early writers of Scotland, and in the way of assisting some way or other their literary remains, I was proposed in 181- as a member of the Antiquaries—but was *black-balled*. A similar result followed at a later time (in 182-) when proposed for the Royal Society of Edinburgh.[1] In the former Society I was elected without my knowledge, in 182[4], and it so happens that I am now the second oldest of the members on the roll—and I might have also [been] admitted to the other, but *declined*. At the time there was a general feeling for reviving

---

[1] One more ball would have carried the election in his favour. See letter from Sir David Brewster (1827) under head 'Correspondents.'

its Literary Department—and I was desirous of some stimulus to make me exert myself. In 18[18] also an opening of a different kind occurred in the vacancy of Librarian to the Faculty of Advocates. I did not offer myself as a candidate till the year following, but there was so much party spirit exhibited, that, even supported by Sir Walter Scott and others, I had no chance—and in this case it was agreed that some of the younger members in my favour were to be at liberty to vote for one of the other candidates. I did regret my want of success, feeling at the time, and ever since, that I could have done much for the Library which it required, and still requires.

'In January 1821 my Father assumed me as his partner, and I so continued till his death in 1833, [it was really in 1832], and indeed till I relinquished business altogether, as I shall mention.

'In February 1823 the Bannatyne Club was instituted, and this had a very important influence on my future life. Although taking a keen interest in setting it agoing, it was only at the special request of Sir Walter Scott, the founder and first President, that I was induced to undertake the responsible office of Honorary Secretary. The amount of time devoted to its various duties no one perhaps would believe; but now I hope the time was not uselessly employed, and in the course of the present year (1866) I tried to see its affairs brought to a prosperous termination, after a lengthened period of forty and three years. In 18[61] the members presented me with a valuable testimonial for my services.'

Thus ends the narrative which, though only a fragment up to the thirtieth year of his age, is yet a precious one. While much more that we would have liked to know is omitted, it gives a succinct and unpretentious account of his early days such as could not otherwise have been presented. It is entirely in his own handwriting in one of his small manuscript volumes, but a copy of it in a recent hand, and not very accurate, has also been found among the papers.

The story of his childhood is artlessly told, as indeed is the whole narrative, bearing the impress of truth and modesty at every turn. Parental aspirations for his future eminence in ecclesiastical life or in professional position other than the ancestral vocation did not come to realisation, and the great book-lover was left to rise to his own special eminence in his own special way. For this I think we should feel grateful; for, though there is no saying to what distinction he might have attained in some other domain of intellectual life, had the Fates so ordained, yet he could not have been the DAVID LAING whom we loved and honoured, and knew to be possessed of a distinction in his own line that was peerless.

Though face to face in his early life with the great outburst of literary activity in Edinburgh in the beginning of last century, of which the poetry of Scott, the Waverley novels, the *Edinburgh Review*, and *Blackwood's Magazine* may be regarded as the most prominent features, Laing makes no reference in his narrative to these intellectual phenomena of the period. Constable has already appeared upon the scene (on a previous page) in casual connection with Laing senior; and James Wilson, brother of 'Christopher North,' and Adam Black, the well-known Edinburgh publisher of the Victorian age, are named as his companions on a Continental tour. William Blackwood, and the origin of *Blackwood's Edinburgh Magazine*, are indeed touched upon, and Sir Walter Scott comes in for notice, not as the 'Great Unknown,' the Wizard of Poetry and Romance, but merely as a friendly supporter in an application for an appointment, and, at a later date, urging him to accept the secretaryship of the Bannatyne Club. But Jeffrey, Brougham, Horner, and Sydney Smith, the moving spirits of the *Edinburgh Review*, and the other stars of the brilliant literary firmament which made Edinburgh a Mecca of light and learning at the time, receive no express notice, though he was coming constantly in contact with many, if not most, of them. Had the narrative been continued to a later date there is no saying what might have been told of the sayings and doings of these celebrities, and of Kirkpatrick Sharpe, Lord Cockburn, and other luminaries of the times which followed. Friendly correspondence with most of these is, however, preserved.

At Laing's first visit to London in 1809 he was, as already mentioned, only sixteen years of age, a proof of his father's implicit faith in his knowledge and business capacity. His presence at the Roxburghe sale in 1812 gives us a glimpse, direct and personal, of a scene which remained unparalleled for a lengthened period until developments in later times with the Mazarin Bible, Caxtons, Shakespeare First Folios, Kilmarnock *Burns*, and such like, opened the eyes of a new generation to marvels of the auction-room surpassing the wildest dreams of former ages.

These business visits to London, for weeks and occasionally more than a month at a time, and the voyages between Leith and London, sometimes occupying eight or ten days, in sailing smacks, present a strange contrast to the railway run of eight hours or thereby, and the hastily dispatched day or two in town, of the present day, and afford a striking illustration of the difference in the conditions of life now prevailing. But London was not the only objective of his expeditions in this time of his youth. In 1810 he was in Dublin, and on the Continent in 1816 and 1819, all in the pursuit of knowledge and the furtherance of business.

His being blackballed by the Society of Antiquaries of Scotland and by the Royal Society of Edinburgh are black spots which might not have been remembered, and over which I would willingly have drawn a veil, but for his own frank avowal of that treatment. It was apparently deemed that the young bookseller was scarcely up to the social level at which the guiding spirits of these bodies estimated themselves. The Antiquaries had leisure to repent, and tried to make amends by subsequently enrolling him as a Fellow without his knowledge. It was well for them that they did so; and his acknowledgment was the magnanimous one of becoming the saviour of the Society at a critical point in its history at a later stage, and of being the greatest and most important contributor to its literary and historical work that it has ever had, or is ever likely to have. He declined to have any connection with the Royal Society.

PERSONAL HISTORY

The private memoir which we have been considering terminating in 1823, it remains for us to see what can be done to supplement the information contained in it, and to continue the story of his life in the years that follow, as far as the materials existing will allow.

The visits to Holland, Flanders, and Paris in 1816, and to Holland, Denmark, and Sweden in 1819, returning by Kiel and Hamburg on the latter occasion, have been briefly touched upon in the memoir. But luckily a full report, in his own handwriting, of the former of these visits is preserved. The passport, dated 11th July 1816, is by the Lord Provost of Edinburgh, then William Arbuthnot, who was created a baronet by George IV. on 24th August 1822 (patent dated 3rd April 1823), to 'David Laing, Esquire of this city,' and bears to have been *viséd* at Rotterdam, Amsterdam, Mons, Brussels, and Paris.

FIRST VOYAGE TO HOLLAND

'1816, July 10th at 5 o'clock on Friday morning (after some days' disappointment owing to the bad weather) the vessel, *The Consul* of Leith, Captain A. Wilson, at length sailed. The only passengers were our party, consisting of Messrs. A. B. [Adam Black], D. B. [David Brown],

J. W. [James Wilson], and myself. On reaching the coast of Yarmouth we lay in the roads three days. On the 9th day we got across the bar at the mouth of the Maase, being for three days beating about, in squally weather. On Sunday sailed up the river, with a contrary wind, and at 10 o'clock the vessel dropped anchor at the Brill, where we took a boat, resolving to walk on towards Rotterdam—met with a Dutch [?], and had some refreshments and schnaps—passed through Flaarding [Vlaardingen], Schiedam, and Delfthaven, arriving at Rotterdam at 6 in the evening.

'On Tuesday morning at 7 set off by the treck boat to Delft—breakfasted at the Stadt logement—saw the two churches [the Old Church (*Oude Kerk*) and the New Church] with the monuments of Van Tromp and the Prince of Orange—also medallion heads of Leuwenhoek and Grotius—ascended the steeple and had an extensive view.

'From there we proceeded to the Hague—saw the Picture Gallery—the House in the Wood [*'T Huis in 't Bosch*], etc. Our next visit was to Leyden, and [we] stopped during the Thursday and part of Friday at the Lion d'Or, nearly opposite the Stadt-house.

'I was very pleased with Leyden—quiet, clean, and reasonable. In the churches, monuments to Boerhaave, Camper, and Meerman. Old pictures in the Town Hall. The lecture-room in the University old, dark, and gloomy. The Theatre of Anatomy, circular and the seats rising one above the other to enable the students to witness the operations or dissections. In the Botanic Garden, a tree planted by Boerhaave, and another a century earlier, by Clusius. In a separate apartment birds let loose, etc. There is a collection of old marble and stone busts and statues, some of them mutilated and but indifferently restored. The University Library, extensive and valuable—the books not well arranged, but containing some early editions, and a large and valuable collection of MSS. The number of printed volumes is reckoned at 70,000 and 4000 manuscripts. They exhibit as a curiosity a set of books to the number of 133 volumes. Each volume is formed of the substance of different trees, shrubs, or flowers, and being ingeniously bound, so that each of the 133 volumes exhibits the various portions of the wood, bark, the fruit, leaves, etc., of so many different kinds.

'We left Leyden on Friday at ½ past 12, and in four hours got to Haerlem. Took a hasty look at the town, and I enquired after the book [the *Donatus*, alleged to have been] printed by Laurence Koster, at the Town House. The keeper told me that the king had it in his custody at present, but expected it would be shortly sent back. Having ordered Dinner, we sent and engaged the Organist to play on the very wonderful instrument so celebrated for its size and wonderful effects. We were so delighted with the performance that we forgot Dinner and our intention to hasten on that night to Amsterdam, until the Organist ceased. For his performance we paid him nine guilders [about 15s. stg.] which he was most careful in reckoning not to lose one doight, from our ignorance of the Dutch money.

'Left Haarlem at 7, and got to Amsterdam that night after a pleasant sail. Next day we visited the chief parts of the city, including the Stadt House, now the Palace—the rooms of a magnificent size and richly furnished. It was built upon stakes [*i.e.* piles] about the middle of the seventeenth century, and there is a large folio volume wholly occupied with its description. The Gallery of Paintings is very numerous and of great value, containing fine specimens by most eminent Dutch Painters. Went in the evening to the French Theatre. On Sunday in the forenoon went to the English Church, then walked through various parts of the town—harbour, docks, etc. In order to save a day, left Amsterdam on Sunday evening at 8 by the Utrecht boat, and arrived next morning at 5. Curious group of characters in the boat—and odd incident of my hat falling overboard, the boatman turning back and endeavouring to recover it. Utrecht a fine town and beautifully situated, an excellent Library belonging to the University—charming walks at this season without the walls.

'Wishing to make the most of our time, James W[ilson] and I resolved to have another night excursion, to regain our companions who had previously set out for Rotterdam. Started at 8 in the evening—saw somewhat of Dutch manners and customs. The boat stopped at Gouda between 5 and 6 in the morning, and thence we came by the *diligence* to Rotterdam by 9. Remained there Tuesday and Wednesday. But [what] of Messrs. B. & B. [Black and Brown]? Had they gone forward to Paris?—but their trunks, etc., were still here. At last they appeared, having, it seems, instead of getting into the Rotterdam boat, took one which carried them back to Leyden!

'Set off by the Antwerp *diligence* on Thursday morning at 5—crossed to Williamstadt—thence to Bergen-op-Zoom—the roads and ferries very unpleasant. Scarcely perceive any indication of the town until we enter the sloping ramparts, apparently cut into fanciful shapes and angles, covered with smooth verdant turf, yet forming an almost impregnable fortress, and to an experienced tactician exhibiting the perfection of military science. No one is allowed to approach too near the ramparts, but notwithstanding this prohibition, having taken the liberty of doing so, the guard turned out and came to take us prisoners. We explained as well as we could, we had trespassed somewhat unintentionally—we were allowed to walk away. From these ramparts the whole flat adjoining country can be swept, to prevent the approach of an enemy within reach of shot.

'Hired a post-chaise at ½ past 4, and reached Antwerp about 10 at night. At Antwerp admired the fine old houses and spacious streets. Very busy all day, making the tour of the churches, the harbour, fortifications, etc. From the top of *L'Eglise de Notre Dame*, ascending to the height of 420 feet by about 620 steps, we had a splendid view of the city and suburbs, with the river and adjacent country. The fine pictures which adorned the Cathedral and some other churches having been removed [1]—but in the Church of St. Jacques I saw Rubens' burial-place with the painting of himself and wives,[2] etc.

[1] By Bonaparte. This was the case with 'Paul Potter's Bull' at The Hague, and may explain Laing's silence regarding that famous picture, and the equally famous 'Descent from the Cross' by Rubens at Antwerp, both, however, restored.

[2] This is a picture by Rubens of the Holy Family, in which he introduces his two wives as Martha and Mary Magdalene, and himself as St. George.

The Church of the Dominicans, with its absurd representation of the Crucifixion, and of figures in purgatory,[1] etc. In the Church of St. Andrew with the Curles' monument,[2] and the small portrait of their unfortunate mistress, Mary Queen of Scots. Saw the Academy exhibition of modern paintings, but above all, in a separate room, those paintings which the French had carried off to Paris, but now restored to the city, although not yet replaced in the churches.

'We left Antwerp on Saturday morning at 6 by the *diligence* and reached Brussels at 11. Passed through Mechlin, apparently a populous and thriving town, and the country in a high state of cultivation. Brussels is indeed a charming place and very gay. The Town House is a remarkably fine building, with a gigantic figure of St. Michael on the top of the spire, or 350 feet, serving for a weathercock. The Park, the Place Royale, etc. Shortly after their arrival my companions resolved upon visiting the field of Waterloo. I declined going, being tempted by the sight of various old books in stalls, etc., and they set off in a chaise, and returned in the afternoon. Next day, Sunday morning, I deter-

---

[1] This is the 'Calvary,' which is visited by all tourists.
[2] Two English ladies of that name who are said to have served Mary Queen of Scots as ladies-in-waiting, one of them receiving her last embrace before the execution.

mined upon also going—but finding no conveyance, after enquiring the road, etc., I started at 7, walked on briskly through the Forest of Soignies, and reached Waterloo at 10—breakfasted, went into the chapel during the hour of service, hired a guide, and for nearly three hours walked about visiting the various localities. On returning to the village of Waterloo, after hesitating about taking some refreshments, I set out on my return from this Pilgrimage to the field, and after a wearisome journey, longing for some conveyance, with sore feet, I was back in time for dinner, to the surprise of every one. I reckoned that I could not have walked less than 28 to 30 miles.

'Remained in Brussels next day, along with Ja[s.] W.—A. B. and D. B. having as usual hurried on to reach Paris. Mr. W. and myself left Brussels by the *diligence* at 4 on Tuesday morning—passed through Hal to Mons and Valenciennes—stopped there for the night. Next morning at 6, by the *diligence* to Cambray, reached it at 10, and remained during the day. The British troops were encamped here. Left Cambray on the Thursday at 11, passed through Peronne, and did not dine till reaching a small place called Roye, at 9, travelled all night and arrived at Paris, about midday on Friday the 9th of August 1816.'

Laing's narrative breaks off abruptly at this point—the arrival of the quartette of young Scotsmen in Paris. But fortunately for us the *Memoirs of Adam Black*,[1] one of the party, come to the rescue, and enable us to follow the travellers to the conclusion of their journey. From this we quote:

'After about six weeks' absence Black and Laing left Paris together, leaving James Wilson at the Jardin des Plantes, where he spent most of his time. Black and Laing had spent theirs chiefly in bookshops and on the Quais, where they secured many valuable books in beautiful old bindings, remains of the noble libraries of princes and aristocrats, confiscated during the great Revolution. David Laing as usual carried away also a quantity of prints. Curiously enough he was the hero of the only adventure that befell them in Paris. "He never liked to hear me mention it," says Black, " but he had no reason to be ashamed of himself." One Sunday evening they had been walking together in the Champs Élysées, and came to the gates of the Tuileries just as they were being shut. Black got through, but Laing was locked in, and had to go round a little to get out. Black walked on to the hotel, and wondered what was keeping

---

[1] *Memoirs of Adam Black*, edited by Alexander Nicolson, LL.D. Edinburgh: Adam and Charles Black, 1885.

his friend. Presently, however, Laing returned, with a flushed face and a scratch on his cheek. The explanation was, that after the gates were closed, he heard the National Guardsmen jabbering to each other, and the word " boxy " repeated. He turned to look at them, when one of the valiant Gauls came up and gave him a whack on the side of the head, knocking off his hat. Fortunately David had learned at the High School how to use his fists, and he now did so. " We continued sparring," he said, " till some women came up and separated us—neither, I dare say, very loath." This practical illustration of the grand Scottish motto, " Nemo me impune lacesset," on the part of one of the most peaceable of men and greatest of Scottish archæologists is delightful.

' On their return home they had, as sometimes happens even to prudent Scotsmen, reserved just enough of money to pay their travelling expenses. At Margate Laing had to pay much more duty on his prints than he anticipated, and borrowed from Black, which left between them enough to pay for dinner, with one shilling over. The landlady took places for them on the coach, to be paid in London, which she said was often done, and they started in glee. At Canterbury they spent their last shilling on a cup of tea. About midnight they arrived at Rochester, where the coach proprietor, "a stout imperious John Bull," insisted that they must pay their fares before going any farther. In this emergency David Laing called to mind that he had some coins in his trunk, which he had collected in Paris, and he dug them out. With some grumbling they were taken for what they were worth, and the deficit that still had to be made up was kindly lent by a fellow-passenger.'

Thus ends the story of Laing's first Continental tour. The second was in 1819 to Holland, Denmark, and Sweden, returning by Kiel, Hamburg, and London, as briefly related in his own memoir. His companion was again James Wilson the naturalist, brother of 'Christopher North.' The passport, dated 25th August 1819, is issued by Kincaid Mackenzie, Lord Provost of Edinburgh, to 'David Laing, Esquire, residing at Lauriston, near this city.' A supplementary passport in Swedish, given at Gothenburg in Sweden, of date 28th September, covers his travelling to Trollhättan, Wenersborg, Jönköping, and Helsingborg in that country. This latter document contains a description of his personal appearance, not found in the British passports, viz.: Age 24 (*sic*), hair black, eyes blue, face (*ansigte*) oval, middle size.

The only other souvenirs remaining of this tour are two letters, on quarto sheets, addressed by Laing to his father from Copenhagen, dated 21st September and 11th October respectively. They are almost exclusively on business matters— the buying, selling, or exchanging books, all of a weighty type, classics, history, science, and religion. Literature of a lighter character does not enter into the cognisance of the grave young traveller of nearly a century ago. Reference is made to the depression of business, and the ruin to libraries and public and private buildings consequent upon the siege and bombardment of Copenhagen (by Nelson). The scenery of Sweden is extolled, and travelling is said to be more expeditious, agreeable, and less expensive there than in most other countries. He and his companion, however, ' found it advisable to buy a small carriage—and, as necessary, to have a guide, or rather an interpreter.' He seems to have had little difficulty in the matter of language in Continental towns, where, as now, English must have been pretty well understood, especially among the educated men with whom, naturally, he came mostly in contact. No mention is made of how the bought carriage was disposed of.

I have not scrupled to deal thus amply with these records of Laing's earlier life since the materials were available. His own accounts of his travels in foreign countries show us not only what he saw, but how he saw it—an index to his mental attitude to art, architecture, books, and history, the subjects to which the attention of his later life was mainly directed. He preferred to hawk about the old book-stalls of Brussels while his friends went off to Waterloo in a conveyance, and walked the next day, Sunday, twenty-eight or thirty miles, to and about the field, and back again, after having started at seven o'clock in the morning, without breakfast, circumstances characteristic of his passionate love of books, and of his persistency in getting to the bed-rock of fact and truth in every matter which he deemed worthy of serious attention. It is also noticeable in reference to Waterloo that, though it had little more than a year before been the scene of the great struggle which settled the destinies of Europe for the time, he moves over it assuredly with keen curiosity and interest but yet without any outburst of sentiment, the fact being that his literary and archæological tastes were more absorbing than even that episode which, tremendous as it was, was all too recent to enlist more than his passing concern.

It was in Holland, on the first of these tours, that Laing fell in with John Gibson Lockhart, Scott's biographer. Lockhart appears to have been so impressed with the personality and talents of Laing that he lost no time in giving expression to his feeling regarding him. In his poem, 'The Mad Banker of Amsterdam, or The Fate of the Brauns,'[1] printed in *Blackwood's Magazine* of July 1818, Laing figures as his companion at a dinner at the Dutchman's house:

> ' But to return—(in this new style of Frere's,
>   A phrase which oft hath been, and oft must be)—
> I dined, when last in Holland, at Mynheer's;
>   No one was there but David Laing and me,
> And a Dutch minister, one Vander Schpiers,
>   Domestic tutor in the family:
> To give Mevrouw the praise that is her due,
> The dinner much invited a set-to.
>
> ' In course of talk the Clergyman and Braun
>   Enlarged upon the charms of Dutch society,
> Its comfort—none that attribute disown—
>   And, what some won't agree to—its variety.
> David and I sucked all their doctrines down,
>   But over-doses generate satiety;
> So we, to pay them back in their own coin,
> Began in praise of Scotland to rejoin.
>
> ' A fruitful topic, it must be confest,
>   And in good hands, I mean in Laing's and mine,
> (David, the most sagacious and the best,
>   As all Old Reekie's erudites opine,
> Of Scottish Bibliopoles, who knows the zest
>   And cream of every title-page *Aldine*;
> A famous Bibliomaniac, and a shrewd,
> Who turns his madness to no little good).

---

[1] ' A Poem in four Cantos. By William Wastle, Esquire.'

'We touched on many topics, I and David;
   He chiefly sung the praise of a Sale dinner;
I on Young's tavern principally ravéd,
   Ore soluto—I'm a glorious spinner,
I painted to the set, in colours vivid,
   The portrait of full many a curious sinner
Who comes, with ready head and readier tongue,
To kill his evenings in thy house, Bill Young!'

Racy and amusing as this is, it was not all. Lockhart returned to the talented young bibliophile, and gave in *Peter's Letters to his Kinsfolk*, published in 1819, a word-picture of the Laings, *père et fils*, which no one dealing with their name can ignore, and which is therefore introduced here. The book was printed by J. Ballantyne & Co., Lockhart, the author, posing under the pseudonym of 'Dr. Peter Morris of Pensharpe Hall, Aberystwith.' The friend 'Wastle,' whose opinions and doings he professes to quote, is himself; and, in describing Creech, Constable, Ballantyne, and other Edinburgh booksellers of the day, he thus descants upon the Laings:

'As for shops of old books, classics, black-letter, foreign literature, and the like, I was never in any great town which possesses so few of them as this. It might indeed be guessed that her riches in this way would not be great, after the account I have given you of the state of scholarship among the *littérateurs* of the North. There is, however, one shop of this sort which might cut a very respectable figure, even in places where attainments of another kind are more in request; and I confess I have visited this shop more frequently, and with more pleasure, than any of its more fashionable neighbours in Edinburgh. It is situated, as it ought to be, in the immediate vicinity of the College, and consequently quite out of the way of all the fashionable promenades and lounges; but indeed, for anything I have seen, it is not much frequented, even by the young gentlemen of the University. The daily visitors of Mr. Laing (for that is the name of its proprietor) seem rather to be a few scattered individuals of various classes and professions, among whom, in spite of the prevailing spirit and customs of the place, some love of classical learning is still found to linger—retired clergymen and the like, who make no great noise in this world, and, indeed, are scarcely known to exist by the most part even of the literary people of Edinburgh. The shop, notwithstanding, is a remarkably neat and comfortable one, and even a lady might lounge in it without having her eye offended or her gown soiled. It consists of two apartments, which are both completely furnished with valuable editions of old authors; and I assure you, the antique vellum bindings or oak boards of these ponderous folios are a very refreshing sight to me after visiting the gaudy and brilliant stores of such a shop as that I have just described [Manners & Miller, High Street]. Mr. Laing himself is a quiet, sedate-looking old gentleman who, although he has contrived to make very rich in his business, has still the air of being somewhat dissatisfied that so much more attention should be paid by his fellow citizens to the flimsy novelties of the day than to the solid and substantial articles which his magazine displays. But his son is the chief enthusiast. Indeed he is by far the most genuine specimen of the true old-fashioned bibliopole that I ever saw exhibited in the person of a young man. My friend Wastle [that is, Lockhart himself] has a prodigious liking for him which originated, I believe, in their once meeting casually in Rotterdam, and travelling together over most part of Holland in the Treckschuyt—and indeed this circumstance has been expressly alluded to by Wastle in one of his poems [see the preceding extract]. Here Wastle commonly spends one or two hours every week he is in Edinburgh, turning over, in company with his young friend [then twenty-five or twenty-six years of age] all the Aldines, the Elzevirs, and Wynkin de Wordes and Caxtons in the collection; nor does he often leave the shop without being tempted to take some little specimen of its treasures home with him. I also, although my days of bibliomania are long since over, have been occasionally induced to transgress my self-denying rule, and have picked up various curious things at a pretty cheap rate, and one book in particular, of which I shall beg your acceptance when we meet—but at present I won't tell you what it is. David Laing is still a very young man; but Wastle tells me (and so far as I have had occasion to see, he is quite correct in doing so) that he possesses a truly wonderful degree of skill and knowledge in almost all departments of bibliography. Since Lunn's death, he says, he does not think there is any of the booksellers in London superior to him in his way; and he often advises him to transfer the shop and all the treasures thither. But I suppose Mr. Laing has very good reason not to be in a hurry in adopting any such advice. He publishes a Catalogue almost every year, and thus carries on a very extensive trade in all parts of the island. Besides, miserable as is the general condition of old learning in Scotland, there is still, I suppose, abundant occasion for one bookseller of this kind, and, I believe, he has no rival in the whole country. For my part, if I lived in Edinburgh,[1] I would go to his shop every now and then, were it only to be put in mind of the happy hours we used to spend together long ago at Mr. Parker's.

[1] He really lived for years in No. 25 Northumberland Street.

'This old gentleman and his son are distinguished by their classical taste in regard to other things besides books—and amongst the rest in regard to wines—a subject touching which it is fully more easy for them to excite the sympathy of the knowing ones of Edinburgh. They give an annual dinner to Wastle, and he carried me with him the other day to one of these anniversaries. I have seldom seen a more luxurious display. We had claret of the most exquisite Lafitte flavour, which foamed in the glass like the cream of strawberries, and went down as cool as the nectar of Olympus. David and Wastle entertained us with an infinite variety of stories about George Buchanan, the Admirable Crichtonius, and all the more forgotten heroes of the Deliciæ Poetarum Scotorum. What precise share of the pleasure might be due to the claret and what to the stories I shall not venture to inquire; but I have rarely spent an evening more pleasantly.

'*P.S.*—They are also very curious in sherry.'

This portraiture of Laing and his father wellnigh a hundred years ago is invaluable for us who desire to perpetuate their memory. In that rich emporium of literature we could imagine their feeling that their ' Books ' were ' their kingdom all,' though true it is, as indicated by Lockhart, that their possessions were not then limited to the stores of learning beside them, but extended to worldly substance of other kinds of no inconsiderable value. And the accuracy of the picture need not be doubted. Underneath the usually cynical style of Lockhart there is, in this case, unmistakable evidence that he has a high appreciation of the qualities of the two learned booksellers—especially of the younger—and a genuine esteem for them personally, an esteem which was fully shared by Scott, of whose sentiments Lockhart usually was a faithful re-echo.

Laing's first literary venture up to this time, so far as known, was his reprint, in 1815, of the *Auctarivm Bibliothecæ Edinbvrgenæ*, a list of the books presented to the University of Edinburgh by William Drummond of Hawthornden, a creditable and characteristic beginning at twenty-two years of age.

It is no wonder if, with the consciousness of his own bibliographic skill, and his reputation in connection therewith, he should by this time have thought of courting eminence in some literary line other than that of merely a dealer. A vacancy occurring in the Librarianship of the Advocates' Library in 1818, he, young as he was, (twenty-five) appeared as one of the candidates for the appointment, but without success, as he has told us in his own narrative, though supported by the powerful influence of Scott; and Dr. David Irving of Edinburgh was elected to the post. Laing's application is so characteristically modest as to deserve reproduction here:

'EDINBURGH, *June* 21, 1819.

'SIR,—I beg leave, respectfully, to present myself to your notice as a Candidate for the Office, which I understand is still vacant, of LIBRARIAN to the Honourable The FACULTY OF ADVOCATES.

'The general tenor of my pursuits, for several years past, encourages me to hope, I might be found not altogether unqualified for this situation. And I offer my services under a full conviction, that the duties of the office are both arduous and important, and such as to require an assiduous and undivided attention.

'I should therefore, were I so fortunate as to be honoured with this appointment, immediately and entirely relinquish my present profession of a Bookseller, so as to enable me to apply myself wholly and zealously to the objects which the Faculty must be supposed to have in view, in the nomination of a Librarian.

'I have the honour to be, very respectfully, Sir, Your faithful humble Servant,

'DAVID LAING.'

Laing's narrative of his early years, as we have seen, brings us to his thirtieth year in 1823; and we have been able, from other material, to supplement the information contained in it up to the present point, 1819, at which it may be permissible to take a brief retrospect.

His own pen has recorded such incidents of his childhood, youth, and early manhood as he thought worthy of note. His experiences at school and college he regarded as unsatisfactory; but whatever his deficiencies in English grammar, or in the Greek language, may have been, in his own sensitive estimate of the proper standard of attainment, there is yet abundant evidence throughout his career that he possessed the scholarly equipment sufficient for his requirements in dealing with history, languages, and literature, ancient and modern, the result of natural capacity and studious care.

Designs for a professional career not taking shape, his tastes quite naturally led to his falling into the routine of his father's business, which was steadily rising into repute and prominence. We have seen how he was sent at an early age on successful missions to London, to Dublin, and to the Continent, in connection with the business; while his reputation for literary taste and knowledge of books has brought him into the circle of the best men in the domain of letters at that time in Edinburgh, and beyond it. He was the genuine antiquary from the beginning, 'born, not made.' We find no trace of early dreams, fancies, frivolities. His boyhood glides into manhood with the love of books, art, and architecture, a veneration for the antiquities of his country, a passion for the preservation of its literary remains. The public knowledge and estimation of his powers began at a surprisingly early age. In a letter of date 6th June 1809 from A. G. Hunter of Blackness to his partner, Archibald Constable, he speaks comically of an expedition being fitted out 'against the English booksellers, from which the greatest hopes are entertained of success.' Among the officers to command, DAVID LAING (then sixteen years of age) is to be 'Deputy Adjutant General'! As will be afterwards seen, testimonies of a more serious kind to the precocity of his knowledge and judgment are not wanting.

But while thus grave and practical were the fundamentals of Laing's character and aims, as were the achievements of his later life, it is interesting to find traces of a lighter vein—some attempts at courting the Muses. Three little manuscript volumes contain mild efforts in the gentle art of poesy, at all events of versification, with specific dates ranging from 1818 to 1840.

Nor did the Drama escape a passing tribute; indeed he appears all along to have had a genuine interest in its reputation and history. In one of the small volumes is found, under date April 1826, ' An Inquiry into the origin of Dramatick Exhibitions in Scotland,' the draft of a communication which he read to the Society of Antiquaries in the following year; and in 1853 he produced, for the Shakespeare Society of London, a reprint of the rare old tract, *A Defence of Poetry, Music, and Stage Plays*, by Thomas Lodge of Lincoln's Inn. He even made an attempt at dramatic composition, entitled *The Scottish Protomartyr*, the scene being at St. Andrews, March 1527-28, and the *personæ* Friar Myll, David Lindesay, and John Wynram, servitor. Its merit for histrionic purposes may be small, but it shows his taste for the Drama, and his judgment of the first tragedy of the Reformation struggle.

The poetical pieces include the following, some of them marked as having been written before twenty-one years of age:

>   Mary Queen of Scots.
>   St. Andrews.
>   A Summer Storm.
>   Jesus Stilleth the Waves of Galilee.
>   The Vision of St. John in Patmos.
>   Copenhagen—The Round Tower (1819).

Psalm 121.
Hymn for the Day of Humiliation.
On Death (1822).
A Dirge. 'The Beauty of Israel is fallen' (November 1817). (On the death of the Princess Charlotte of Wales).
A Darien Song.
On hearing the Forenoon Service in the Church of Skara in Sweden, Sunday, 3 October 1819.
Winter. Ode.
On visiting the English burying-ground at Leghorn (Livorno), Sunday morning, 6 September 1840.
The Return of the Traveller.
James Renwick—to those who are Sufferers for the Faith.
The Exile's Lament.
On the Poems of Dunbar, the Scottish Makkar.
A Bannatyne Song for the Anniversary Meeting, 1825. *To be sung to its own proper accompaniment.*
Ah! Marian dear.
Blow yee Gentle Breezes.
Ah! Fickle Love.
On the Death of his Brother, Sunday, 1 November 1846.

Of these pieces several are in blank verse, not always formally regular, while others are in different metrical styles. They are interesting as illustrations of his state of mind and feeling at the time of writing, but it has been thought that their merits do not justify reproduction here. One in particular, addressed to 'Marian dear,' might be interpreted as possibly a tribute of tender regard; but if it be the case that the attractions of this 'Marian' inspired the lay, she cannot be identified now, and their attachment cannot have gone beyond the Platonic stage. It is conceivable that Marian herself might have been responsible for this, if the piece, 'Ah, Fickle Love,' may also apply to her. But, however this may have been, he remained a bachelor, wedded to his books and antiquities to the end of his days. At a much later date, in 1857, when he was sixty-four years of age, he wrote appreciatingly to his sister Jessie of some ladies in whose company he had been, to which she replied, 'I would rather hear of one lady being attractive than all, *i.e.* if mutual.' But the result remained the same. He was, in short, one of the men who had found his true vocation, as the lover and historian of Scottish literature and antiquities, and he was able to exercise his powers to the full in the sphere for which they were so well adapted.

One of the poems, 'On hearing the Forenoon Service in the Church of Skara in Sweden,' in 1819, gives evidence, as do others, of his devout frame of mind; and it also indicates a Catholicity of sentiment greatly at variance with the narrowness prevalent in Church circles in Scotland at the time. In the same way, when he is travelling in Catholic countries we look in vain for disdainful reprobation of the religious forms and sentiments which he found in existence around him.

There is nothing in the literary material left to us to indicate anything of a convivial tendency on Laing's part, though one brief note in regard to the ' Spelunca,' seemingly a social club or fraternity of some kind, would imply that he was a member. It is as follows :

' 1 December 1819.

' At the session of the Spelunca held this day it was resolved that the time of meeting should be changed during the Winter, and that for the next six weeks Dinner shall be on the table at a quarter past Four o'clock exactly.'

No such club as the Spelunca appears in the Sketch of Clubs given by Mr. Harry A. Cockburn in the *Book of the Old Edinburgh Club*, vol. iii. (1910), or in any other list known to me. It was probably small, and restricted in membership to men interested in books, or in objects of kindred character. But at the anniversary dinners of the Bannatyne Club there is every likelihood that he thoroughly entered into its festivities, along with the distinguished men around him. Scott presided from 1823 to 1831, and composed the song for the first dinner, which was sung by James Ballantyne; while, as we have seen, Laing has left us the draft of one for the meeting of 1825. It is patched and mended, and does not lend itself to transcription, but of the five stanzas one, addressed to the once ' Great Unknown,' may be quoted :

> 'Hail! chief of the Minstrel race,
> Our lakes and hills thou hast made dear;
> Hail! much loved Scott! and, in this place,
> May we assemble many a year.
> What stream or river flows along
> Thy noble Tweed but hath its song;
> Or silver trout, in Tay or Yarrow,
> And tales of love, or joy or sorrow?'

Whatever attractions literary society may have had, nothing could tempt him away from his own work and studies to enter the arena of politics, municipal or parliamentary, or to be moved by the ecclesiastical dissensions which agitated life in Scotland in his day. He all along stands entirely aloof, absorbed in worthy and enduring labours, which have enriched the historical literature of his country to an extent which is almost inconceivable.

About this time he arranged and catalogued the library of the Earl of Minto, the cost of which, £150, was paid by his lordship in 1839, ten or twelve years having then elapsed since the work

PERSONAL HISTORY

was done, he having delayed to ask for settlement all that time.

Laing continued to act as assistant to his father until 1821, when he was admitted to partnership. The firm then became W. AND D. LAING, and there can be little doubt that in its ordinary work, and especially in its publications, he became the moving spirit. True it is that, in his personal memoir, he gives no hint, up to its close in 1823, of his early adventures in literature, but prior to that date he had already earned distinction by a series of publications of quite a remarkable kind, viz. :

- 1815. *Auctarium Bibliothecæ Edinburgenæ.* (Reprint of the rare original of 1627.) Already referred to.
- 1821. *Poems by Alexander Scott.* (Print of a MS. of the year 1568.)
- 1821. *Epithalamium* (of Sir Thomas Craig) *on the Marriage of Queen Mary and Lord Darnley.* (Reprint of the rare original of 1565.)
- 1821. *Poems of Alexander Montgomery, 1597-1631.* (Reprint.)
- 1822. *Select Remains of the Ancient Popular Poetry of Scotland.*
- 1822. *A Pleasant History of Roswall and Lillian.* (Reprint of the original of 1663.)

1822. *Sir David Lyndsay's Heraldry.* (Facsimile of the original of 1542.)

This is assuredly a remarkable record for a man still in comparative youth.

1823-66

In 1823 the BANNATYNE CLUB for printing works illustrative of the history, antiquities, and literature of Scotland, was instituted by Sir Walter Scott and the prominent men whom he drew around him; and at Sir Walter's special request Laing was induced to accept the onerous post of secretary. That post involved him in the most prolonged and arduous labours of his life, in instigating, guiding, and supervising the great number of important publications—several of them edited by himself—which were issued under its auspices during the whole term of the existence of the club, up to its dissolution in 1860, when he received a handsome testimonial in recognition of his services.

In 1824 he was admitted a Fellow of the Society of Antiquaries of Scotland, under circumstances which have already been described. He soon became an indispensable member and officebearer; and from that time till almost the end of his life scarcely a year passed without valuable services, and important contributions, in the shape of historical papers or donations of interest, being received from him.

In resuming Laing's personal history, we must understand that little material exists to illuminate the last half-century or more of his private life. There is little more than the accounts of some of his travels at home and abroad, and the monumental record of his works, and it is mainly from these that we must form, as best we may, our estimate of his temperament and genius, and of his inner life.

Previous to his election to the Society of Antiquaries in 1824 he had, in 1821, made his first donation to its library, viz., *Poems by Alexander Scott*, from a manuscript written in MDLXVIII, 8vo, edited by him in 1821. Immediately after his admission he recommended a publication of the *Numismata Scotiæ* by the Society, and he was appointed to act from time to time on committees charged with administering various affairs of the Society. After contributing important historical papers, and doing valuable services in other ways, he became treasurer in 1836, and continued an officebearer, in other capacities, to the end of his life, besides being the most extensive and most variedly suggestive exponent of national history, art, and antiquities ever connected with the Society.

Equally important was his connection with the Bannatyne Club, to which, in 1823, the year of its institution, he presented a reprint, in black letter, of the curious old Scottish brochure, *The Buke of the Howlat,* with an elaborate 'Introduction,' the first of his literary labours on behalf of the Club. But this is all referred to merely in passing to illustrate the commencement of his career in the byways of Scottish literature. The details of his life-work are narrated in a subsequent chapter.

In 1826 he issued his volume of *Early Metrical Tales,* and the *Album of the Bannatyne Club.* In 1827 came *The Knightly Tale of Golagrus and Gawane and other Ancient Poems,* and the *Miscellany* No. 1. of the Bannatyne Club, with a succession of curious reprints, and learned communications to the Society of Antiquaries during the years 1828 to 1832. In 1825 George Chalmers, author of *Caledonia,* came to Scotland, visiting Archibald Constable at Polton House, and Laing was recommended to act as his friendly guide. In 1825 and 1827 he was engaged in connection with transferring the books of the University Library from their old quarters to the present building, his labours at which were highly prized by the Senatus; and in the latter year he was elected an Honorary Member of the Society of Antiquaries of Newcastle-on-Tyne.

In 1832 his father died, leaving him head of the family, and in sole command of the bookselling and publishing business. In 1834 the ABBOTSFORD CLUB was founded, largely as a tribute to the memory of Scott, and that too claimed Laing's assistance, which was accorded at a later date. Meanwhile, in the years 1833-37, a number of important publications, mostly reprints of early Scottish pieces, came from his hand.

In 1837, on 21st June, Laing received the appointment of LIBRARIAN to the Society of Writers to the Signet, which, though altering his position, gave only greater scope for the exercise of his tastes and talents. His election was moved by Sir James Gibson Craig, Bart., seconded by James Tytler of Woodhouselee.

In support of his application he submitted twenty-two testimonials from 'gentlemen distinguished in the Literary World, and officially connected with other Public Libraries.' A few excerpts from these testimonials may not inappropriately be introduced here (printed by Laing, Edinburgh, April 1837).

Sir William Hamilton, Professor of Logic in the University, thought any evidence from him superfluous, as Laing's character and acquirements must have been already sufficiently known to most of the members of the Society, but he goes on to say :

> 'In reference to his acquaintance with the money value and comparative rarity of books in general, I presume that in this country he is unequalled. But his Bibliographical skill is not merely professional. He has made a liberal study of some departments of Literature, and in a general knowledge of Scottish authors and their works, if Dr. Lee be excepted, he is, I am convinced, if equalled by any, excelled by none. In regard to his character and disposition I need say nothing : the one is known to be honourable, the other to be obliging,' etc.

Rev. John Jamieson, D.D., author of the *Etymological Dictionary of the Scottish Language* :

> 'You have been bred from your infancy in the midst of books. You have shown that you, as it were, instinctively viewed the *papyrus* as your natural aliment. Your personal acquaintance, by no means limited, with men of letters, many of the first character, not in Britain only, but on the Con-

tinent, must have greatly increased your literary information. Your attention and deep research have been well known to me, from your having been, from its very formation, Secretary to the BANNATYNE CLUB, of which I have the honour of being a member; as well as from being a zealous *Fellow* of our Society of Scottish Antiquaries. The public has been much indebted to you for the proofs you have given of your unwearied diligence in various publications connected with our National literature, and meant to preserve our classical remains;—for the production of which few of your compeers were qualified. These you have in a great measure rescued from oblivion.'

Rev. JOHN LEE, D.D., afterwards Principal of the University of Edinburgh:

'I can safely say, with the utmost confidence, after a very intimate acquaintance of nearly twenty years, that I have never known any one who, in my opinion, was in every respect more amply qualified than you for the charge of a large public Library, and who would be more steadily and enthusiastically devoted to the discharge of all the duties of such an office. Indeed, I think your fitness quite pre-eminent.'

ROBERT SOUTHEY, LL.D., Keswick :

'It would be impossible to find any person better qualified, and very few indeed are those who can possibly be qualified so well.'

Southey gives the same assurance from Wordsworth, the poet, who was then on the Continent.

SAMUEL HIBBERT WARE, M.D., York, author of *A Description of the Shetland Islands.*

'I consider that your pretentions to the office which you seek are of no common kind. To these qualifications I speak from a long and intimate acquaintance with them. . . . I remember but too well how agreeably surprised I was to find an individual so familiar . . . with the valuable manuscripts of your Country which still subsist, and with the history of your National press from its very dawn or rudest state. Nor was I less gratified with the simple and unostentatious liberality with which your knowledge was communicated. . . . Your extensive and correct Bibliographical information has been acknowledged by Authors whose past labours are deservedly recorded in the brightest pages of the literary history of Scotland ; and in making this assertion, I need only refer to the friendly intercourse which you have so long maintained with illustrious *savants*, such as Mr. George Chalmers, Dr. Jamieson, and Sir Walter Scott.'

T. F. DIBDIN, D.D., author of the *Bibliographical Decameron*, etc. :

'I have been acquainted with Mr. David Laing since his boyhood; and have witnessed, with peculiar gratification, his enthusiasm and zeal for books and general literature in youth, confirmed and regulated by the discretion and judgment of his riper years. But favourable as my opinion of his Bibliographical attainments might have been, living at the distance of our respective residences, I have had recent occasion, during my visit at Edinburgh, to have it abundantly confirmed and enlarged; and I should affirm, with the most thorough conviction of the truth, that it would be difficult, throughout Scotland, to select a fitter candidate, in all respects, for the situation in view. His talents, also, as an editor of antiquarian relics, entitle him to very respectful consideration.'

SIR HENRY ELLIS, K.H., Principal Librarian of the British Museum :

'I cannot have the slightest hesitation in stating my belief that your well-known literary attainments, your having so long held the office of Secretary to the Bannatyne Club, and your long experience in collecting and selling books, are as full proofs as can be required for your fitness to fill the office,' etc.

JOHN GIBSON LOCKHART, son-in-law of Sir Walter Scott, and author of the celebrated *Life*:

'I should have supposed it impossible that there could be, in any quarter where you are so well known, any doubt as to your being in all respects suited by taste, habits, and acquirements, to do the highest honour to your patrons in any position of this class which you might deem worthy of your acceptance.'

SIR FREDERIC MADDEN, K.H., Assistant Keeper of the MSS. in the British Museum, editor of *Havelock the Dane*, etc.:

'I can only say, and with truth, that from my personal acquaintance with you, and my knowledge of your zeal to preserve and illustrate the remains of early Scottish Literature, as well as from the literary reputation you have justly earned by various publications, I have no hesitation in thinking you peculiarly qualified for such an appointment.'

PATRICK FRASER TYTLER, Advocate, author of the *History of Scotland*:

'An acquaintance of more than twenty years enables me to speak in the highest terms of your qualifications for the office. Your ardent love of literature, your bibliographical knowledge, and your long experience in all the minuter details connected with the purchase, arrangement, and classification of Libraries must be so well known . . . that I am sure you need not fear any competition upon the fair ground of merit. In addition to these qualities . . . you are ever ready to communicate your stores of information, and to assist men of letters in their studies and researches.'

Other testimonials received were from:
THE RIGHT HON. WILLIAM ADAM, Lord Chief Commissioner of the Jury Court.
ALEXANDER BRUNTON, D.D., Professor of Oriental Languages.
SENATUS ACADEMICUS OF THE UNIVERSITY.
DAVID IRVING, LL.D., Keeper of the Advocates' Library.
THOMAS MAITLAND, Advocate (afterwards Lord Dundrennan).
MACVEY NAPIER, Professor of Conveyancing.
JOHN RIDDELL, Advocate.

Reverend PHILIP BLISS, D.C.L., Registrar of the University of Oxford.

JAMES CHALMERS, London, nephew of the author of *Caledonia*.

ALLAN CUNNINGHAM, London, author of *Lives of British Painters*, etc.

JOHN MILLER, K.C., Lincoln's Inn, London.

In this important appointment he was now equipped with the opportunities, as with the means, of finding, and securing for the W.S. Library or for himself, rare and valuable books; and, at the same time, for undertaking and accomplishing the literary and historical projects, for the benefit of students and scholars, to which the remainder of his life was dedicated.

In 1838 Laing again visited France and other countries, armed with a passport from the French Embassy in London, of date 2nd August, in which he is described, with a perversity common to some foreigners, as 'Natif d'Angleterre,' with the usual personal description—forty-five years of age, height five feet eight inches, etc., etc. It is *visé* at Paris, Geneva, Berne, Basle, Strasbourg, etc. An account of the tour, in his own handwriting, is preserved, but considerations of space forbid its being treated otherwise than by way of brief outline.

Leaving Leith on 28th July by the *Royal Adelaide*, he reached London on the 30th, lodged in 12 Cecil Street, Strand, remaining for a week, in the course of which he dined with Dr. Kerrison at Hampstead, Alexander Dyer in Gray's Inn, and with the Woodburns at Richmond, and visited 'repeatedly' the National Gallery, the British Institution (Old Masters), etc. At the British Museum he was introduced to Mr. Panizzi (afterwards Sir Antony Panizzi, the famous librarian), whom he found exceedingly agreeable. He met young Kemble and another, who inquired about the Poems of William of Shoreham. By Evening Mail [coach] to Brighton, arriving there next morning. The Pavilion [erected by George IV.] a most fantastic-looking building with its towers—crowds of gay people to view a Regatta. Disagreeable passage to Dieppe, where he put up at Durand's *Hôtel aux Armes de France*. On Sunday he heard High Mass in the great church of St. Jacques, 'crowded chiefly with females.' Shops all open, but little appearance of business; quantity of engravings, caricatures and devotional prints. He here thought of John Knox and the letters he addressed 'To his afflicted brethren' from this place in 1554. With an English gentleman he went to the Castle of Arques. Dinner at 5—looked in at the conclusion of service in another church—the town now much frequented by Parisians in the summer months. The next move was to Rouen, staying at the *Hôtel d'Albion* (Smith's). The town, the cathedral, and the great churches, the Museum of Antiquities, the Town Library and the Gallery of Pictures, the monument to Joan of Arc, etc., etc., described. Then by steamer on the Seine, but had to disembark at the narrow windings and proceed by the 'railway coaches' to Paris. In the *Grand Hôtel de Tours* (Place de la Bourse), he encountered Mr. P. from Edinburgh. All the sights were of course seen—the Tuileries, the Louvre, its art criticised, the Venus of Milo, its finest statue, 'although the eye does not easily accommodate itself to a female statue of heroic size,' the Bibliothèque du Roi [now, of course, the 'Bibliothèque Nationale'], where he was introduced to the several librarians—marvellous collection of MSS., etc., etc. Attended service in Notre Dame, Jardin des Plantes visited—Père Lachaise, greatly peopled in last 20 years—at the Opéra Comique—M. Francisque Michel one of his Parisian friends, etc. On 23rd August he left by *diligence* at 8 o'clock in the morning, for Switzerland and the Rhine. Dijon, Poligny, Champagne halted at, and briefly described. One Sunday morning about four o'clock he left the *diligence* and walked up a steep ascent, where he was surprised, at so early an hour as five o'clock, to

PERSONAL HISTORY

hear a church bell summoning the people of the scattered villages of these mountainous districts to devotion.

Here the story ends, but we know from the passports, as duly *viséd* (*gesehn*, seen, in Germany) that the tour extended to Geneva, through Switzerland, and back by the Rhenish provinces; and from a letter of the Rev. William Steven, minister of the Scots Church, Rotterdam, we learn that he was also in that city in the early part of the month of September.

This year, 1838, and 1843, are noteworthy as the only years of Laing's long literary career during which no work of consequence is recorded as having been issued by him. Can it be supposed that the convulsions in Edinburgh about the termination of the ' Ten Years' Conflict ' in the ' Disruption ' of the latter year had any influence in *quieting* his activities? Even if it were so, we may be assured that his private labours were but little affected during that stormy period. He maintained his connection with the Church of Scotland to the end; but his brother Gilbert seceded in the Disruption time.

Little is known of Laing's life and movements during the next few years beyond the materials of his literary activity steadily issuing from the press, and contributed to scientific societies, from time to time, and his again making a tour on the Continent in 1840, this time to Italy. Portions of this tour, particularly his stay in Florence and Venice, and the return journey through Germany, are elaborately described in a narrative by himself which is preserved. The stay in Florence occupies twenty-two pages, while to Venice and the return journey no less than fifty pages are devoted, with descriptions of churches, convents, architecture, libraries, picture galleries, and natural scenery. Seeing that all this was carefully committed to paper by his own hand, I naturally hesitate to dismiss it summarily without partial reproduction, or explanation regarding it. But the whole is only in *pencil*, difficult to read at best, and not improved in that respect by the lapse of seventy-two years since it was put together. I regret that for this reason, and for consideration of space, I must pass it with a scant notice.

There is no record of his proceedings at Rome, which is specially regrettable. But there is no doubt of his having been there, because there is now before me the passport (in French) issued by the British Consular Agent at Rome, of date 18th September 1840, to Laing, described as 'Sujet Anglais allant à Florence (seul)'—age forty-six, middle height, nose small, mouth middling (*moyenne*), etc. It is *viséd* at Florence, Bologna, Venice, Verona, Munich, Augsburg, Coblentz, and Brussels. While nothing is told of Rome, and much of detail about Venice, there is found on separate slips a generalisation of the character of these two cities, which may be transcribed :

Of Rome—' It has been remarked, with some truth, that modern Rome, with its churches, priests, and vulgar streets, prevents one from ever realising the idea of the ancient capital of the world. . . . I cannot say I was disappointed—it is perhaps on the whole the most remarkable city in the world,' etc., etc. (illegible).

Of Venice—' In the great square, with St. Mark's at the other extremity, I stood some time fixed to the spot with admiration. I don't recollect any view that seemed to me more striking—the long and regular ranges of piazzas on either side, the Doge's Palace, the Campanile, and, above all, the oriental character of St. Mark's. The interior of the latter is not less imposing, not imposing by its dimensions or symmetry, but by its peculiar uniqueness of style and decoration. The town has much the appearance of decay, yet I understand that a slow but gradual improvement in its trade is taking place since the time it was made a free port, and if the proposed railway to the town is completed, it may produce a still more decided improvement. It does not appear to me just to charge the people with laziness—on the contrary, there was as much activity and enterprise as is usually found in a city of this kind, not starting into greatness with the spirit of youthful maturity, but one which had ceased to retain its greatness.'

Laing withdrew in 1843 from membership of the Abbotsford Club on account of his many engagements otherwise, but principally because 'it was resolved to abstain from printing Old Poetry and Romances,' which he thought was its proper object. This same year Thomas Carlyle, who at this early time valued Laing's acquaintance, was in Edinburgh and called upon him, as he informs his wife in a letter from Haddington of 4th September, when he was going to survey the battlefield of Dunbar:

> 'Before quitting Edinburgh I had gone to David Laing's and refreshed my recollection by looking at his books, one of which he even lent me out hither.'

This friendly acquaintance was continued to the end.

In 1845 Laing took a tour to Orkney, Shetland, and the north of Scotland. We only know this from a letter of Dr. Hibbert Ware, of 21st

December 1845, congratulating him on his *iter septentrionale* to those regions.

In this same year the family residence of Ramsay Lodge, which had been occupied by them for forty years, was disposed of to the city as a site for the Sheep and Cattle Market, for the sum of £1925. The ground is now the site of the Edinburgh Fire Brigade Station. The city at the same time acquired the adjoining property of Willow Grove, entering from Lady Lawson's Wynd (now ' Street '), the total price for the two being £3000. The latter property is now the site and grounds of the Edinburgh College of Art. The Ramsay Lodge property, having its principal entrance from Lauriston Place, consisted of the dwelling-house, with coach-house and stable, and garden and parks extending to about two acres. A feu-duty of £3, 5s. 4d. was payable to the Corporation of Shoemakers of Portsburgh (a separate burgh now swallowed up in the city), and £13, 4s. 10d. to another superior. The eldest brother, James, then in Ceylon, was the seller.

Laing now removed to the house No. 12 James Street, Portobello, which he purchased from Elizabeth Sievwright of Southhouse, and in which he remained to the end of his life. It was a comfortable house of moderate dimensions, with some considerable garden ground; but, crowded with books, pictures, and objects of antiquity and *virtu*, it in the course of time became inadequate for the requirements, and a lofty and handsome library building was added at one end, as shown in the accompanying view.

The new library was scarcely finished at the time of his death, and his stores of rare and valuable books had not been arranged in the new quarters when the time came for the whole to be disposed of. When Ramsay Lodge was left, the inventory of furniture and other effects within it amounted to £405, 1s., showing a considerable increase in the estimated value of the silver plate compared with the figures in his father's inventory of 1832.

Laing's reputation as an authority in literature and antiquities had now extended beyond the limits of his own country, and in 1847 he was elected a member of *Det Kongelige Oldskrift Selskab* (the Royal Society of Northern Antiquaries) of Copenhagen. The diploma, bearing the signature of Frederick, then Crown Prince, is dated 13th November.

In 1848 Dr. Irving retired from the keepership of the Advocates' Library, and Laing, after having been for several years in charge of the Signet Library, again submitted an application for the appointment. The somewhat delicate circumstances under which he did so are explained in the opening paragraph of his letter of application as follows :

'SIGNET LIBRARY, *27th December* 1848.

' SIR,—At the suggestion of several members of the Honourable the FACULTY OF ADVOCATES I beg respectfully to offer myself as a Candidate for the Office of Keeper of your Library. If I hesitated in doing so immediately upon the announcement of DR. IRVING'S proposed retirement from this responsible and distinguished situation, it proceeded from a feeling of delicacy in regard both to my learned friend and to the SOCIETY OF WRITERS TO H.M. SIGNET. The courtesy I have experienced from the Curators of the Signet Library, and from the Members of the Society generally, during the eleven years in which I have acted as their PRINCIPAL LIBRARIAN would render it very unbecoming in me to appear solicitous to relinquish the Office for any similar appointment ; and my chief inducement in desiring the change is the hope of finding it to be a sphere of greater usefulness,' etc., etc.

The testimonials put forward were simply those which accompanied the application to the Curators of the Signet Library in 1837, with two additions—from Thomas Thomson, Advocate, and William Tennant, LL.D., Professor of Oriental Languages in the University of St. Andrews. The appointment was, however, given to another very remarkable man, Mr. Samuel Halkett.

Along with Laing's official duties as the head of the Signet Library, his historical researches and literary labours continued without intermission during the years which followed, leaving little record of his private life. We find, however, traces which enable us to follow him in a variety of journeys at home and abroad. In 1852 he was in London and Oxford; in 1854 in Germany, Denmark, Sweden, and Norway; in September 1856, after attending the meetings of the British Association at Cheltenham, he revisited Holland, and in 1860 was again in Belgium and France.

Of these travels the information we have is derived from the passports he carried, and from fragmentary notes, of which those relating to his visit to Holland are the fullest. From these the following particulars may be given:

In 1852 he set off on Good Friday, 9th April, by the mail train (now no more journeyings by mail coach or by packets from Leith), *via* Berwick to Derby, thence to Leamington,

Warwick, and on to London; there, of course, he frequented the British Museum, also going to the new Houses of Parliament, and noting the Bills which were under consideration by both Houses. On his way to London characteristic incidents occurred, which I quote in his own words :

> 'Strange to say, twice left behind by the train—once by sitting still when the carriages were changed, the other not observing that they were starting—but got my luggage at Euston Station and proceeded to Paddington Station, and on to Britwell,[1] in time for dinner.'

From London he went to Oxford, where he met some of the Professors, and the return journey to Edinburgh was made by Carlisle. There is nothing to show that he was induced to go to London in 1851 to see the first great 'International Exhibition' to which all the world repaired.

In 1854 a passport by Duncan M'Laren, Lord Provost of Edinburgh, dated 9th August, was issued to 'David Laing, Esquire, Keeper of the Signet Library, Edinburgh,' empowering him to

[1] Britwell House, Buckinghamshire, the seat of William Henry Miller of Craigentinny, Edinburgh, where there was a great library, a catalogue of which Laing printed.

pass, without molestation, to 'Hamburgh,' to travel on the Continent of Europe, and to return to Great Britain. This passport is marked as valid (*gültig*) at Vienna, Prague, Dresden, and Lübeck; and also at Rotterdam; at Copenhagen for Norway and Sweden, and at Christiania for Kiel and Hamburg. Of this extensive journey the passport is the only witness left, and we are therefore deprived of what would have been an extremely interesting account of his views of life and art in those countries at the time.

The year 1856 possesses a more ample record. Here we have a brief narrative of a visit to Cheltenham and other places in England, and of his visit again to Holland.

The ostensible object of the run to England (in the month of August) was to attend the meetings of the British Association at Cheltenham, but his notes contain no reference to its proceedings. On the day of his arrival he proceeded to Gloucester, where he attended morning and afternoon service in the Cathedral; and, returning to Cheltenham, he attended evening service in St. Mary's Church. On Tuesday following he went by coach to Great Malvern, where he 'walked over the Malvern Hills, enjoying the prospects,' returning next day to Cheltenham by Worcester, where he revisited the Cathedral, joining an excursion train to Chepstow, Tintern Abbey, etc.

He also went to Hereford to see the Cathedral, where he heard service. On the return journey to Scotland, he was again at Oxford, where he spent two days; and, passing on to Harrogate, he went to Ilkley, to Ripon, Studley Park, and Fountains Abbey, where we can follow him in his profound appreciation of the surpassing interest of those places.

The visit to Holland in the following month, September, is vouched by a brief description in his own handwriting, as already indicated. It is as follows:

'Sep$^{tr.}$ 1856. After an interval of many years, having at length revisited Holland, I find my old recollections renewed, and former impressions strengthened, as I proceed nearly in the same track as when, not less than *forty years ago!* I first landed on the Continent. Having at the time kept a kind of journal, I have extracted very briefly some notes, chiefly of dates and names of places visited, before destroying the said journal.

'On Saturday the 11th Sep$^{tr.}$ went on board the *Balmoral* steamer at Leith, Capt. Greig, for Rotterdam, with the view of spending a fortnight in Holland. Sailed at 2 in the afternoon, weather favourable—passed Scarborough next morning before breakfast. Reached Helvoet [sluys] about noon on Monday, but had to pass through the Canal and landed about 7 in the evening [at Rotterdam]. Went to the New Bath Hotel, so much spoken of—but quite full—put up at the York Hotel—not a first-class house, but very civil and moderate. It was too dark to think of going out. Next day, visited the Gallery of Paintings, and all parts of the town, harbour, etc. Wednesday the 17th took the Railway to the Hague. Went to the *Belle Vue*, a large, fashionable, and well conducted Hotel. The old landlord or proprietor regularly took his place as the Maître of the Table d'Hôte, enjoying his dinner and bottle of wine, without opening his mouth to any one. He had some recollection of the party who attended the Meerman sale in 1824. His son, the active landlord, a nice, civil, gentlemanly fellow. The house is rebuilt and much enlarged [since his former visit], and merits its present reputation. First visited the Gallery of Paintings, then to the Royal Library. Thursday chiefly in the Library, and examined its rarities, MSS. and general arrangement, through the kindness of the Assistant Librarian, Mr. Campbell. In the evening to the French Opera. Friday was chiefly spent in searching for old books in the warerooms of M. Nishoff & Jacob. The day very wet, but walked to Scheveningen [three miles distant] before dinner. Had the day been fine I should have bathed in the sea, but the cold wind and roughness of the water made it prudent to give up such a notion. Saturday I meant to have set off towards Leyden, but delayed in consequence of making an application to [see] the collection in the house left to the town by my old friend the Baron Westreeran de Fiellandt. Although against the rules of admission (the house being only visible two days in the month) Mr. Campbell went, and he spent two hours in looking over the really extensive and valuable collection of early printed books and MSS. The strange old man who had been collecting all sorts of things for upwards of 50 years, allowed no one to see his books, and he was scarcely credited when he talked of possessing such and such early editions. He was a near relation and one of the legatees of Meerman, and made many important acquisitions at the sale—but one or two precious MSS. were found after his death which had been bought by Meerman, but did not cast up during the sale, nor were in the Catalogue. Whether they had been a gift to the Baron, or had been lent or deposited in his hands, no one knows. One volume, a Latin Bible, executed with miniature of Charles the Fifth of France (bought at the . . . sale) is in the most beautiful and perfect style of illumination, with the artist's name and date. Another is a volume of

Augustin's *Cité de Dieu*, the other volume, it appears, being preserved in France.'

In addition to the above there is scratched upon the back of an old quarto letter an account, apparently of proceedings at Leyden, from which he went to Amsterdam, but it is not decipherable. He was also at Utrecht, because he informed Sir Frederic Madden, of the British Museum, in a letter dated 27th November 1856, that he had then discovered in the University Library at Utrecht a Cottonian MS. which at that time had been missing for one hundred and sixty years.

When the annual meeting of the Archæological Institute of Great Britain and Ireland was held in Edinburgh in 1856, it was thought desirable to have an Exhibition of Scottish Historical Relics at the same time; and in this, as might be supposed, Laing had a principal hand. He exhibited portraits of value, as was shown in the catalogue, to which he contributed ' Notices of the Civic Insignia of Edinburgh, 1616-1632.'

In November 1857 he was elected an Honorary Member of the Glasgow Archæological Society.

The next year, 1858, he once more crossed the North Sea. In the draft of a letter of 7th August he spoke of being 'just on the eve of setting out for Denmark,' and likely to be a few weeks from home. On 4th October he reported his having returned 'from the North of Europe a few weeks since,' a trip of which the only other record is a letter of his from Christiansand in Norway, dated 16th September, in which reference is made to his also having been at Stockholm and Upsala in Sweden.

In 1860 he again found his way to the Continent, of which the only evidence is a passport, signed by Lord John Russell, dated 16th August, to 'David Laing, British subject, going to Antwerp,' countersigned also for France, for one year, at the French Consulate General in London, on the 27th of the month. The absence of an account of this tour is disappointing. But we have seen enough of his travels in foreign parts to convince us that, with all his devotion to art and literature, he was yet by no means a solitary bookworm, indifferent to all other interests, but that, on the contrary, he was fully alive to the claims of cultured life and of human friendship.

Prior to this, in 1854, the honour had been done to him of his election to the position of Honorary Professor of Antiquities to the Royal Scottish Academy; and in the year 1861 he, as their 'Professor of Ancient History,' delivered a lecture to 'a select and brilliant company' invited by the President and Council, within their Gallery on the Mound, on 'The State of the Arts of Design in Scotland at an Early Period,' upon which perhaps no one was better qualified to speak. Another lecture was delivered in the same year on 'Scottish Artists who flourished between the Union of the Crowns in 1603 and the Present Century.' A third lecture on the same subject was given in 1862.

THE BANNATYNE CLUB, founded in 1823, was dissolved, and its last formal meeting held in the apartments of the Society of Antiquaries of Scotland on 27th February 1861, after an existence of thirty-eight years, during which it had issued at least one hundred and seventeen different works, several of which were in two or more volumes.[1] Of these works at least thirty-nine were edited entirely, or in a few cases jointly with another, by Laing; while at the same time there is little doubt that *every* volume passed under the supervision of his well-trained eye.

Lord Neaves was in the chair on the occasion of this closing meeting; and at the termination of the business he said that he 'took the oppor-

---

[1] A complete set of the Club's publications, one hundred and twenty-six volumes, realised £200 at the Laing sale.

tunity of presenting to Mr. Laing, in name of the Club, a handsome piece of silver plate, purchased from a contribution among the members, amounting to three hundred and fifty guineas, as a mark of their high sense of the admirable manner and disinterested spirit in which the proceedings of the Club had been assisted, and its publications superintended, by Mr. Laing, as its Honorary Secretary, from its institution in 1823 till its dissolution at this time. During that long period Mr. Laing had possessed the entire confidence of the many distinguished Antiquaries, and other eminent men who had been connected with the Club, including Sir Walter Scott, its founder and first President, Mr. Thomas Thomson, and Lords Cockburn and Rutherfurd, who succeeded as Presidents, Lord Chief-Commissioner Adam, Lord Jeffrey, and Lord Dundrennan. It was certain that, without Mr. Laing's services, which had all along been wholly gratuitous, and involved sacrifices of no light description, the Club could not have subsisted for so great a length of time, and could not have given to the light, with so much care, accuracy, and judgment, the many valuable publications of manuscript records, works, and documents, by which it has helped to illustrate the whole range of Scottish history and literature.'

Laing, in accepting the testimonial, made a long but characteristically modest speech dealing with the whole situation; but, as we are here concerned only incidentally with the Bannatyne Club, it is sufficient to quote only so much as bears upon his own connection with it.

'I had not the least desire,' he said, ' to assume any prominent part in its management: Sir Walter Scott, however, insisted that I should, at the outset at least, act as Secretary. But it was soon found that an office like this, to be efficient, was not one to pass annually into different hands, and this rendered it necessary that I should continue. Being at the time a young man engaged in business as a bookseller, I determined therefore to act in a manner to evince that I was not influenced by any mercenary motives, and to be above all suspicion of what is called jobbing.

'I have no wish to exaggerate the extent of my continuous labour; but no one can imagine how much of my time was so spent—days and nights, with frequent and sometimes distant journeys—on matters more or less connected with the Club; and wearisome enough work besides, with doubts occasionally springing up in my mind whether a person like myself, having always a very limited income, was justified year after year in thus spending the best part of his life. Persuaded, however, that the object in itself was laudable, and one to which I had early devoted myself, I now feel thankful, at the close of such a lengthened period, to be able to say that, during these thirty-eight years, neither seeking praise nor receiving reward, I never faltered from my work, nor drew my hand back from the plough. No doubt, like other editors, I might have fairly claimed remuneration for extra work, but, to the best of my knowledge and belief, beyond repayment of expenses actually incurred, I never received from the Club funds, or from individual contributors, any pecuniary advantage whatever.'

The testimonial was a handsome silver vase, ornamented with three emblematical figures of History, Poetry, and Music, and surmounted with a statuette of Sir Walter Scott, the founder of the Club. It bears the following inscription :

PRESENTED
BY
THE MEMBERS OF THE BANNATYNE CLUB
TO
DAVID LAING, ESQUIRE
IN GRATEFUL ACKNOWLEDGMENT
OF HIS SERVICES
AS HONORARY SECRETARY
SINCE THE INSTITUTION OF THE CLUB
IN THE YEAR
1823

The testimonial was exhibited at the commemoration in Edinburgh, in July and August 1871, of the birth of Scott, when Laing gave the following explanation in regard to it :

'The form that this testimonial might assume was left to myself; and I could not but desire, in grateful and pleasing recollections, to have the chief portion associated with the name of the founder of the Club. A composition designed and modelled [as above described] by Mr. Peter Slater was adopted, surmounted with a statuette of Sir Walter,' etc.

In 1863 a portrait of Laing, 'Honorary Professor of Ancient Literature to the Royal Scottish Academy,' was painted by his friend Sir William Fettes Douglas, and is now in the National Gallery of Scotland. The picture, in which the Bannatyne Club testimonial is a prominent feature, is reproduced as the frontispiece of this volume.

Exhibited in the Academy's Exhibition of the following year, the *Scotsman's* notice of it is as follows :

'It is a delightful small cabinet portrait of Mr. David Laing in his sanctum. The likeness is good; and the missals, old books, and curiosities, are painted to perfection; but Mr. Laing's attitude, though we are aware it is a common one with him, when looking over a book, is not very happily chosen, and does not do justice to the learned bibliographer. One should always represent his friends under the best aspect; and Mr. Laing's general bearing is erect and dignified.'

A bust of Laing, by W. D. Stevenson, will be found in the National Portrait Gallery, Queen Street. Another is in the possession of the Society of Antiquaries, who also have a small portrait in oil.

While the indebtedness of the Bannatyne Club to Laing was thus gratefully and handsomely acknowledged, the Society of Antiquaries, in whose interests he had also so long laboured, had placed him in the honourable position of Vice-President; and on his retiring, by rotation, he, on the 9th December of this same year 1861, gave an important Address on the State of the Society from 1831 to 1861 (printed in the *Archæologia Scotica*, vol. v. part I.). In this, notwithstanding his studied reserve, it was impossible to conceal the importance of his services, especially at a critical time in the Society's history, as was well understood by those who had intimate knowledge of its affairs.

The only other incident in Laing's personal history to chronicle for this year 1861, is a visit to Peterborough and its neighbourhood in the month of July, apparently in connection with the meeting of some scientific society not named. The almost illegible jottings on a scrap of paper show an admiring inspection of the Cathedral (chiefly of the twelfth century), and especially the fan tracery, of a later period, of the apse roof. There were also excursions to Stamford, Crowland Abbey, Fotheringay, Northampton, etc., with reception and entertainment in several country houses.

In 1864 the University of Edinburgh, all too tardily, when he was seventy-one years of age, bestowed upon Laing its honorary degree of Doctor of Laws. (He, however, always objected to being addressed as 'Dr.', preferring the simple 'Mr.') At the graduation ceremony on 20th April, Sir David Brewster presiding, he was presented for laureation by Professor Cosmo Innes, whose remarks, asserting the work and claims of the presentee, deserve to find unabridged reproduction here. He said:

> 'Master Vice-Chancellor, In the name of the Faculty of Law I present to you Mr. David Laing as one upon whom the Faculty and Senatus of our University think it fit to confer the honour of a degree of Doctor of Laws. Mr. Laing is one of the Foreign

Secretaries of the Society of Antiquaries of Scotland, Honorary Professor of Ancient History in the Royal Scottish Academy, and a gentleman accurately learned in several departments of literature and art. Mr. Laing has made a peculiar study of the early poets and poetry of Scotland, and has devoted much labour and research to our national history, especially the history of the Reformed Church in Scotland. If you desire specimens of his work, he has given an admirable edition of the Poems of Dunbar, our Scotch Chaucer—and his elaborate edition of Knox has at length placed the writings of that great Reformer on a sound foundation. Mr. Laing's qualifications have been long known to men of kindred studies. At the institution of the Bannatyne Club, a society for promoting the study of early Scotch literature—a society in which Sir Walter Scott took great delight—he selected Mr. Laing for the office of Honorary Secretary; and Mr. Laing held that office and discharged the duties in a most efficient manner from the birth to the end of the Club, for forty years. During that long period, I may say, his hand was never idle. Besides the official work of Secretary, he arranged and gave to the Club a continuous series of works of history, antiquities, art, and literature—the most important of which, perhaps, is the *Collected Correspondence of Principal Baillie* [of Glasgow]. Mr. Laing has some peculiar claims upon the gratitude of our University. To him we owe the full catalogue of our graduates from the foundation. We are also indebted to him for the arrangement of our library preparatory to its being moved into the present noble room. It was a task for which he was pre-eminently qualified, and which he performed as a labour of love. In Mr. Laing's knowledge of art, both native and foreign, if he has equals, he has no superior among his countrymen. . . . He is a workman who knows his tools, and where to find them. To many a young student he has saved the dreary and discouraging labour of informing himself where information is to be found. His love for all letters, his willingness to assist all study, have brought it to pass that, sitting in that fine Signet Library, of which he holds the keys, he is consulted by everybody in every emergency. No wise man will undertake a literary work in Scotland without taking counsel with **Mr. Laing**.'

Those of us remaining who knew Laing, and benefited by his generous help, will recognise in this an apt and faithful picture.

In going over Laing's correspondence I found letters from Principal Tulloch, St. Andrews, offering him this same honorary degree of LL.D. from that university, in 1862, which he declined. The reason assigned was his ' insuperable aversion to the idea of being called Doctor, and to all public appearances.'

In 1865 Carlyle was elected Lord Rector of the University of Edinburgh, and it is worthy of note, as showing his special appreciation of Laing, that he then selected him as his Assessor in the University Court.

In 1866, at some time of comparative leisure, he put together, with his own pen, the short sketch of his life up to 1823, when the Bannatyne Club was founded, which has already been given. The record of his literary output during all these years, as shown under a subsequent heading, is very remarkable.

1866-78

For some years after this date there is little material to illustrate Laing's private life. His literary labours were still unremitting, and a number of small expeditions were undertaken to places of historic interest, to famous libraries, and to meetings of scientific bodies. But all the time it must not be forgotten that the taper of life, however well husbanded, was now beginning to burn low. At our last-named date, 1866, he was seventy-three years of age; and at the close of the various summer tourings which we are about to note, up to 1874, he had reached the eighty-first year of his laborious life. At this stage he might well have courted rest. But his work was not yet done, and while he lived his life was work; and in that life there were no paradoxes or contradictions, but one undeviating onward course of duty, honour, labour.

Accordingly in 1869 we find him pursuing investigations, in his usual way, at Peterborough, Cambridge, and Harrogate; in 1870 at Liverpool, at the meeting of the British Association, in some of the proceedings of which he was greatly interested; and thence to the Isle of Man, Kenilworth, and Harrogate. In 1871 Leeds, Huddersfield, and Manchester were visited, and in 1874 there was a trip to Ripon. Of all these tours a few brief scrappy notes are left.

In 1871 he was elected a corresponding member of the New England Historic Genealogical Society.

It appears from correspondence preserved that

he was instrumental in a movement in 1872 for a monument in Edinburgh to John Knox.

In 1874, when he had been a Fellow of the Society of Antiquaries for fifty years, opportunity was taken, at the annual meeting, to recognise the profound appreciation by the Society of his great and unwearied services on its behalf during all those years, and of 'the respect, esteem, and love of the members for him as a man, an antiquary, and a friend.' A personal testimonial had not been acceptable to him, but he had consented to sit for his portrait, to meet the wish that he might be at all times in view in loving remembrance. The painter was Robert Herdman, R.S.A., and the picture, which is now in the National Portrait Gallery, was presented to the Society in an appropriate speech by Dr. John Alexander Smith, one of the then leading office-bearers. Dr. (afterwards Sir Arthur) Mitchell, who was in the chair, added (*inter alia*) that the picture ' would be a source of interest to the Society for centuries to come. . . . It records our grateful remembrance of a hundred acts of usefulness to the Society at a time when it needed help. It expresses our admiration of work which is almost as remarkable for its amount as for the learning and ability it displays, and for the dignified manner of its performance. It gives expression to the feelings of personal regard and affection which we entertain towards a high-minded and kind-hearted gentleman. We honour him as a man of learning, but he is endeared to us by his pleasant, helpful, loyal, unselfish, and unostentatious ways.'

It may be mentioned that Laing had been for fifteen years Treasurer, more than once Vice-President, and for twenty years one of the Foreign Secretaries of the Society,—all this in addition to his invaluable literary contributions and donations.

Next year, 1875, he paid another visit to London, and, though no account of his doings there is preserved, yet from scraps of waste paper certain notes can be gathered of his being at Canterbury and Durham, the glorious cathedrals at these and other places always possessing a fascinating interest for him. As these jottings so nearly approach to the close of the chapter of his life, they are entered here verbatim.

'July 1875. Left Granton by the Steamer —— Captain Wilson, on Saturday the —— at 3, and reached London on Monday the —— without stopping; took the Railway direct to Canterbury; put up at the Fountain Hotel.—Sunday, July 25. At morning and afternoon service in the Cathedral [texts of sermons noted]. . . .—August 1875,

DAVID LAING

*After the Portrait by Robert Herdman, R S A,
in the Scottish National Portrait Gallery*

Saturday 7th. Left London and reached Durham in time for dinner—the weather very close and hot. The Stations, not only at King's Cross, but at York and Durham, crowded with passengers—and an awful mass of luggage. Having resolved to stay a day or two at *Durham* rather than *York*, was surprised to find the streets swarming with people, it happening to be the *fair-day*—although the streets wet.

'The Cathedral Church. . . . Sermon in the Nave, by the Archdean Brown—reference to the absence, from bad health abroad, of Mr. Dykes, one of the Minor Canons, and author of various Anthems, etc. In the afternoon, but there was no sermon—a custom it seems in several Cathedral churches—walked round the building, etc., but weather unfavourable. Next morning, instead of remaining all day, set off by the Express—the day being wet, foggy, and disagreeable.'

So much for the last English tour; but next month, September, we find him on the Borders with a description which he heads—

'I may well call all the following "A weary Night's travel in Roxburghshire."'

The writing is vigorous but shaky, as it might well be at eighty-two years of age; and it is revised, with emendations in pencil, in ordinary style, as if in preparation for the press! As it is his last effort of the kind, I have attempted its transcription:

'Friday, September 3rd, 1875. Left Edinr. for Jedburgh by the N.B. train at 1.15, intending to spend a few days in revisiting some places after an interval of probably half a century. Reached Jedburgh at —— and stopped at the Spread Eagle Hotel. After dinner took a stroll through the town, but found that the interest was almost entirely limited to the Abbey.

'Next morning the object was to attend the Centenary Commemoration of Dr. John Leyden at his Birthplace. Having failed the previous day in finding at the other Hotels any conveyance to the place, as they were all pre-engaged, I set out on foot, walking leisurely and refreshing my memory with the fine scenery, passing the Dunian, and keeping a look-out for Ruberslaw [two hills of Teviotdale]. I reached Denholm in good time (about 2), a couple of hours before the banquet; the whole population being in a state of excitement, with Music, Games, Banners, Processions, and Speeches. Lord Neaves was Chairman of the meeting; and, while harangues outside of the Banquet Hall prolonged the time, I went and sat down for a time, and had some pleasant talk with him. The meeting went off extremely well, although Lord Neaves's voice

PERSONAL HISTORY 103

was rather weak for such an assemblage. An acquaintance from Edinburgh, who was to leave for the Railway to start by the train from Hawick, arranged, as I hoped, with some of his Jedburgh friends, to carry me back with them. But lo! about 8, I was informed they could not take me. I therefore looked about me, round the Green, to see if some other conveyance were to be had. Nothing of the kind was available, and as the distance was only six or seven miles, and, as I thought, a road that could not be mistaken, I set out, reckoning it might be between 10 and 11 before I should reach the Hotel.

'On therefore I went, occasionally looking back at the illuminations, and keeping free of conveyances, loaded outside and in, hailing them as they drove past, as if it were a race, until I came to a toll-bar which I had passed in the early part of the day. There was nothing for it but to push on, as the night was getting fearfully dark, and fancying I had passed the Dunian, and in sight of a large hotel. Well, said I to myself, the worst of the journey is now past, and another half-hour will bring me to my destination. But behold, what I took for a large house on the rising ground looking down on Jedburgh was only a clump of trees, while lights in the distance, what seemed to be on the other side of the River, went out or disappeared. Well, here is a precious mess! I could not stand still; I did not know which way to turn. Even if it were to go back to Denholm, this was quite out of the question.

'After some further weary wandering I saw lights in a large house to which access seemed to be by an unfinished road. I tapped at the window of apparently a dining-room, when "Who is there?" etc. The gentleman, coming to the door, on [my] explaining matters, told me I had come three miles out of the road, and kindly asked me to enter and take some refreshment. I thanked him, of course, for such an unexpected invitation, but I said my object was to get to Jedburgh with as little delay as might be. He gave me some directions as to the course, and added he would get a lanthorn and show me a somewhat shorter way to the high road. But this proved rather unfortunate, as, when I found myself in the darkness, I was worse off than ever as to the direction to take. Still pushing on, I came to another house. Here the door was open, like a toll-bar keeper's house. He also came out to put me on the right path—but with no better results. I next came to other cottages. Knocking, a man in bed near a small open window, in reply to my application, persisted in repeating *keep straucht on*, but whether to the right or left of what he called a " pump wall " [well] I could not learn. It was always *straucht on*.

'The conviction at length forced itself on my mind that the chance of reaching the Hotel that night was quite hopeless. Yet what could I do except to keep moving, whether right or wrong, in the possibility of stumbling on some cottage, or house of refuge, where I might pass the night. It was all in vain. I could find nothing like shelter, not even a stone at the road side on which I might sit down and rest me. The darkness was so intense that a score of times I could have sworn a stone wall obstructed the way until I pushed out my hand or umbrella to prove otherwise. So true is the saying " He that walketh in darkness knoweth not whither he goeth " (John xii. 35). By this time I knew it was past midnight; and in the words of the well-known Hymn, now sung in our churches, I might have said "*Lead, kindly light, amid the encircling gloom. . . . I ask not light to see the distant scene, one step enough for me*"! It was, indeed, all I then wished—step by step—to hasten on to some place of shelter. It was well I was not *very* nervous, as strange fancies were crossing my mind. At one time I really imagined, for instance, there was a person silently walking at my side. At another time that I had got inside of the ruins of a splendid Cathedral church. Again this would change to the ruins of a small parish kirk such as Alloa Kirk,[1] with its burial-ground; and, by some optical illusion, or passing gleam of light, there seemed to be two or three female figures on the other side of the trees, in long white garments, floating in the air, in a contrary direction. But the chief delusion was that of being close to a stone wall stopping my progress.

'As I was scarcely able to keep on my feet, sauntering on, on, and half asleep, my course was to find myself at the foot of a tree where I might sit down for at least a couple of hours, instead of keeping on the cold wet ground of what seemed to be the high road. Having reached one, after various attempts, that had a number of small branches at the foot, I did what was possible to twist them together as a kind of seat. I had scarcely done so when a number of midges, or small insects, came buzzing about my face, and kept me awake for the first half-hour, when they disappeared, or became quiet. In this position I remained for, I suppose, two hours, occasionally dozing, until, feeling rather stiff, I attempted to rise, but fairly tumbled over; yet it was idle to think of resuming my walk in the continued darkness, and [I] thought it best,

---

[1] Alloway Kirk in Ayrshire, with Tam o' Shanter and the witches, is evidently in view here.

for another hour, to sit down, at the risk of my black trousers coming to grief from the broken branches. Rising again and coming to what seemed the high road, I set out leisurely, looking at the sky when the first faint symptoms of dawn appeared, and watching its increase, until I could actually see the road on which I was proceeding in an Easterly direction. This continued for about an hour, until I passed the iron gate of a gentleman's residence on a rising ground, but apparently no porter's lodge; and here I sat down on one of the curb-stones for nearly another hour.

'The daylight at length was sufficient for me, on meeting any person on the road, to appear a *bona fide* traveller (and not a night wanderer), and I considered what I should ask or say. The best plan seemed to be, not to talk of Jedburgh, but simply to enquire which was the nearest Railway Station. By and bye, still walking leisurely, about six o'clock, I saw a foot-passenger coming along, and, accosting him, he said the next station was Kirkbank, about a mile and a half towards the left. (This I knew was about half-way between St. Boswells and Jedburgh.) This being Sunday morning, he said there would be no train there till after ten o'clock. He was a nice, intelligent man, and his direction left me in no difficulty in reaching it before 7. Had it been in the dark I might have gone wide enough, and come to Roxburgh. Having not the least desire for further walking, I sat down on the platform till some of the Railway people would be stirring. There was no house near for refreshments, but [I] was recommended to try one of those near at hand, occupied by a Shepherd who kept a cow, and where I might get a bowl of milk. He was not at home, but his Wife, who was dressing two young girls, asked me to come in and sit down at a comfortable fire, and brought me milk, which was very refreshing. She would not take any payment—but I left a trifle to give the girls, having nothing suitable to offer.

'The train at length arrived, with few passengers; but there was no *omnibus* at the terminus [at Jedburgh], so I had still to walk half a mile or so, while the kirk bells were ringing, and several carriages came driving past with the gentry going to church. In the street leading to the Hotel I met some of yesterday's visitors at the Leyden banquet, who invited me to come in to their (the U.P.) Church. This I declined, naturally preferring, without saying so, to get back to the Hotel, and have some breakfast, after which I lay down (in my clothes) for an hour's nap. By this time the forenoon services were over, and, as there was no afternoon service, I lingered amidst the Abbey ruins.

'In the evening I went in good time to the New Church, erected by the Marquess of Lothian when the old parish Church, connected with and disfiguring the remains of the old Abbey, was handed over to him by the Presbytery. It is a large spacious building, erected in good style, and fitted up handsomely—and more than compensates for having the other cleared away, [of] which no alteration or renovation, could have proved satisfactory.'

This story might, no doubt, have been compressed within shorter limits; but it is a memorable adventure for a man of advanced years; and, since Laing thought it worth while to chronicle it so fully, his biographer is justified in rendering it here verbatim. It gives a vivid and entirely realistic impression, at first hand, of the man himself, his aims, his moods, and his indomitable perseverance in circumstances of exertion and exposure which might have cost him his life. One extraordinary feature is, how, amid his multifarious literary labours, he found time, or cared, to indite a small personal narrative of this kind, at such an age, and with such amplitude of detail at every turn of the story.

Notwithstanding all these laborious journeyings, both in England and in Scotland, he found time this year (1875) to issue at least three important volumes—(1) *Etchings by Sir David Wilkie*, (2) *The Poetical Works of Patrick Hannay, 1622*, and (3) *Correspondence of Sir Robert Kerr, First Earl of Ancram.*

In the next year, 1876, Laing was able to see completed, mainly at his own expense, the restoration of the monument in Greyfriars Churchyard, erected in 1727 in memory of the famous Principal Carstares, the friend and adviser of King William III. But for his exertions on this occasion the monument would have crumbled away into a nameless ruin. His account of the restoration appears in vol. xi. pp. 525 *et seq.* of the *Proceedings* of the Society of Antiquaries of Scotland.

Laing was also very desirous that suitable monuments should have been erected in the city to John Knox and George Buchanan. But his efforts were not seconded, and it is to himself that we are indebted for the small tablet—

I. K.
1572

let into the causeway (though the exact spot of interment is uncertain) in the old burying-ground of St. Giles, to mark the last resting-place of Knox; and for the monument to Buchanan which now stands in Greyfriars Churchyard. The cost of the latter was defrayed by the trustees after his death.

At this time, 1876, at the advanced age of eighty-three, signs of weakness might naturally be looked for. But, though his race was well-nigh run, his activities were not relaxed; while his works testify that his intellect remained clear, and that his striving for accuracy was as keen as ever.

In July of this year he was in London, for the last time. The occasion was his being called to give evidence before a Committee of the House of Lords, in the Annandale Peerage case, in regard to the authenticity of the Asloan Manuscript and the Auchinleck Chronicle. In the year 1844 he had been an important witness in the same matter in the interests of Sir Frederick Johnstone, Bart., who urged him again to appear at this time much against his (Laing's) own will, as shown by correspondence preserved.

To the Society of Antiquaries he read, on 10th January, an exceedingly interesting paper on 'The Forrester Monuments in the Church of Corstorphine,' followed in 1877, on 8th January, 14th May, and 11th June, by other communications exhibiting his old qualities of erudition and lucid exposition. His last appearance before the Society was on 13th May 1878, five months before his decease, his subject being 'Notice of John, Duke of Lauderdale, and the Dispersion of his Library and Correspondence,' too sadly premonitory of the breaking up of his own treasures within a short time thereafter. In the course of the year he had issued two important works; and at the time of his decease he was engaged on the production of four others, as described under his 'Literary Work,' *infra*.

Among these works was Wyntoun's *Orygynale Cronykil of Scotland*, upon the third volume of which he was intently occupying himself when the end was drawing near. The *Cronykil* is preserved in eight different MSS., one of which, the 'Wemyss' copy, was discovered in Wemyss Castle by Laing himself in 1822, when he was making a valuation of the library, the paintings, etc., there. When the new edition was in progress he desired this MS. for collation purposes, but was informed that 'no such book could be discovered.' A fire had taken place since the first discovery, and destroyed a number of books in that part of the library where it stood, and it was apprehended that it must have perished. But Mrs. Wemyss afterwards came upon it, tied up with other books, and placed it at Laing's disposal.

This is Laing's account, as given in the Appendix to his Preface to volume III.; but a more circumstantial story was related by himself, at a later date, to the effect that when Mrs. Wemyss wrote that the MS. was not preserved in the castle, he insisted that it should be found between certain windows in the library. She replied that at that place everything had been destroyed by the fire. Then, said he, it may be in the staircase to a certain turret, where he remembered having had it in his hand, intending its being taken to Edinburgh to be repaired. *That was fifty years before, and there it was found.* When it reached him in town he, with great delight, pressed it to his breast. My informant is Laing's now aged friend, Mr. David Douglas, the publisher of *Wyntoun*, who got the story from his own lips.

In the course of the next year, 1878, he had again in hand the scheme for a statue of John Knox in Edinburgh. In the draft of a letter in the month of July to a nobleman whose name is not given, he suggested that the statue should be of bronze, not inside any church or building in the Old Town, but under the great east window of St. Giles, ' at the entrance to Parliament Square, so that the figure might be looking down the High Street.'

The building of the new library at the house in Portobello being completed about this time,

H

and some of his choicest books arranged in it, he, in the month of August, on the occasion of a visit of his friend Sir Daniel Wilson from Canada, had a number of his old friends beside him, when some of his rare literary treasures were exhibited. But by this time he must have been failing, though the only direct indication of this is a reference to the state of his health in one of his letters to the Marquess of Lothian, who, in his reply of the 30th of August, said, ' I trust you are well again. I am very sorry to hear you have been ailing'; and again, on 4th September, ' I trust your health is now quite restored.' All the while he was closely engaged in his usual editorial work, two volumes being issued during the year, and Wyntoun's *Cronykil*, Lyndsay's *Heraldry*, and other works in course of preparation.

THE END

The end came all too sadly soon after this. In the Signet Library, at his usual duties, he was struck down with paralysis. When awakening to consciousness he, looking around, promptly inquired whether the proof of *Wyntoun* had been sent up by the printer. After a short lingering in his own house, he expired on 18th October 1878 in his eighty-sixth year.

Thus passed away, in the midst of his labours, the grand old bibliophile and antiquary; a man of honour, truth, and righteousness, the centre of a universal esteem.

THE FUNERAL

The funeral took place on the 23rd to the family tomb in the New Calton Burying Ground. It was a dull and cold October day, but a very large company assembled both in the house and at the cemetery. In the religious services the Rev. Dr. William Robertson of New Greyfriars officiated in the dining-room, the Rev. William Makellar in the drawing-room. The cortège consisted of a hearse drawn by four horses, and thirty carriages. Among those attending were the council of the Society of Antiquaries, the office-bearers of the Royal Society and of the Society of Writers to the Signet, and the members of the New Greyfriars Kirk Session, Dr. Laing having been connected with that congregation. The pall-bearers were—Mr. William Reid, Pittentian, Perthshire (married to a niece, and the only relative present), James T. Gibson-Craig, W.S,. William Fettes Douglas (afterwards Sir William, President of the Royal Scottish Academy), James Hope, D.K.S., Dr. John Alexander Smith, Sir Daniel Macnee, P.R.S.A.,

William Brodie, R.S.A., Rev. Dr. Robertson, and Rev. William Makellar.

The general company included Dr. John Hill Burton, Professors Mackay, Masson, and Laurie, John Hutchison, R.S.A., George Hay, R.S.A., J. M. Barclay, R.S.A., Robert Herdman, R.S.A., Gourlay Steell, R.S.A., W. Beattie Brown, A.R.S.A., William Horne, Advocate, Henry Moffat of Eldin, S.S.C., James Macdonald, W.S., M. Montgomerie Bell, W.S., John Milligan, W.S., John Cook, W.S., J. D. Marwick (afterwards Sir James, Town Clerk of Glasgow), James S. Tytler, W.S., William Skinner, W.S., Charles Jenner, David Douglas, J. Menzies, Samuel Edmonston, Thomas Dickson (afterwards LL.D.), Register House, Dr. Bedford, T. B. Johnston, geographer, Rev. Dr. Begg, Rev. G. W. Sprott, North Berwick, Rev. Dr. Struthers, Prestonpans, Dr. Stevenson Macadam, James Dymock, William Paterson and T. G. Stevenson, booksellers, D. Hunter of Blackness, and the writer of these memoirs; with many more, almost all of whom are now departed.

OBITUARY NOTICES

Of pulpit references to the deceased it may be sufficient to quote a portion of the remarks of the Rev. Dr. Robertson of New Greyfriars, whose testimony was based upon intimate knowledge. He said :

'He departed full of years and full of honours. Many friends and not one enemy has he left behind. As one said to me while we followed his remains to their last resting-place, " Not one enemy, for surely one so gentle, so genial, so amiable, so kindly, could hardly ever have made an enemy, and could not have left one." And many friends, most truly, for those who knew him best loved him best. Honoured and admired also was he by all who knew his personal work, or were acquainted ever so little with the high place in Scottish literature which he has left, so far as I know, absolutely untenanted. He lived in great measure withdrawn from the eyes of the world, and, owing to his modesty and retiring disposition, few, except those who were themselves walking in the same path of literature, or were interested in its results, were acquainted with the singular talents he displayed in his own department, with the successful labours which he prosecuted, and the untiring zeal almost up to the moment when the sands of his glass were to be counted by grains, or with the singularly voluminous evidence of his genius and his industry which he has left behind him. Widely known beyond the brilliant circle of literary men and archæologists he was not. It is strange how completely his own retiring habits excluded him from general fame, and it may be that comparatively few even of this congregation were at all aware that the grave unpretending old gentleman whom they were accustomed to see for long years in his place among them, was unquestionably in his own selected walk the most distinguished man of his generation. An eminent professor in our University [1] has just, in presence of his students, declared David Laing to have been the prince of Scottish literary antiquarians of the century. And how few were cognisant of the long period over which his labours extended! He was the link which connected the brightest days of Scottish literature with our own; only twenty-two years the junior of Sir Walter Scott, and having his first contribution to Scottish literature in the press the very year that *Waverley* appeared, and yet surviving the author of *Waverley* for nearly two generations. The works which he gave to the press are reckoned at no fewer than 250 volumes. . . . He did not work either

---

[1] Professor David Masson, LL.D.

for money or for fame. . . . Not only his latter end, but his whole life was peace. . . . " Is Christ our Redeemer with you now, and comforting you ? " was asked almost at the very moment of his death. " I feel Him to be very near," was his reply. With these last words he passed away.'

Newspaper notices of Dr. Laing were numerous in all quarters of the country. The statements of his literary labours, which fall to be treated more exhaustively in this memoir, do not call for recapitulation in this place, and a few extracts of a general character, as corroborative of the estimate of his life and work which has been set forth in these pages, may be sufficient for our purpose.

The *Scotsman* :

'There will be a general feeling that Scotland has sustained a notable loss in the demise of Mr. David Laing. The event has come, in the fulness of time, to close a life as long as it has been useful, but none the less on that account will it be felt that a sad blank is left in Scottish literary society. Indeed the sense of deprivation must be all the greater that the deceased had come to be regarded as a sort of literary Nestor. . . . In addition to his labours in connection with the Bannatyne, the Abbotsford, the Spalding, and Hunterian Clubs, his services, and the ample stores of his curious erudition, were freely placed at the disposal of all who could show the slightest claim to them. No one in Scotland thought of undertaking literary work in any way connected with historical research without consulting him as to available materials and previous efforts in the same direction. And not in Scotland only, but by correspondents in many lands, he was the authority always resorted to, and never in vain, on any bibliographical question or any doubtful point of Scottish history. . . . Nor were his services of this kind confined to private individuals, for, in July 1876, he gave, before the Committee of the House of Lords on the claims to the " Earldom of Annandale," highly important evidence in regard to the " Asloan Manuscript " and the " Auchinleck Chronicle " of the reign of James II., proving the authenticity of the manuscript, and its value as an original historical document. It almost follows from what has been said that among his friends and correspondents were numbered most of the eminent men of learning and letters of his time, from Thomas Carlyle downwards.'

The *Athenæum* :
'His knowledge of bibliography was immense. Hardly anything of importance since the invention of printing had escaped his notice. . . . His chief interest, however, lay in the ecclesiastical and literary history of Scotland. . . . It was only the other day that he gave a dinner to a number of his brethren of the Society of Antiquaries on the occasion of the visit of his friend Professor Daniel Wilson of Toronto to Edinburgh, and it was curious to see the old man sipping his Madeira with as much relish, and enjoying the old-world talk as keenly as Lockhart in his *Peter's Letters* records his doing some sixty or more years ago.'

The tribute of his old friends the Society of Antiquaries of Scotland deserves to be specially noted. At the meeting of 30th November 1878 it was resolved to record their sense of the loss sustained, and the minute proceeds :
' From the time when he joined the Society in 1824 Mr. Laing had been one of its most active members, and for nearly the whole

period of his connection with the Society, extending over fifty-four years, he took a leading part in the management of its affairs, first as Treasurer for sixteen years during the most critical period of its existence, subsequently as one of the editors of its *Proceedings*, as Vice-President and as Foreign Secretary, and in each of these departments contributed largely to its prosperity and usefulness. From first to last he was a constant contributor of papers at the meetings; and the number, variety, and importance of these contributions are altogether unparalleled in the history of the Society. His readiness to communicate freely from his unexampled stores of information was felt to be an invaluable aid to historical research, while his genial presence and counsel in connection with the Society's affairs was at all times highly prized, and the Society is deeply sensible that no loss which it has sustained will be longer felt or more deeply regretted than that of its oldest and most respected member, David Laing.'

His important services to the Church of Scotland were recognised by minute of the General Assembly, passed on 2nd June 1879, in which they express 'their deep sense of the loss this Church has sustained in the removal by death of David Laing, Esquire, LL.D., whose tried attachment to the Church through a long and eventful life was evinced by the many services he rendered in connection with her history and literature, and especially by his valuable editions of the works of her great reformer, and of the letters and journals of one of her representatives at the Westminster Assembly' [Robert Baillie, 1637-62].

It may be noted that besides his long connection with the church of New Greyfriars, already referred to, Laing was for many years an attached member of St. Luke's Congregation, Young Street, of which his friend the Rev. Ranald Macpherson was minister.

His great knowledge of art, both native and foreign, and his services in the interests of Scottish art, were very cordially recognised in the Report of the Council of the Royal Scottish Academy for the year 1878.

In closing these obituary notices of Dr. Laing, it may perhaps not be unbecoming that I, as his biographer, should add my own small testimony to what has gone before. Admitted a Fellow of the Society of Antiquaries in 1869, I soon became acquainted with him, and learned how supremely important his services were, both in its management and as a contributor of valuable matter to its publications. During the period of nearly ten years till his death, I had several occasions of consulting him on historical points obscure to me, and was always received with unfailing courtesy, and helpful and unaffected kindliness. Once, when I was inquiring whether it were possible to have a loan from the Signet Library of a certain volume for a literary friend at a distance, he explained the difficulty of doing so in the case of a stranger, though, 'had it been for yourself, the case would have been different.' Trifling as this was, I yet took the reply as a note of confidence in myself, then but a youth, and have treasured it ever since with gratitude and veneration.

Dr. Laing was survived by his sisters, Mrs. Sanson, of Hawthorn Brae, Duddingston, and Miss Euphemia Laing. The latter had all along been in residence with him, and continued in occupancy of the house until her death on 4th March 1896, keeping up its character and traditions as long as her health permitted. Many were the pleasant afternoon gatherings

HOUSE OF DAVID LAING
JAMES STREET, PORTOBELLO

of friends in the famous library, when interesting and instructive addresses of various kinds were delivered by Professor Blackie, Mr. Guthrie, Advocate (now the Honourable Lord Guthrie), Sir Arthur Mitchell, K.C.B., and others. On other occasions musical entertainments were provided. The house and grounds were sold by the trustees after her decease for £1960, after occupancy by the family for fifty-three years. The whole is now covered by a large and ungainly tenement, at the foot of James Street, its eastern windows looking out upon the wide expanse of the Forth; and the associations of the place perished for ever.

III

TESTAMENTARY BEQUESTS

Dr. Laing's will (holograph) was dated 12th March 1864, with codicil of 19th June 1875. After family arrangements and special bequests, it was provided that there should be left to the University of Edinburgh the entire MANUSCRIPT portion of his books and papers, ancient and modern, bound or unbound, and in various languages; old CHARTERS, autograph letters, and other written documents; also such of his own papers, memoranda, and bibliographical notes, and letters addressed to himself, as may be worth preserving; with a carved oak bookcase (this at a valuation) for the purpose of holding a portion of the same, etc., etc.—all to be kept in a separate and distinct class in the library, with a distinguishing book-stamp, and a descriptive catalogue to be prepared at the expense of the University.

Failing the acceptance by the University of this bequest, a similar offer was directed to be made to the Society of Antiquaries of Scotland;

TESTAMENTARY BEQUESTS

and this failing, the entire collection to be sent to London for sale by public auction. The bequest is prefaced by the following pathetic recital:

'Having during the course of a long period at considerable expense and trouble, formed an extensive Collection of Books and other materials intended to illustrate the History and Literature of Scotland, and although I never can accomplish this object, I cannot but regret to have the Collection altogether broken up and dispersed; I therefore,' etc., etc. (as before stated).

A descriptive catalogue of the CHARTERS, no less than 3326 in number, extending from A.D. 854 (an English writ) to 1837, was published by the University in 1899, in a volume of 1053 pp., under the title *Calendar of the Laing Charters*, edited by the late Rev. John Anderson of the General Register House.

In addition to these the bequest to the University comprised an immense quantity of other manuscripts in the shape of books and papers of various kinds. A separate catalogue of these was prepared, entitled *List of Manuscript Books* (etc., etc.), *in the Collection of David Laing, LL.D.*, 135 pp. This list, which bears no date or imprint, contains about 1800 items, consisting of copies of the Scriptures, or portions thereof, breviaries, missals, etc.; works on theology, philosophy, history, law, medical science, biography, heraldry, poetry, music, travels, oriental MSS.; autographic letters and signatures of foreign monarchs, and of noblemen, statesmen and others, British and foreign; besides a mass of miscellaneous historical and other documents. A selection of those of historical interest has been made by the Rev. Henry Paton, M.A., of the General Register House, for the Royal Commissioners on Historical Manuscripts, and is now being printed. Many of the historical letters and papers are given at length, and the whole selection is arranged in chronological order. This extraordinary bequest of charters, books, and other MSS., when completed in print, cannot fail to be of great value in the elucidation of Scottish history and genealogy.

The means by which so vast a collection of legal and other documents came to Laing's hands it is difficult to comprehend. It is well known that obsolete papers, the supposed 'refuse' of many law offices, are scattered as 'waste' on the demise of old practitioners, and these largely found their way to him through diverse channels. One of these, and the most prolific, was Mr. Gilbert Adcock, (Waste-)Paper Merchant, well known to many of the last, and still remembered by some of the present, generation for his grave demeanour and knowing eye, as if all the secrets of Edinburgh were within his ken. For thirty or forty years he was constantly bringing to Laing's cognisance everything of moment that came his way—the fortunate means of saving many valuable documents from imminent destruction.

The first letter of Adcock's preserved is dated 1st June 1841, from 81 South Bridge, in reference to a painting supposed to be by Rubens; one in 1847 sends ' a few more parchments and old papers for your perusal '; another, from 50 High Street, is about ' a quantity of old Parchments, etc.'; and on 2nd June of that year he grants receipt of twenty shillings for ' about 5 lb. weight of the old deeds, sasines, etc., above mentioned.' On 1st May 1851 he begs Laing to call ' and look over some old books and papers which I have got to-day from the house of the late Lord —— ' (I suppress the name). The last letter preserved is from his office, 11 South St. Andrew Street, dated 11th July 1869, asking Laing to call. At another time a ' great quantity of letters ' was sent to Adcock from the representatives of a well-known Highland lady ' in perfect confidence of their being destroyed or torn up without meeting my other eye than your own '—*i.e.* Adcock's. Among these were letters from

Laing's friend, George Chalmers of *Caledonia*, which Adcock thought 'might be coveted' by Laing, as doubtless they were.

The likelihood is that Laing at an early date became known as an omnivorous collector, and that, in consequence, every person in possession, by whatever means, of ancient documents or manuscript scraps of any kind which they desired to dispose of, came to him as the likely purchaser. But, even with these explanations, the extraordinary extent of such manuscript material, gathered together by one man, remains somewhat of a mystery, as yet unsolved, and perhaps unsolvable. Many, no doubt, of the more precious items were secured in the course of his numerous visits to the Continent in his earlier and later days.

Besides all this there is a large collection of manuscript papers of a personal kind—notes of travel, poetical, biographical, and other sketches; letters from noblemen and other correspondents; title-pages and facsimiles of ancient Scottish books and notices of the authors, illustrations of Edinburgh antiquities, and such like. These have been utilised in the preparation of the present memoir, and will be handed over to the University as soon as my purpose with them is served.

TESTAMENTARY BEQUESTS

To the SOCIETY OF ANTIQUARIES OF SCOTLAND were left:
1. Two 'Stirling Heads.'
2. Testimonial (silver) from the Bannatyne Club.
3. Painted portraits, to be held, or 'stowed away,' in view of a National Portrait Gallery of Scotland being formed.
4. Antique intaglios and engraved gems, with other articles suitable for the museum, 'that my Executors may choose to add.'

To the NATIONAL GALLERY OF SCOTLAND the following pictures, viz.:
1. 'King Lear in the Storm,' by Runciman.
2. 'The Holy Family,' attributed to Domenico Ghirlandajo; and another—
3. 'Holy Family,' small, by Lorenzo de Credi.
   'Likewise two additional paintings by the Old Masters, suitable for the Gallery, to be selected at the discretion of the Keeper or Director, or by any two persons to be named by the Board of Trustees.'

To the ROYAL SCOTTISH ACADEMY:
'a large miscellaneous Collection of Drawings and Sketches by the Old Masters,

provided the Academy agree to have the whole classed and bound in volumes, excluding such as may be reckoned not worth preservation.'

The engraved GEMS, bequeathed to the SOCIETY OF ANTIQUARIES, are thus described by Henry Laing, author of *Scottish Seals* :

'The collection, though not very extensive, or containing any that can be placed in the highest class of such engravings, is yet very interesting as containing some examples of the earliest as well as of the more advanced state of that beautiful art, and may well be appreciated as fairly representative of the art which attained such excellence in the best periods of Greece and Rome, and which still remains unsurpassed.

'The whole number of the collection is thirty-nine, of which four are cameos and the remainder are intaglios, mostly small, the stones of good quality, and many mounted in gold for rings.' The particulars of the gems individually need not be quoted.

At the same time there came to the Society—

Four volumes of the publications of the Bannatyne Club that were wanting in the set in the Society's Library.

Copy on vellum of the facsimile of an ancient heraldic manuscript, emblazoned by Sir

TESTAMENTARY BEQUESTS

David Lindsay of the Mount, Lyon King of Arms, engraved by W. H. Lizars, and edited by David Laing, 1822.

The Bannatyne Club silver plate testimonial to Laing.

At subsequent dates the following were received for the Museum of Antiquities from the trustees :

The two 'Stirling Heads,' described as 'two large circular Panels of carved oak, 28 inches diameter, from the old Palace at Stirling, supposed to represent James v. and his Queen, Mary of Guise. Each panel contains a bust within an ornamental border, carved in a rude style of art.'

Vase, with handle, of black Chiusan ware, $8\frac{1}{2}$ inches high, ornamented with figures of chimeræ in relief.

Three small miniatures on paper. One is intended for Queen Mary, the other two are in lockets.

Marble slab with an inscription which seems to be : '*Faustilla Flavi Clementis serva pia (quae) vixit annos viginti hic sepulta est. Hermeros Cæsaris nostri servus tabellarum conjugi piæ fecit.*'

Portrait in water-colour on ivory of the Earl of

Moira, Commander-in-Chief of the Forces in Scotland.

Miniature portraits of William Low, Portrait Painter, by John Kay; of Lady Leslie, and Nisbet of Dirleton, also on ivory.

The Minute-Book of the Abbotsford Club.

Gordon of Rothiemay's 'View of Edinburgh.' An impression of the original engraving, by De Witt.

Bundles of Bannatyne Club papers.

A copy of Atkinson's *Gold Mines in Scotland*.

Nineteen pamphlets, proclamations, and other printed papers.

Laing had long contemplated the formation of a NATIONAL PORTRAIT GALLERY OF SCOTLAND, and, though he did not live to see it, the erection of a suitable building for the purpose was accomplished some years after his decease through the munificence of Mr. John Ritchie Findlay of Aberlour. In view of a national collection being formed, the following PORTRAITS, chiefly in oils, were bequeathed to the Society of Antiquaries, to be held by them until such time as they could be properly exhibited as a contribution to such a collection, as already stated:

Full-length portrait of—
Adam Smith, author of the *Wealth of Nations*.

Half-lengths of—

Reverend Dr. Henry, of Greyfriars, author of *A History of Great Britain.*
Sir Hans Sloane, Physician and Naturalist.
Sir Patrick Hume, Earl of Marchmont.
William Purves, by Sir P. Lely.
Field-Marshal Wade.
John Runciman, Artist, by himself.
Alexander Runciman and John Brown disputing, by John Runciman (now in the National Gallery).
James Tassie, Artist.
Sir W. Chambers, Architect.
Professor John Playfair.
Honble. A. Murray, by Allan Ramsay.
Allan Ramsay, by himself (probably a copy by Lilie).
David Anderson, Architect, Aberdeen.
Andrew Geddes, Artist.
Professor Mackay (Civil Law), Edinburgh.
Rev. Gilbert Burnet, D.D., Bishop of Salisbury.
Rev. Dr. Thomas Drummond.
Sir David Murray.
Rev. Robert White.

There was also a miniature head of—

Sir Walter Scott, in infancy, painted in water-colour on ivory, and
Five portraits, two of which are supposed to be

likenesses of Lord Darnley and King James VI. when a boy : the others uncertain.

The 'two additional paintings by Old Masters' selected for the NATIONAL GALLERY OF SCOTLAND under the bequest to that collection were :

'Winter Scene,' by Hendrick Avercaup.
'Flight into Egypt,' by John Runciman.

The collection of DRAWINGS AND SKETCHES bequeathed to the ROYAL SCOTTISH ACADEMY were arranged by a committee of the Academy, and bound in nineteen large folio volumes. These remained in the library of the Academy until 1910, when they were transferred to the trustees of the National Gallery. Many of the most important are now on view in the room devoted to drawings by old masters in the National Gallery, and the others are preserved in the library there, as I am informed by Mr. James L. Caw, the director of the National Galleries of Scotland.

The PRIVATE PAPERS already referred to, falling under the bequest to the University, along with the whole of the private correspondence, were sent by the trustees to Dr. (afterwards Sir) Arthur Mitchell, with a view to a biography of Laing being prepared by him, Mr. (afterwards Sir) William Fettes Douglas, R.S.A., agreeing to help in the references to art, and Professor Æneas

J. G. Mackay, LL.D., in those to historical literature. It is noted in the minute of trustees of 19th December 1879 that Sir Arthur ' had made considerable progress in arranging and examining ' the papers ; but beyond that arranging and examining, however important, nothing was ever accomplished ; and Sir Arthur dying in 1909, thirty years later, the execution of the work came, after considerable delay, to be entrusted to me. The friends who undertook to be helpers have passed to the majority.

The total personal estate, apart from the dwelling-house in Portobello, was originally put in the inventory at £11,967, including the library, prints, and drawings, estimated at £3095, but which actually realised, on sale, £16,807, 12s., as will be afterwards shown. The total funds eventually amounted to £29,167, 9s. 8d.

IV
THE LIBRARY

THE settlement provided that, after the books and manuscripts had been selected and brought together for the special bequest to the University:

> '—the whole of my printed Books shall be sent to London for sale by public auction, in two separate divisions, where such books are more highly appreciated, and more carefully catalogued than in this place. The first Division or Part to contain all Books connected with Scottish History and Literature in various languages; the second Division or Part, printed Books of all Classes; also a small collection of Engravings or Etchings for a separate Day's Sale.'

Elaborate catalogues of the different portions were accordingly prepared, occupying 753 pp. and containing no less than 11,743 lots; and the whole, along with the prints, were disposed of by Messrs Sotheby, Wilkinson & Hodge, London; the sale extending over thirty-one days, on four different occasions.

THE LIBRARY

Laing having been, as we have seen, an ardent collector from boyhood, he had spared neither research nor money in gathering together an extraordinary number of exceedingly rare books, many probably unique and unknown to bibliographers, and the dispersal of such a large and well-known library brought together a great number of purchasers, the leading booksellers mustering so largely that private enterprise had small chance of success. Some who attended with the idea of picking up a stray souvenir of the collection went away disappointed and empty-handed, for there was the keenest competition for every lot. Several Scottish booksellers were present, but their London brethren were the more active buyers. Quaritch had the lion's share, and created some surprise by his prodigal bidding, though it was surmised at the time that he held important commissions, and it is believed that the British Museum and the Bodleian Library had their respective collections enriched by his care on this occasion. As an indication of the keenness of the competition, and the high range of prices, it may be noted that the first day's sale realised £1099, 15s. and the second £1593, 6s., without including any single volume of very large figure.

The order of sale was as follows, viz.:

The first portion,	3799 lots, on 1st December 1879 and ten following days, realising	£13,288	8	6
,, second ,,	4082 lots, on 5th April 1880, and ten following days	1,738	3	0
,, third ,,	2443 lots, on 20th July 1880, and four following days	771	9	6
,, fourth ,,	1419 lots, on 21st February 1881, and three following days	738	18	0
	In all 11,743 lots.	£16,536	19	0
The prints realised	. . . . . .	270	13	0
	Total	£16,807	12	0

From this amount there fell to be deducted the cost of the preparation of the catalogues and other expenses, and the commission of the auctioneers.

It would be in vain, and perhaps not very profitable at this time of day, to attempt a detailed account of this great sale, one of the most memorable in the annals of bibliography; but it presented some romantic incidents in the unprecedented upward movement of prices, and a few of the principal items, with the figures which they commanded, may be noted, *e.g.*—

Barbour's 'Actys and Life of Robert Bruce,' printed at Edinburgh in 1571, and believed to be unique, went to Quaritch for £142.

The Bannatyne Club publications, 126 volumes, fell to William Paterson, Edinburgh, for £200.

THE LIBRARY

Brand's 'Description of Orkney and Zetland, 1701, £2, 12s. 6d.

Zachary Boyd's 'Last Battel of the Soule in Death,' Edinburgh, Andro Hart, 1629, brought the large price of £52, 10s.

'Don Quixote,' 1st edition, Madrid, 1608, began at £25, and was at last got by Quaritch for £192.

The Kilmarnock edition of Burns's Poems, 1786, in fine condition, with a snatch of song in the poet's handwriting, the usual price averaging about £40, went to Quaritch for what would now be considered the ridiculously low price of £90, £1000 being a more likely figure at the present day.

Bodrugan's 'Epitome of the Title that the Kynges Maiestie of Englande hath to the Sovereigntie of Scotlande,' black-letter, 1548, brought £27, 10s.

Chalmers's 'Caledonia,' in quarto, £18.

'The Earl of Bute's Botanical Tables' (1785), characterised by Lowndes as 'more splendid than useful,' was bought by M'Gregor of Dundee for £77. It is said that only 12 copies were printed, at a cost of £10,000, and the copperplates destroyed.

'Breviarium secundum Ritum Romanæ Ecclesiæ cum Calendario,' an exquisite edition in two volumes, printed at Venice in 1482 — only one other copy known to exist, that in the National Library, Paris — to Richardson, Glasgow, for £93.

'Biblia Latina,' published at Nuremberg in 1477, in the original oak boards, covered in stamped pigskin, £84.

A 'Breeches Bible,' Andro Hart, Edinburgh, 1610, £10, 15s.

Hector Boece's 'Scotorum Historia,' Paris, 1526, dedication copy of the 1st edition to King James v. of Scotland, £71.

'The Shyp of Folys of the Worlde,' Barclay's translation, R. Pynson, 1509, £19, 10s.

'Booke of Common Prayer for the Church of Scotland' (Laud's Service Book), Edinburgh, 1637, with 'Psalmes' translated by King James (in verse), 1636, £9, 5s.

'Confessione of Fayth and Doctrin,' Edinburgh, 1561 (sold for £5, 15s. 6d. at the Chalmers sale), £62, 10s.

'True Relation of the Apparition of one Mrs. Veal,' £3, 10s.

Sir J. Dalrymple's 'Institutions of the Law of Scotland,' a magnificent specimen of contemporary Scottish binding, Edinr., 1681, £295.

Foxe's 'Book of Martyrs,' 2 vols., black-letter, 1562-63, £50.

Drummond of Hawthornden's 'Poems,' second

impression, Andro Hart, Edinburgh, 1616, excessively rare, £50.

'The Forme and Maner of Examination Befoir the Admission to ye Tabill of ye Lord,' Edinburgh, 1581 ('presumed probably to be unique'), black-letter, to Quaritch, £70.

De Foe's 'Adventures of Robinson Crusoe,' 1st edition, portrait, very rare, 1719-20, £31.

Ferguson's 'Scottish Proverbs,' 1st edition, Edin., 1641, £20.

D'Urfey's 'Wit and Mirth or Pills to Purge Melancholy,' 1719-20, £13.

Aberdeen 'Cantus,' John Forbes, 1666, 2nd edition, £37.

Fraser's 'Memorials of the Montgomeries,' £21.

Sir William Dick's 'Lamentable Estate and Distressed Case,' 1632, £6, 10s.

Facsimiles of National Manuscripts of Scotland, 1867-70, £11, 5s.

Sir John Froissart's 'Cronycles of Englande, etc., etc.,' 1525, £28.

'Buke of the Howlat,' edited by Laing, Bannatyne Club, black-letter, printed on vellum, and illuminated by W. Penney, Mid-Calder, Edinr., 1823, £119.

Archbishop Hamilton's 'Catechisme,' black-letter, St. Andrews, 1552, excessively rare, £148.

A Horn Book, E. Raban, Aberdeen, n.d., £15.

'Edinburgh Celebrities,' by J. Jenkins, 150

coloured plates, with MS. key, extremely scarce, 1799-1805, £26.

Hunterian Club Publications, £10, 15s.

A. Gordon's 'Itinerarium Septentrionale,' 1726-32, £13, 5s.

Hakluyt's 'Voiages,' 3 vols., black-letter, 1598-1600, £31.

John Knox's 'Admonition or warning that the faithful Christians in London, Newcastle, Barwycke and others may avoide God's Vengence,' black-letter, Wittenburge, 1554. Excessively rare, if not unique. This copy, purchased by Laing at Heber's sale for £6, 11s. and since bound, went for £65.

John Knox's 'First Blast of the Trumpet against the monstrous Regiment of Women,' 1568— (the Roxburghe copy sold for £4, 5s.)— £16, 10s.

John Knox's 'Answer to a Letter of a Jesuit named Tyrie,' St. Andrews, printed by R. Lekpreuik, 1572, £53.

J. La Fontaine's 'Fables Choisies,' 1st edition, Paris, 1668, £101. (Quoted in the newspaper report of the day as '£161.')

Kay's 'Collection of Portraits of Eminent Scotch Persons,' 1784-1828, £43.

'Liturgy,' approved by John Calvin (usually termed 'John Knox's Liturgy'), Geneva, 1641, £45, 10s.

THE LIBRARY

John Kello, Minister of Spot, 'Confessioun togidder with his ernist. Repentance maid upon the Scaffold befoir his Suffering,' Edinburgh, R. Lekpreuik, 1570, £25, 10s.

'Basilikon Doron,' by King James I. (VI.), Edinburgh, 1603, £8, 2s. 6d.

Theodore Beza's 'Confessione della Fede Christiana,' vellum, in morocco case, 1560. Stated to have belonged to Mary Queen of Scots, one of the few remaining specimens of her library, an extraordinary rarity. Began at 20 guineas, and finally secured by Richardson, Glasgow, for £149.

'Histoire et Martyre de la Royne d'Escosse,' with four folding woodcuts. Paris, 1589, £28.

Sir David Lyndesay, 'Ane Dialog betuix Experience and ane Courteour, off the miserabyll estait of the Warld,' n.d. (St. Andrews, John Scott). The extraordinary sum of £121 paid by Walford, bookseller, Strand. The highest price previously quoted is £30.

A. Montgomery's 'Cherrie and the Slae,' etc., 1668-73, £27.

A. Montgomery's 'The Flyting betwixt Montgomery and Polwart,' Edinr., heirs of Andro Hart, excessively rare, £52, 10s.

John Milton's 'Paradise Lost,' 1st edition, 1669, £12, 5s.

Napier's 'Logarithms,' 1619, £15, 10s.

'Psalmes in Meter, with Prayers and Catechisme for the Kirk of Scotland, with sundrie other things,' Edinr., 1596, £43.

Spenser's 'Faerie Queene,' 1st edition, 1590, £120.

Spenser's 'Colin Clout's come Home Againe,' 1595, £5, 10s.

'Lyfe and Actis of Wallace,' 1601, only £6, 6s. Said to have realised £31 at the Roxburghe sale.

'Virgil' of Gawin Douglas, Edinburgh, 1710, £23.

Blind Harry's 'Wallace,' Edinburgh, 1661, £15, 15s.

The above are only a fraction of the nearly 12,000 lots brought to the hammer; and it may be thought matter for regret that we have been unable to describe some of the most rare and costly, and the keen contests which took place for their possession. This the limits of the present work do not permit; but it is hoped that those noted are sufficiently indicative of the nature generally of the treasures submitted, and of the expert estimates of their value at the time. One general remark may be made, viz. that, while the collection contained no single volumes fabulously large in price, it was of unusually

THE LIBRARY

high character for rarity and excellence, and that a very high range of prices prevailed throughout. All the circumstances call for veneration of the collector, whose long life was devoted to the accumulation of such an extraordinary mass of precious literature; and a feeling of regret, almost of personal loss, especially to those who were acquainted with him and his stores, in contemplating the process of its wide dispersal.

V
LITERARY WORK

WE have endeavoured in the foregoing pages to trace the main events in the career of the honoured antiquary, with some particulars of the closing scenes and of the dispersal of the famous library. In similar cases it is not infrequently the privilege of the biographer to be able to draw upon a more or less extensive private correspondence for illustrations of the inner life and mental qualities of the deceased. There is little or nothing of the kind here, and all has had to be built up from casual incident or accidental record. Wide as Laing's circle of correspondents was, he kept few copies of the letters he himself dispatched, though a large quantity of drafts of his replies, on old envelopes and scraps of paper, are preserved, for most part in such a patched and fragmentary condition as to be unsuitable for biographical purposes. But when we come to his literary work we find it carrying its own credentials, and needing no further testimony. *Si monumentum requiris, circumspice.*

In the great library of which for forty-one years he was the head, the number of volumes is stated to have been increased from about 40,000 when he took charge, to no less than 70,000 when he left it. His great private collection was gradually augmented at the same time, until it reached the figure of nearly 12,000 books, as has already been shown. And all the while he was at the call of inquirers in all departments of literature and history, involving personal attention and a very large correspondence with scholars and men of literary and artistic tastes at home and abroad.

But it was in the domain of Scottish literature and antiquities that his instincts and powers found full scope and expression. As Secretary to the Bannatyne Club from its formation to its dissolution, it may be safely affirmed that not one of its publications, numbering one hundred and seventeen in all, saw the light without the penetrating scrutiny of his eye, and the correcting influence of his wide knowledge; while of these no less than thirty-nine, traced through unimagined by-ways and found in obscure recesses, were edited by himself (or occasionally jointly with another), with scrupulous care and amplitude of explanatory comment. In the same way, as a Fellow for fifty-four years of the Society of Antiquaries of Scotland, and occupying during almost all that time responsible positions in its management, his devotion to its interests was one of the outstanding features of his life; and to its *Proceedings* he contributed an astounding number of important papers on a great variety of Scottish historical and literary subjects. But his literary labours were not confined to these two bodies. He was a member also of the Wodrow, the Hunterian, and other societies, and did valuable editorial work for them; besides all which, several books of value to students and lovers of their country were the product of his laborious researches and his prolific pen.

Among the mass of material left are endless gatherings of rare title-pages, fragmentary portions of old authors, and specimens of typography of different dates, with historical and biographical notes, all presumably accumulated with a definite design, and which may yet be of value for bibliographical purposes supplementary to the laborious work of Mr. Aldis.[1] His collections in regard to the history and antiquities of Edinburgh are also large, and evince the devotion of a lifetime to the interests of the city which he loved so well.

In attempting to set out Laing's literary per-

---

[1] *A List of Books printed in Scotland before 1700, including those printed furth of the Realm.* By Harry G. Aldis (Edinburgh Bibliographical Society, 1904).

formances I propose to proceed in chronological order, so as to show the gradual development of his tastes and his studies as the years sped on. We may be enabled in that way to synchronise and correlate his literary achievements with the outward tenor of his life as sketched in the preceding pages.

It is reasonable to assume from what we know of his character and tastes that, from the time when he came to participate in the management of his father's business, no book bearing the imprint of William Laing or of W. & D. Laing passed into circulation without his critical revision : but in the following list of works, whatever the extent of his unacknowledged labours may have been, I propose to include nothing but what bears his name as editor or author, or such as can safely be ascribed to him on other grounds. Unfortunately in some of his books he preferred the rôle of anonymity. In consequence of this, and of so many of his books being CLUB publications, the list of works under his name to be found in library catalogues is limited, bearing no comparison to the amount of literature which proceeded from his pen, and therefore inadequate and misleading for the inquirer. He is understood, besides, to have contributed articles to encyclopædias, reviews, and magazines from time to time, without name ; so that there is probably a good deal of his composition in existence which will never be known as his. In the meantime the following list may perhaps be regarded as being as near to completeness as is possible in the present state of our knowledge. In preparing it I have availed myself of reference to what is contained in the British Museum, in the Advocates' Library, the Signet and University Libraries, of Edinburgh, and the Library of the Society of Antiquaries of Scotland, utilising at the same time all other sources of information accessible. The result is extraordinary—such an amount of literary output, as regards its extent, its variety, and its quality as, I apprehend, could be placed to the credit of very few men who ever lived.

The first to attempt an enumeration of Laing's publications was Thomas George Stevenson in his *Notices* of Laing, printed at the time of his death. The number of books briefly noted by him is eighty-two, and though neither complete nor always accurate, it is yet a useful record. The books and treatises of all kinds brought together in the following list reach the number of two hundred and fourteen.

1815

1. AUCTARIVM BIBLIOTHECÆ EDINBVRGENÆ sive Catalogus Librorum quos Gulielmus

Drummondus ab Hawthornden Bibliothecæ D.D.Q. Anno 1627. Edinburgi. Excudebant Hæredes Andreæ Hart. 1627. (*Verso.*) Edinburgh. Reprinted by James Ballantyne & Co. for William Laing and William Blackwood : and John Murray, London. 1815.

This account of the books presented by Drummond to the Library of the University of Edinburgh, though issued anonymously, is unquestionably, as a reprint, the work of Laing, and possibly his earliest. In the copy preserved in the University Library there is given in his handwriting, after the Preface, a ' List of Books presented to the Library by William Drummond of Hawthornden subsequent to the publication of the printed *Auctarivm*, 1627.' Seventy volumes are then described on inserted leaves, under the letters A, B, C, and D up to ' Disputatio,' etc., etc., where the list abruptly ends. The Library references of every book in the printed list, and also in Laing's supplementary manuscript list, are noted on the margins in his handwriting. It is entirely in keeping with the efforts of his later life to find him at this early age, twenty-two, addressing himself to the reproduction of such a work as this.

1821

2. POEMS BY ALEXANDER SCOTT. From a Manuscript written in the year MDLXVIII. (*Verso.*) 'Printed by Balfour and Clarke, 1821.' (Dedication) ' In token of Respect and Friendship and in acknowledgement of

the manifold services which he has rendered to the History and the Literature of Scotland, this little volume is inscribed to George Chalmers, Esq., by the Editor.' An 'Introductory Notice' of 12 pp. is signed 'David Laing, Edinburgh, 12th October 1821.' There are also copious 'Notes' at the end, with a musical accompaniment to one of the poems.

3. THOMÆ CRAIGI [Sir Thomas Craig of Riccarton] EPITHALAMIUM QUO HENRICI DARNLEII ET MARIÆ SCOTORUM REGINÆ NUPTIAS CELEBRAVIT. Impressum Edinburgi M.D.LXV. Denuo Editum Anno M.D.CCC.XXI.

This is the reprint of *twelve copies,* with a Latin Preface, issued by Laing, in 1821, of the following, the only known copy of which is in the Library of the University of Edinburgh :

HENRICI ILLVSTRISSIMI DVCIS ALBANIÆ COMITIS ROSSIÆ ET MARIÆ SERENISSIMÆ SCOTORUM REGINÆ EPITHALAMIUM. PER THOMAM CRAIGVM. IMPRESSUM EDINBURGI PER ROBERTUM LEKPREVIK. ANNO 1565. 8vo.

4. THE POEMS OF ALEXANDER MONTGOMERY [1597-1631] : WITH BIOGRAPHICAL NOTICES. By David Irving, LL.D. Edinburgh:

Printed by James Ballantyne & Co. For W. and C. Tait, Princes Street, 1821.

Laing's name nowhere appears in connection with the title; but in a footnote on p. xvii. of the introductory ' Biographical Notices ' Dr. Irving says :

' It is necessary to state that neither the credit nor the responsibility of editorship belongs to me : the poems were collected, arranged, and conducted through the press by Mr. David Laing, who likewise contributed the notes on the reverse of the different pages, and at the end of the volume '—an early instance of Laing's lifelong modesty, and his desire not to obtrude himself upon public notice.

1821-22

5. SELECT REMAINS OF THE ANCIENT POPULAR POETRY OF SCOTLAND. Printed at Edinburgh MDCCCXXII. (Quarto, about 108 copies issued.)

At the beginning there is an explanatory note, termed ' The Advertisement,' without signature, dated at Edinburgh 6th November 1822. Twenty-eight pieces, or ' tracts,' are reprinted, with an introductory note to each showing full and accurate knowledge of early Scottish writers. The book bears to be ' Printed for Wm. & D. Laing, by Balfour & Clarke, MDCCCXXI-MDCCCXXII.' Laing shrouds his identity as editor, but in the ' Advertisement' says, that ' with all due feeling of grateful esteem he would inscribe it as a slight but sincere tribute of respect to THE DISTINGUISHED AUTHOR to whom, of all others, the literature of his native country is most deeply beholden ' (Scott, of course).

The issue of this work by a young man, single-handed, was a great undertaking. It has since been reissued 'with Memorial Introduction and Additions' by John Small, M.A., in 1885, and again in 1895 by W. Carew Hazlitt. The copy in Laing's sale brought £12, 15s., the original stated to have been 'collected and edited by David Laing, 1822.'

6. A PLEASANT HISTORY OF ROSWALL AND LILLIAN. Declaring the occasion of *Roswall* his removing from his Native Kingdom to the Kingdom of *Bealm*, and what befell him in his journey from his Steward; the entertainment he met with from an Aged Wife; His Education at School; With his fortunate admission to be Servant to Lillian the King's only Daughter, with whom he fell deeply in love. The reward of the three Lords by whom he attained the honour of the three dayes justing before the Marriage of the Steward, who was known to be a Traitor and therefore justly executed; with the renewed wished-for Marriage betwixt *Roswall* and *Lillian* : His thankful remembrance of his friends; the number of his children, and their good fortune, all worthy reading. EDINBURGH : Printed by I. H. Anno 1663.

The original, in the Advocates' Library, was purchased at the Roxburghe sale in 1813, for £9, 9s. It consists of fourteen leaves. Laing's reprint (75 copies), n.d. [1822], contains a short Introduction, without signature.

7. FAC SIMILE OF AN ANCIENT HERALDIC MANUSCRIPT EMBLAZONED BY SIR DAVID LYNDSAY OF THE MOUNT, LYON KING OF ARMS; 1542. Edinburgh: Published by W. & D. Laing, MDCCCXXII.

Has 'Advertisement' and Introduction of 12 pp. without signature. A second edition, bearing on the title-page 'Edited by David Laing, LL.D.,' was published by William Paterson, Edinburgh, in 1878.

1823

8. THE BUKE OF THE HOWLAT. BY HOLLAND. Printed at EDINBURGH MDCCCXXIII. Black-letter, with frontispiece. 'This Edition of "The Buke of the Howlat" is respectfully dedicated and presented to the President and Members of the Bannatyne Club by their faithful servant, David Laing.' 23rd October, 1823. A Preface of 24 pp.

The author is assumed to be Sir Richard Holland, whose name occurs in an Act of the Scottish Parliament of March 1482. The poem was first printed in 1792, in Pinkerton's *Collection of Scottish Poems*, from the copy preserved in Bannatyne's manuscript.

1824

9. LETTER TO DR. HIBBERT, SECRETARY TO THE SOCIETY OF ANTIQUARIES OF SCOTLAND,

recommending the publication by the Society of the *Numismata Scotiæ*.

Read to the Society 22nd March 1824.

10. THE POEMS OF GEORGE BANNATYNE, MDLXVIII. Edinburgh, 1824, pp. 21, 8vo.

It ends with ' Finis, quoth Mr. Secretary,' *i.e.* Laing. The original manuscript is in the Advocates' Library.

1825

11. THE DISCOVERIE AND HISTORIE OF THE GOLD MYNES IN SCOTLAND. BY STEPHEN ATKINSON. Written in the year M.DC.XIX. EDINBURGH. PRINTED BY JAMES BALLANTYNE AND CO.

Printed from a MS. in the Advocates' Library. The text revised, and an Appendix added by Laing, but without his name or initials. 72 copies printed. (Bannatyne Club.)

12. VARIOUS PIECES OF FUGITIVE SCOTTISH POETRY, principally of the seventeenth century. EDINBURGH: PRINTED FOR W. & D. LAING. Small 8vo.

Contains forty-two separate pieces. A Preface of pp. 32 is dated at Edinburgh January MDCCCXXV, but without signature. The copy in the Advocates' Library is inscribed in Laing's handwriting, ' For the Library of the Faculty of Advocates from the Editor.'

LITERARY WORK

13. ETCHINGS, CHIEFLY OF VIEWS IN SCOTLAND. BY JOHN CLERK, ESQ., OF ELDIN, MDCCLXXIII-MDCCLXXIX (Bannatyne Club). MDCCCXXV.

Twenty-seven etchings. Only 40 copies printed. An enlarged edition, edited by Laing, was issued in 1855. This first volume, we may unhesitatingly assume, went through his hands in the same way.

14. ALBUM OF THE BANNATYNE CLUB. NO. I. 1825.

Contains a list of works recommended to the Club for publication.

1826

15. EARLY METRICAL TALES, INCLUDING THE HISTORY OF SIR EGEIR, SIR GRYME, AND SIR GRAY STEILL. Frontispiece by Charles Kirkpatrick Sharpe; portrait of the Earl of Eglinton, and tail-piece by Geikie, Edinburgh, 1826.

A Preface, Edinburgh, June 1825, with lengthy Introduction by Laing, but without his name. Printed for W. & D. Laing, and J. Duncan, London. 12mo. Only 175 copies printed.

16. LETTER addressed to the Secretary to the Society of Antiquaries of Scotland respecting Callander of Craigforth's Manuscript Notes on Milton in the possession of the Society.

Read 27th March 1826, and printed in *Archæologia Scotica*, vol. III. p. 83.

17. A REPORT on the unpublished 'Annotations on Milton's Paradise Lost,' written by the late John Callander, Esq., of Craigforth, presented by him to the Society in August 1781.

Read 10th April 1826, and printed in *Archæologia Scotica*, vol. iii. p. 84.

1827

18. THE KNIGHTLY TALE OF GOLAGRUS AND GAWANE AND OTHER ANCIENT POEMS. Printed at Edinburgh by W. Chepman and A. Myllar in the Year MDVIII. Reprinted MDCCCXXVII.

Black-letter. Edited by Laing, but without his name either on the title-page or to the Introduction. The original, preserved in the Advocates' Library, is the only known copy, and is one of the first books printed in Scotland.

According to the Laing sale catalogue, 'All the copies on paper, with one exception, were damaged by fire in the bookbinder's shop. Eighty copies were distributed, all of which were partially inlaid, thus only five perfect copies exist.'

19. THE BANNATYNE MISCELLANY, CONTAINING ORIGINAL PAPERS AND TRACTS, CHIEFLY RELATING TO THE HISTORY AND LITERATURE OF SCOTLAND. Volume I. Printed at Edinburgh M.DCCC.XXVII. (Bannatyne Club.)

No Introduction, but copy of minute of the Club, of

LITERARY WORK

4th July 1823, resolving that this miscellany ' be printed in successive numbers or parts, under the joint superintendence of the President and Secretary.' Signed by ' David Laing, Secretary.' We can readily understand how much labour in this form could be looked for from Scott at this, or indeed at any other time; and the ascription of the gathering and issue of the miscellany to Laing may be accepted as incontrovertible. The contents are so varied, curious, and valuable, that I am constrained to quote the list for the benefit of students.

> A Proposal for Uniting Scotland with England, addressed to King Henry VIII. by John Elder Clerke, a Reddshanke [1542.]
>
> The Progress of the Regent of Scotland, with certain of his Nobility, June 1568.
>
> An Account of a Pretended Conference held by the Regent, Earl of Murray, with the Lord Lindsay, and others, January 1570.
>
> An Opinion of the Present State, Faction, Religion, and Power of the Nobility of Scotland, 1583.
>
> Instructions from Henry III., King of France, to the Sieur de la Mothe Fenelon, Ambassador at the Court of Scotland, 1583.
>
> The Heads of a Conference betwixt King James VI. and Sir Francis Walsingham, September 1583.
>
> Notes presented by Mr. John Colville to Lord Hunsdon, 1584.
>
> The Manner and Form of the Examination and Death of William, Earl of Gowrye, May 1584.
>
> The Apology of Mr. Patrick Galloway, Minister of Perth, when he fled to England, 1585.
>
> Relation by the Master of Gray, concerning the

- Surprise of the King at Stirling, November 1585.
- The Application of Three Several Discourses delivered on Occasion of the Gowrye Conspiracy, August 1600.
- Narrative by Mr. Robert Bruce, one of the Ministers of Edinburgh, concerning his Troubles in the year 1600.
- Edinburgi Regiæ Scotorum Urbis Descriptio, per Alexandrum Alesium Scotum, S.T.D., 1550.
- Elegy on Sir Robert Kerr of Cessford, first Earl of Roxburghe, 1650.
- A Relation of the Imprisonment and Examination of James Cathkin, Bookseller, June 1619.
- Letter from Robert of Dunhelm, Monk of Kelso, to the Prior and Convent of Tynemouth, 1257.
- Reasons against the reception of King James's Metaphrase of the Psalms, 1631.
- Declarator in the Court of the Superintendent of Fife, 1561, upon the Articles and Sentence against Sir John Borthwick, Knight, by Cardinal Beaton, 1540.
- A Diary of the Expedition of King Edward i. into Scotland, 1296.
- Extracts from the Obituary of the Rev. Robert Boyd of Trochrig, Principal of the College of Edinburgh, 1609-1625.
- Poems by Sir Robert Ayton.
- Letters of Florentius Volusenus.
- Meditation faite par Marie Royne d'Ecosse et Dovariere de France, 1572.
- Letters of John Earl of Gowrye, 1595.

In every case these interesting historical papers are introduced by an explanatory article supplied by Laing.

20. DELIVERIE FROM THE SPANISH ARMADA, 1588. PRINTED AT EDINBURGH BY THE HEIRS OF ANDRO HART. 1628.

Read to the Society of Antiquaries 15th January 1827.

21. THE FIRST PART OF AN INQUIRY INTO THE ORIGIN AND PROGRESS OF DRAMATICK EXHIBITIONS IN SCOTLAND.

Read to the Society of Antiquaries 9th April 1827.

1828

22. A BRIEF ACCOUNT OF THE HAWTHORNDEN MSS. IN THE POSSESSION OF THE SOCIETY OF ANTIQUARIES, with Extracts containing several unpublished Letters and Poems of William Drummond of Hawthornden. By David Laing, F.S.A.Scot., and Hon. Member Society of Antiquaries, Newcastle-upon-Tyne.

Read to the Society of Antiquaries 14th January 1828, and printed in *Archæologia Scotica,* vol. iv. p. 57.

1829

23. MEMORIALS OF GEORGE BANNATYNE, M.D.XLV-M.DC.VIII. Printed at Edinburgh, M.DCCC.XXIX.

These *Memorials* consist of a ' Memoir ' by Sir Walter Scott; an ' Account of the Contents of George Bannatyne's Manuscript 1568 ' by Mr. David Laing, etc., etc.

Also 'Poems by George Bannatyne, From his manuscript M.D.LXVIII.'

1830

24. A RELATION OF PROCEEDINGS CONCERNING THE AFFAIRS OF THE KIRK OF SCOTLAND. From August 1637 to July 1638. BY JOHN EARL OF ROTHES. Edinburgh: Printed M.DCCC.XXX.

Presented to the Bannatyne Club by James Nairne (W.S.). An introductory 'Notice' of four pages is initialed 'J. N.' and dated 'Picardy Place,' August 1830 (his house was No. 18). In it he makes acknowledgment to Laing for 'relieving me of the details of the publication, for which my professional avocations ill fitted me'; also for 'the Articles and Notes which form the Appendix,' except one item. The book contains three plates, and a portrait of Rothes, *ætatis* twenty-five.

25. AN ACCOUNT OF THE VISIT OF A COMPANY OF ENGLISH COMEDIANS TO THE COURT OF JAMES VI. IN THE YEAR 1599, WITH INTRODUCTORY NOTICES OF THE PROGRESS OF THE EARLY DRAMA IN SCOTLAND.

Read to the Society of Antiquaries 30th December 1830.

1831

26. THE GENEALOGY OF THE MOST NOBLE AND ANCIENT HOUSE OF DRUMMOND. BY THE HONOURABLE WILLIAM DRUMMOND, AFTERWARDS FIRST VISCOUNT OF STRATHALLAN.

M.DC.LXXXI.   EDINBURGH,   M.DCCC.XXXI.
PRINTED BY A. BALFOUR & CO.

A large quarto volume of 331 pages, with an elaborate Appendix and Notes without signature or initial, but all in Laing's careful style (100 copies). The work was again privately printed in Glasgow in 1889, declaring itself to be 'The Fac-Simile Reprint of Dr. David Laing's Edition of 1831, which has now become rare,' etc. (Again 100 copies only.) Laing's print was from a copy made by Mr. David Drummond, Advocate, anno 1689, of the Viscount's original manuscript of 1681.

27. THE BUIK OF THE NOBLE AND VAILZEAND CONQUEROUR ALEXANDER THE GREAT. EDINBURGH. PRINTED M.DCCC.XXXI.

This, originally printed by Bassandyne in 1580, was presented to the Bannatyne Club by William Henry Miller of Craigentinny, and bears no Preface, Introduction, or explanatory Note. But Laing had prepared an elaborate Preface, which was approved by Scott (with an appendix), and Miller took exception to certain clauses in it, particularly the form of acknowledgment to Lord Panmure, from whose unique copy the book had been reprinted. Laing would not consent to the alterations proposed, and the Preface and Appendix were withdrawn. This explanation is disclosed in the correspondence which is preserved, and is now, after the lapse of more than eighty years, probably unknown to bibliographers.

28. REMARKS ON THE ANCIENT SCULPTURES AT THE NETHERBOW, EDINBURGH, SUPPOSED

TO BE THE HEADS OF LUCIUS SEPTIMIUS SEVERUS AND HIS WIFE JULIA.

Read to the Society of Antiquaries 24th January 1831, and printed in *Archæologia Scotica*, vol. iii. p. 287.

29. REMARKS UPON THE STATE OF THE FINE ARTS IN SCOTLAND DURING THE 15TH, 16TH AND 17TH CENTURIES.

Read to the Society of Antiquaries 28th February 1831.

30. ALBUM OF THE BANNATYNE CLUB. NO. II. 1831.

Contains a list of works recommended to the Club for publication.

31. REMARKS ON THE SCOTTISH ARTISTS OF THE LAST CENTURY, in continuation of the previous communication.

Read to the Society of Antiquaries 14th March 1831.

1832

32. EXTRACTS FROM CONVERSATIONS BETWEEN DRUMMOND OF HAWTHORNDEN AND BEN JONSON IN THE YEAR 1619. Communicated from an unpublished MS. in the Advocates' Library.

Read to the Society of Antiquaries 9th January 1832, and printed in *Archæologia Scotica*, vol. iv. p. 241. These extracts, according to Professor Masson, were ' a flash of light on the literary and social history of England in the reign of James I., and on the lives of Ben Jonson and Drummond in particular.'

1833

33. COLLECTION OF ANCIENT SCOTTISH PROPHECIES IN ALLITERATIVE VERSE. REPRINTED FROM WALDEGRAVE'S EDITION. M.DC.III. EDINBURGH. PRINTED BY Ballantyne & Co. M.DCCC.XXXIII. (Black-letter.)

This was edited by Laing for the Bannatyne Club, with a Preface by Thomas Thomson, the Vice-President.

34. A BRIEF MEMOIR OF THE LIFE AND WRITINGS OF SIR DAVID DALRYMPLE, BART., LORD HAILES. From the *Encyclopædia Britannica*, Seventh Edition. Edinburgh, May 1833. 19 pp.

This is evidently one of Laing's contributions to the *Encyclopædia*. The copy possessed by Sir Arthur Mitchell, now in the Advocates' Library, bears 'corrections in the handwriting of David Laing.'

35. BRIEF NOTICE OF THE SMALL FIGURE CUT IN IVORY, SUPPOSED BY PENNANT TO REPRESENT THE KING OF SCOTLAND IN HIS CORONATION CHAIR, AND WHICH WAS DISCOVERED IN DUNSTAFFNAGE CASTLE.

Read to the Society of Antiquaries 11th March 1833, and printed in *Archæologia Scotica*, vol. iv. p. 366.

1834

36. THE POEMS OF WILLIAM DUNBAR, NOW FIRST COLLECTED. WITH NOTES AND A MEMOIR OF HIS LIFE. BY DAVID LAING. 2 vols. EDINBURGH. MDCCCXXXIV. Printed for Laing and Forbes, Princes Street; and William Pickering, London.

Preface signed ' D. Laing. Edinburgh, January 1834.' A small supplement followed in 1865, sm. 8vo.

Laing's care and accuracy in his use of the different MSS. upon which this work is based, is highly commended by an Austrian scholar, Professor Schipper, in his edition of Dunbar's *Poems*, published in Vienna in 1894.

1835

37. CERTANE TRACTATIS FOR REFORMATIOUN OF DOCTRYNE AND MANERIS, SET FURTH AT THE DESYRE, AND IN YE NAME OF YE AFFLICTIT CATHOLIKIS, OF INFERIOUR ORDOUR OF CLERGIE, AND LENJIT MEN IN SCOTLAND BE NINIANE WINZET, ANE CATHOLIKE PREIST BORNE IN RENFREW. Quhilkis be name this leif turnit sall schaw. *Murus aheneus sana Conscientia.* Edinburgi, 21 May 1562.

Reprinted at Edinburgh MDCCCXXXV (black-letter), with other contemporary tracts by Winzet (Maitland Club). Preface by Laing, without signature, with *Life of Ninian Winzet,* 13 pp., described in the Introduction to the Scottish Text Society's edition of 1888 as—'though meagre, concise and generally accurate,' and admitted to have been 'useful in suggesting sources of information for this edition.'

Winzet (or Wingate), this valiant defender of the ancient Church, had a hard time of it in his own country. Expelled from the schoolmastership of Linlithgow, he was some time in Edinburgh under the protection of Queen Mary, but fled abroad for safety, and eventually became Abbot of the Scottish Monastery at Ratisbon in Germany.

1836

38. THE BANNATYNE MISCELLANY; CONTAINING ORIGINAL PAPERS AND TRACTS, CHIEFLY RELATING TO THE HISTORY AND LITERATURE OF SCOTLAND. Volume II. Printed at Edinburgh, M.DCCC.XXXVI.

This volume was to be printed 'under the joint superintendence of the President and Secretary,' which is equivalent to saying that it became, practically, the work of the Secretary (Laing).

Its contents are—

Strena ad Jacobum v. Scotorum Regem de Suscepto Regni Regimine [1528], with Translation into English verse.
Historia Miraculose Fundationis Monasterii Sancte Crucis prope Edinburgh [1128]. Historia Fundationis Prioratus Insule de Traile, etc., etc.
Negotiations of the Scottish Commissioners at Nottingham, September 1484.

Oratio Scotorum ad Regem Ricardum Tertium pro Pace firmanda inter Anglos et Scotos, 1484.

List of Contributions to the Senators of the College of Justice, April 1586, etc.

A Survey of the Castle and Town of Edinburgh, January 1573. Journal of the Siege of the Castle of Edinburgh, April and May 1573.

The Opinion of George Buchanan concerning the Reformation of the University of St. Andrews [1563].

Testamentum Domini Jacobi de Douglas Domini de Dalkeith Militis, 30th September 1390. Testamentum Ejusdem, 19th December 1392.

The Spectakle of Luf, translated from the Latin by G. Myll, at St. Andrews, 1492.

Catalogus Librorum Manuscriptorum e Bibliotheca D. Joannis Ducis de Lauderdale, 1692.

The Quair of Jelousy, a Poem by [James] Auchinleck, written about the year 1480.

Collection of the Wills of Printers and Booksellers in Edinburgh between the years 1577 and 1687. [30 persons named, with the requisite particulars, beginning with Thomas Bassandyne, 1579, and ending with James Watson, 1687].

An Obituary from the Rental Book of the Preceptory of St. Anthony, near Leith, 1526.

Collection of Papers relating to the *Theatrum Scotiæ* and *History and Present State of Scotland*, by Captain John Slezer, 1693-1707.

Collection of Papers relating to the Geographical Description, Maps, and Charts of Scotland, by John Adair, F.R.S., Geographer for the Kingdom of Scotland, 1686-1723.

Urbis Edinburgi Descriptio, per Davidem Buchananum, circa A.D. 1648.

39. A Diary of Public Transactions and other Occurrences, chiefly in Scotland, from January 1650 to June 1667. By John Nicoll. Printed at Edinburgh, M.DCCC.XXXVI.

Preface signed 'D. Laing, Septr. 1836.' (Bannatyne Club.) The original MS. is in the Advocates' Library.

1837

40. The Seven Sages, in Scottish Metre. By John Rolland of Dalkeith. Edinburgh : Reprinted from the Edition of M.D.LXXVII. M.DCCC.XXXVII.

Preface signed by 'D. Laing, Edinburgh, December MD.CCC.XXXVII.' Rolland was a notary in Dalkeith. (Bannatyne Club.)

41. Testimonials in favour of Mr. David Laing as a Candidate for the office of Principal Librarian to the Society of Writers to His Majesty's Signet, Edinburgh, 1837.

I would not have entered this among Laing's literary works were it not that it is to be found so quoted in library catalogues.

42. Owain Miles, and other inedited Fragments of Ancient English Poetry (selected from the Auchinleck Manuscript).

A copy of this is in the British Museum, but I have

not been able to trace it in any Edinburgh library. One copy appeared at the Laing sale, where it brought £2, 11s. The catalogue states that only 32 copies were printed for private distribution. Laing's co-editor was W. B. D. D. Turnbull, Advocate. (12mo.)

1839

43. THE SCOTS MUSICAL MUSEUM, London, 1787-1803. NEW EDITION, WITH NOTES AND ILLUSTRATIONS OF THE LYRIC POETRY OF SCOTLAND, BY THE LATE WILLIAM STENHOUSE, AND ADDITIONAL ILLUSTRATIONS. EDITED BY D. LAING, ESQ., EDINBURGH, 1839. 8VO. 6 volumes.

Quoted by Lowndes as above, but a copy is difficult to find.

The Preface by Laing, dated 'Signet Library, Edinburgh, MDCCCXXXIX,' is issued verbatim with the subsequent edition of 1853; with an 'Advertisement,' also signed by him, 'Edinburgh, May 1853.'

1840

44. HISTORICAL OBSERVES OF MEMORABLE OCCURRENTS IN CHURCH AND STATE. FROM OCTOBER 1680 TO APRIL 1686. BY SIR JOHN LAUDER OF FOUNTAINHALL. PRINTED AT EDINBURGH. M.DCCC.XL.

On 8th July 1836 it was resolved by the Bannatyne Club that these 'Observations,' as they call them, should be printed 'under the joint-superintendence of Adam Urquhart, Esq., and the Secretary of the Club';

and again, on 3rd July 1840, that the volume of *Historical Observes of Memorable Occurrents*, which was circulated among the members in January 1838, should now be completed as a separate work—that quoted above.

45. JACOBITE CORRESPONDENCE OF THE ATHOLL FAMILY DURING THE REBELLION, M.DCC.XLV-M.DCC.XLVI. FROM THE ORIGINALS IN THE POSSESSION OF JAMES ERSKINE OF ABERDONA, ESQ. EDINBURGH. PRINTED FOR THE ABBOTSFORD CLUB. M.DCCCXL. 4to.

The existence of this correspondence, and its offer to the Club for publication, was intimated at a meeting on 26th November 1838; and the editing of the work was confided to John Hill Burton and Laing. The 'Introductory Notice,' which bears no signature, is dated from '7 Howard Place, Edinburgh, 7 March 1840,' apparently Burton's residence at the time. It proceeds in name of 'the Editor,' thus ignoring Laing's co-operation; but it may be confidently assumed that he did not fail to discharge the full share entrusted to him in the preparation of the volume.

46. NOTICE OF AN ORIGINAL DEED RELATING TO THE DOWRY OF MARGARET, WIDOW OF PRINCE ALEXANDER OF SCOTLAND. The original deed, dated at Namur in the year 1286, in the possession of Mr. Laing, was exhibited.

Read to the Society of Antiquaries 30th March 1840.

1841

47. THE LETTERS AND JOURNALS OF ROBERT BAILLIE, A.M., PRINCIPAL OF THE UNIVERSITY OF GLASGOW, M.DC.XXXVII-M.DC.LXII. In Three Volumes. Volumes First and Second (pp. 492 and 516) *Edinburgh* M.DCCC.XLI. Volume Third (pp. 627) M.DCCC.XLII. (Bannatyne Club.) 4to.

On 3rd December 1838 it was resolved by the committee of the Club that these letters and journals, from the original manuscript preserved in the archives of the Church of Scotland, be printed under the superintendence of the secretary of the Club. The Preface is signed by Laing, 'Signet Library, June 1841,' and to it is appended a memoir (63 pp.) of the life of Robert Baillie initialed ' D. L.,' the whole work a great and laborious undertaking. Carlyle reviewed it very favourably in the *London and Westminster Review*, remarking that Laing had exhibited his usual industry, sagacity, and correctness, with notes brief, illuminative, ever in the right place, not over plenteous nor more than needed. A separate edition, royal 8vo., was issued at the same time.

48. NOTICES AND EXTRACTS FROM A MS. VOLUME OF OLD ENGLISH POEMS AND ROMANCES, WRITTEN IN THE YEAR 1457 (INCLUDING SIR BEVIS OF HAMPTON, THE LEGEND OF SAINT ALEX OF ROME, LIBEOUS DISCONIOUS, AND CHAUCER'S TALE OF GRISELDIS), preserved

in the 'Reale Biblioteca Borbonica' at Naples.

Read to the Society of Antiquaries 22nd February 1841, and printed in Wright and Halliwell's *Reliquiæ Antiquæ*, vol. ii., London, 1843.

49. A LETTER OR PRECEPT BY FRANCIS THE FIRST, FOR CERTAIN PAYMENTS TO BE MADE TO FRANCIS DE LONGANNAY, AND THREE OTHER PERSONS, ARCHERS IN THE COMPANY OF THE DUKE OF ALBANY, NOTWITHSTANDING THEIR BEING LAID UP WITH SICKNESS SINCE THEIR RETURN FROM THE KINGDOM OF NAPLES. Dated at Rouen, 27 Feb. 1558.

Read to the Society of Antiquaries 22nd February 1841.

50. A SHORT DIARY OR JOURNAL BY SOME PERSON, SUPPOSED TO BE ONE AYLMER, A WRITER OR NOTARY-PUBLIC IN EDINBURGH, from November 1681 to November 1684.

Read to the Society of Antiquaries 29th March 1841.

51. WARRANT BY THE REGENT MURRAY APPOINTING SIR ANDREW MURRAY OF ARNGASK, KNIGHT, TO BE PRINCIPAL KEEPER OF THE KING'S PARK OF HOLYROOD HOUSE, dated at Edinburgh, 12 February 1567; from the original in the possession of William Smythe, Esq., Advocate.

Read to the Society of Antiquaries 29th March

1841, and printed in *Archæologia Scotica*, vol. iv. p. 401.

52. NOTICE OF THREE PORTRAITS OF JOHN DUKE OF ALBANY, MARY QUEEN OF SCOTS, AND OF SIBILLA BETOUN, ONE OF THE QUEEN'S ATTENDANTS, BEING FAC-SIMILES OF ORIGINAL DRAWINGS IN THE ROYAL LIBRARY AT PARIS.

Read to the Society of Antiquaries 21st June 1841, when the portraits were exhibited.

53. A SCHEME OR MEMORIAL FOR CIVILIZING THE HIGHLANDS OF SCOTLAND, FROM A MS. PURPORTING TO HAVE BEEN WRITTEN BY SIMON FRASER, LORD LOVAT, IN THE YEAR 1716.

Read to the Society of Antiquaries 21st June 1841.

1841

54. THE HISTORY OF THE KIRK OF SCOTLAND. FROM THE YEAR 1558 TO AUGUST 1637. BY JOHN ROW, MINISTER OF CARNOCK : WITH A CONTINUATION TO JULY 1639, BY HIS SON, JOHN ROW, PRINCIPAL OF KING'S COLLEGE, ABERDEEN. EDINBURGH: PRINTED FOR THE WODROW SOCIETY. M.DCCC.XLII.

The Preface is signed ' DAVID LAING, SIGNET LIBRARY. EDINBURGH, November 1842,' with an ' Account ' of Row's life, ' Notices ' respecting him, and a Note of the manuscript copies of his *History*, 62 pages in all.

1842

55. NOTICES REGARDING THE METRICAL VERSION OF THE PSALMS RECEIVED BY THE CHURCH OF SCOTLAND. EDINBURGH. M.DCCC.XLII. (*Verso.*) FROM THE APPENDIX TO PRINCIPAL BAILLIE'S LETTERS AND JOURNALS.

A small octavo volume, 53 pp., with the initials ' D. L.' and the date ' April 1842.' Privately printed.

56. NOTES OF BEN JONSON'S CONVERSATIONS WITH WILLIAM DRUMMOND OF HAWTHORNDEN. JANUARY M.DC.XIX. LONDON: PRINTED FOR THE SHAKESPEARE SOCIETY. 1842.

A Preface of 20 pages signed ' David Laing, Signet Library. Edinburgh.'

1844

57. THE MISCELLANY OF THE WODROW SOCIETY : CONTAINING TRACTS AND ORIGINAL LETTERS, CHIEFLY RELATING TO THE ECCLESIASTICAL AFFAIRS OF SCOTLAND DURING THE SIXTEENTH AND SEVENTEENTH CENTURIES. SELECTED AND EDITED BY DAVID LAING, ESQ. VOLUME FIRST. EDINBURGH: PRINTED FOR THE WODROW SOCIETY. M.DCCC.XLIV.

The contents of this *Miscellany,* like that of the

Bannatyne Club, are so important that I am again constrained to transfer a list of them to these pages:

> The Confession of Faith of the Churches of Switzerland; Translated from the Latin by George Wishart, 1536.
> Certamen cum Lutheranis, Saxoniæ Habitum, per Jacobum Melvil, Scotum, Bononiæ, 1530.
> Historie of the Estate of Scotland, From July 1558 to April 1560.
> Ane Compendius Tractive, etc., set furth be Maister Quintine Kennedy, Abbot of Crossraguell, in the ʒeir of God 1558.
> Ane Answer to the Compendius Tractive set furth in the ʒeir of God 1558, be Maister Quintine Kennedy, Abbot of Crossraguell: Be Maister Johne Davidsone, Maister of the Paedagog of Glasgow. Edinburgh, 1563.
> Letter from Mr. Quintine Kennedy, Abbot of Crossraguell, to James Archbishop of Glasgow, together with the Correspondence of the Abbot and John Willock, at Ayr, 1559.
> Letters to John Campbell of Kinyeancleuch, Ayrshire.
> The Forme and Maner of Buriall used in the Kirk of Montrois.
> Roberti Pontani Parvus Catechismus, Carmine Iambico, Andreapoli, 1573.
> Register of Ministers and Readers in the Kirk of Scotland, From the Book of the Assignation of Stipends, 1574.
> Supplication of the General Assembly to the Regent Earl of Morton, April 1578.
> The Presbytery of Haddington's Subscription to the Second Book of Discipline, September 1591.

Act of Presbytery, appointing two Ministers to the Lords at Falkirk, 12th August 1578.

Letters and Papers of Mr. James Carmichael, Minister of Haddington, 1584-1586.

Account of the Death and Funeral of Mr. James Lawson, Minister of Edinburgh, 1584.

Visitations of the Kirk of Holyroodhouse, by the Presbytery of Edinburgh.

Vindication of the Church of Scotland, in reply to Dr. Bancroft's Sermon at Paul's Cross, London, February 1588-9.

Ane Forme of Sindrie Maters to be usit in the Elderschip, 1589-1592.

A Short Forme of Evening and Morning Prayer, By John Davidson, 1595.

Letters of Mr. John Welsch, Minister of Ayr, to Robert Boyd of Trochrig, 1607-1619.

Ane Afold Admonition to the Ministerie of Scotland, By Mr. Alexander Hume, Minister of Logie, 1609.

The Forme and Maner of Ordaining Ministers, and Consecrating of Archbishops and Bishops, used in the Church of Scotland, 1620.

1844

58. MEMOIRS OF THE CHURCH OF SCOTLAND, IN FOUR PERIODS, FROM THE REFORMATION TO THE UNION, WITH AN APPENDIX OF SOME TRANSACTIONS SINCE THE UNION. BY DANIEL DE FOE. CAREFULLY REPRINTED FROM THE ORIGINAL EDITION OF 1717. (Knox portrait—Beza's.) EDINBURGH :

Robert Ogle and Oliver & Boyd. 1848. Royal 8vo.

This work is entered here, in place of under the year 1848, because the 'Introductory Notice,' bearing the initial 'L.,' is dated 'Feb. 28, 1844,' showing that the issue of the book was postponed for some years after its preparation by Laing for the press. The original bears that it was printed in London ' for Eman. Matthews at the *Bible*, and T. Warner at the *Black Boy*, both in Paternoster Row, 1717.'

59. Extracts from an unpublished Journal of the Rebellion of 1715, from a MS. written by Peter Clarke, in the possession of Mr. Laing, the Treasurer.

Read to the Society of Antiquaries 15th April 1844, and printed in Dr. Hibbert Ware's *Lancashire Memorials of the Rebellion of 1715*, for the Chetham Society, 1845.

60. Copy of a Letter written from Rome in January 1721, giving an account of the Birth of 'The Young Pretender.'

Read to the Society of Antiquaries 27th May 1844.

61. Notices relating to the History of Trinity College Church, Edinburgh, with a copy of the Petition presented in name of the Society to the Lord Provost and Magistrates of Edin-

BURGH IN MAY LAST AGAINST THE PROPOSED DEMOLITION OF THAT VENERABLE EDIFICE.

Read to the Society of Antiquaries 23rd December 1844. At the same time Mr. Laing exhibited, by permission of the Treasurer of Trinity Church Hospital, an Original Document, dated in the year 1461, respecting the Foundation of the Church of the Queen-Dowager of Scotland.

62. A TRAGICALL BLAST OF THE PAPISTICALL TROMPETTE FOR MAINTENAUNCE OF THE POPES KINGDOME IN ENGLAND. [BY T. E. 1555.]

Six pages, with introductory Note, and initials 'D. L. Edinburgh, 11 January 1844.' 18 copies printed. 'A very poor affair.'

1845

63. NOTICE OF A LETTER FROM LADY BALMERINACH, IN WHICH THE EXECUTION OF HER HUSBAND IS ANNOUNCED.

Read to the Society of Antiquaries 7th April 1845. Arthur, sixth Lord Balmerino, was tried for high treason, and executed on Tower Hill, London, 18th August 1746.

64. LETTER FROM THOMAS, BISHOP OF ORCADIE AND ZETLAND, TO THE KING OF NORWEGE, DATED AT KIRKWALL, THE 1ST DAY OF JULY 1446, RESPECTING THE GENEALOGY OF WILLIAM ST. CLAIR, EARL OF ORCADIE.

TRANSLATED FROM THE LATIN INTO SCOTTIS BE DEANE THOMAS GWLD, MONK OF NEWBOTTIL, IN THE YEAR 1554.

From a MS. in the library at Abbotsford. With an Introductory Notice. Read to the Society of Antiquaries 7th April 1845, and printed in the *Bannatyne Miscellany*, vol. iii.

1846

65. THE WORKS OF JOHN KNOX; COLLECTED AND EDITED BY DAVID LAING. EDINBURGH. VOLUME I. PRINTED FOR THE BANNATYNE CLUB. MDCCCXLVI.

The *History of the Reformation in Scotland*, the letters and miscellaneous writings, including the *Book of Common Order or the Form of Prayers*, for the Church of Scotland, *The First Blast of the Trumpet against the Monstrous Regiment of Women*, etc., etc., form an elaborate work of seven volumes. By resolution of the committee of the Bannatyne Club of 19th June 1845, other 112 copies were printed for the use of the members of the Wodrow Society, under the same date, 1846.

Three manuscript copies of the *History*, and a portion of a fourth, were in Laing's own possession, besides ten copies in other hands which he describes in the ' Introductory Notice.' The earliest of these manuscripts is preserved in the University of Edinburgh, and is that mainly followed by Laing.

66. AN APOLOGETICAL NARRATION OF THE STATE AND GOVERNMENT OF THE KIRK OF SCOT-

LAND SINCE THE REFORMATION. BY WILLIAM SCOTT, MINISTER OF CUPAR. CERTAIN RECORDS TOUCHING THE ESTATE OF THE KIRK IN THE YEARS M.DC.V. & M.DC.VI. BY JOHN FORBES, MINISTER OF ALFORD. EDINBURGH; Printed for the Wodrow Society. MDCCCXLVI.

Printed for the first time. The 'Preface,' signed by Laing 'Signet Library, 10 July 1846,' acknowledges the co-operation of the Reverend James Anderson in transcribing and collating the manuscripts, and correcting the proof sheets. The Preface is followed by a Life of the two authors, Scott and Forbes, all apparently the result of Laing's unwearied researches.

67. INQUIRIES RESPECTING SOME OF THE EARLY HISTORICAL WRITERS OF SCOTLAND. NO. 1— FRIAR ADAM ABEL, OF JEDBURGH, AUTHOR OF THE 'ROTA TEMPORUM'; NO. 2—JOHN LAW, CANON OF ST. ANDREWS, ONE OF THE ABBREVIATORS OF THE 'SCOTICHRONICON.'

Read to the Society of Antiquaries 23rd February 1846, and printed in the *Proceedings* of the Society, vol. xii. p. 73.

68. NOTICES OF VARIOUS PILGRIMAGES BY KING JAMES IV. TO THE SHRINE OF ST. DUTHAC AT TAYN, IN ROSS-SHIRE BETWEEN THE YEARS 1494 AND 1513.

Read to the Society of Antiquaries 23rd February 1846.

69. NOTICES OF KING JAMES V.'S VOYAGE ROUND SCOTLAND TO THE WESTERN ISLES IN THE YEAR 1540.

Read to the Society of Antiquaries 30th March 1846.

70. SOME NOTICES FROM THE COUNCIL RECORDS OF ST. ANDREWS RESPECTING THE MURDER OF ARCHBISHOP SHARP, 1679.

Read to the Society of Antiquaries 1st June 1846, and printed in *Archæologia Scotica*, vol. iv. p. 409.

71. NOTICES RESPECTING THE TUMULT IN EDINBURGH ON THE ANNIVERSARY OF ST. GILES, 1ST SEPTEMBER 1588, AND THE SUBSEQUENT DISPOSAL OF THE JEWELS AND KIRK WORK, INCLUDING THE CELEBRATED RELIQUE 'THE ARME BANE OF SANCT GEILL.'

Read to the Society of Antiquaries 22nd June 1846.

72. AN ORIGINAL DEED RESPECTING THE DOWRY OF MARGARET, DAUGHTER OF GUY, EARL OF FLANDERS, AND WIDOW OF PRINCE ALEXANDER, SON OF ALEXANDER III., KING OF SCOTLAND, DATED AT BRUGES ON THE WEDNESDAY AFTER THE EXALTATION OF THE HOLY CROSS (Sept. 1285).

Exhibited to the Society of Antiquaries, with an Introductory Notice, 19th June 1846.

1847

73. THE BUKE OF THE ORDER OF KNIGHTHOOD. TRANSLATED FROM THE FRENCH, BY SIR GILBERT HAY, KNIGHT. FROM THE MANUSCRIPT IN THE LIBRARY AT ABBOTSFORD. EDINBURGH. M.DCCC.XLVII. PRESENTED TO THE ABBOTSFORD CLUB BY BERIAH BOTFIELD.

This book is attributed to Laing by T. G. Stevenson, but his name does not appear in connection with it. John Small says it was edited by Laing ' for the Bannatyne Club.' There is no doubt every probability that it was issued under Laing's supervision, though Botfield's Preface gives no intimation of this.

74. INQUIRIES CONCERNING SOME OF THE EARLY HISTORICAL WRITERS OF SCOTLAND. NO. 3—MR. JOHN COLVILLE, THE SUPPOSED AUTHOR OF THE 'HISTORIE AND LIFE OF KING JAMES THE SEXT.' PUBLISHED BY THE BANNATYNE CLUB IN 1825.

Read to the Society of Antiquaries 25th January 1847, and printed in the *Proceedings* of the Society, vol. xii. p. 72.

75. CONTINUATION OF NOTICES OF JOHN COLVILLE.

Read to the Society of Antiquaries 8th February 1847.

76. ORIGINAL DEED, CONTAINING THE 'RULES OF THE EDINBURGH SCHOOL OF ST. LUKE,' 1729, SIGNED BY THE MEMBERS (29 IN NUMBER), PAINTERS OR LOVERS OF PAINTING.

Read to the Society of Antiquaries 24th May 1847.

77. AN ACCOUNT OF THE NAMES OF SOME OF THE PERSONS WHO HAVE ORIGINAL COPIES OF OUR COVENANTS, 'NATIONAL AND SOLEMN LEAGUE,' IN MS. WRITTEN ABOUT THE YEAR 1730; WITH REMARKS.

Read to the Society of Antiquaries 24th May 1847, and printed in their *Proceedings,* vol. iv. p. 238.

78. COPY OF AN OLD DEED IN THE SCOTTISH LANGUAGE, DATED AT KIRKWAW (OR KIRKWALL) IN ORKNEY, 20 JANUARY 1438, FROM THE ORIGINAL IN THE POSSESSION OF W. H. FOTHERINGHAME, ESQ., KIRKWALL.

Read to the Society of Antiquaries 24th May 1847.

1848

79. HISTORICAL NOTICES OF SCOTTISH AFFAIRS, SELECTED FROM THE MANUSCRIPTS OF SIR JOHN LAUDER OF FOUNTAINHALL, BART., ONE OF THE SENATORS OF THE COLLEGE OF JUSTICE. VOLUME FIRST, 1661-1683. VOL-

ume Second, 1683-1688. (Bannatyne Club.) Printed at Edinburgh, MDCCCXLVIII.

On 10th April 1848 the committee of the Club resolved that this work, of nearly 900 pages, edited by the Secretary (Laing), be forthwith completed in two volumes. The Preface by Laing, of fourteen pages, does not bear his name or initials.

80. The Works of John Knox. Collected and Edited by David Laing. Volume II. Bannatyne Club. MDCCCXLVIII.

81. A Decree of Spulzie granted by the Lords of Counsell to William Bruce of Symbister in Zetland, against Patrick Earl of Orkney in 1609 (the original Extract, signed by the Clerk Register, was exhibited by Captain Thomas Fraser, R.A., Portobello), accompanied with Remarks illustrative of the proceedings and fate of the Earl of Orkney.

Read to the Society of Antiquaries 24th January 1848, and printed in *Archæologia Scotica*, vol. iv.

82. Two Bannatyne Garlands from Abbotsford. By D. L.
    1. Captain Ward and the Rainbow.
    2. The River's Penance. (Black-letter.) 1848.

A copy is in the British Museum, but I have not found a copy preserved in Edinburgh.

83. NOTICE OF A SCHEME PROJECTED IN 1686, AND CONFIRMED BY THE ROYAL WARRANT OF KING JAMES VII. (which was exhibited) FOR WEIGHING UP AND RECOVERING SHIPS IN THE SCOTTISH SEAS.

Read to the Society of Antiquaries 13th March 1848, and printed in *Archæologia Scotica,* vol. iv.

84. LETTERS RELATIVE TO THE SEARCH FOR THE REMAINS OF THE QUEEN, MARY OF GUELDRES, AND THEIR REMOVAL TO HOLYROOD CHAPEL.

Read to the Society of Antiquaries 13th March 1848.

85. NOTICES OF THE PLACES OF SEPULTURE OF THE ROYAL FAMILY OF THE STUARTS PREVIOUS TO THE UNION OF THE CROWNS OF ENGLAND AND SCOTLAND.

Read to the Society of Antiquaries 1st June 1848.

86. NOTICES OF FREEMASONRY FOR THE GOVERNMENT OF THE FREEMASONS, DERIVED FROM THE ORIGINAL MS. CODE OF LAWS, ENACTED AT THE PALACES OF HOLYROOD AND FALKLAND AT THE BEGINNING OF THE SEVENTEENTH CENTURY.

Read to the Society of Antiquaries, from the MS. Register of St. John's Lodge, Aitcheson's Haven, 1st June 1848.

87. REMARKS ON THE CHARACTER OF MARY OF GUELDRES, CONSORT OF KING JAMES II. OF SCOTLAND, IN CONNECTION WITH AN ATTEMPT TO DETERMINE THE PLACE OF HER INTERMENT IN THE TRINITY COLLEGE CHURCH.

Read to the Society of Antiquaries 18th December 1848.

1849

88. SIRE DEGARRE, A METRICAL ROMANCE OF THE END OF THE THIRTEENTH CENTURY. EDINBURGH. M.DCCC.XLIX. PRESENTED TO THE ABBOTSFORD CLUB AS A CONTRIBUTION FROM THE LATE WILLIAM HENRY MILLER, ESQUIRE.

This work is without Laing's name; but, looking to his intimacy with Miller, as disclosed in the correspondence between them, and to the fact that its issue after Miller's death was ' carrying his wishes and intentions into effect . . . as a pleasing memorial of his devoted attachment to our Early Poetical Literature,' we may feel assured that its preparation for the press would be by his friend Laing, and by him only. It is therefore without hesitation entered here. A gift of a copy from him is acknowledged by the Rev. A. Dyce, London, on 17th July 1849.

89. CALDERWOOD'S HISTORY OF THE KIRK OF SCOTLAND. 8 volumes. PRINTED FOR THE WODROW SOCIETY, 1842-1849.

The eighth and last volume, containing the Appendix

and General Index, was issued under the superintendence of Laing, who contributed a Preface signed 'David Laing, February 1849,' in which he stated that it had proved 'a much more tedious and irksome labour than I could have anticipated.'

90. AN UNPUBLISHED LETTER OF HORACE WALPOLE TO THE EARL OF BUCHAN, DATED 'STRAWBERRY HILL, NOVEMBER 5TH, 1782.'

Read to the Society of Antiquaries 5th March 1849.

91. REMARKS ON THE EARLIER DESCRIPTIONS OF IONA, OR ICOLMKILL, AND ON THE PRESENT STATE OF ITS ANCIENT SCULPTURED MONUMENTS, SUGGESTED BY A RECENT VISIT TO THAT ISLAND.

Read to the Society of Antiquaries 10th December 1849.

1850

92. LETTER OF JAMES EARL OF PERTH, WRITTEN IN 1675, FURNISHING A GRAPHIC PICTURE OF THE PREDATORY HABITS OF THE HIGHLANDERS AT THAT DATE; ALSO AN OLD DOCUMENT, CONTAINING AN OBLIGATION BY JOHN CAMPBELL, THEN PRISONER UNDER SENTENCE OF DEATH, TO UNDERTAKE THE OFFICE OF EXECUTIONER IN THE STEWARTRY OF STRATHEARN IN 1675.

Read to the Society of Antiquaries 6th May 1850.

93. REPORTS ON EXCURSIONS TO EAST LOTHIAN, ETC. NO. 1—PRESTON TOWER, CHURCH OF PENCAITLAND, and WINTOUN HOUSE.

Read to the Society of Antiquaries 9th December 1850.

THE POEMS AND SONGS OF WILLIAM HAMILTON OF BANGOUR; COLLATED WITH THE MS. VOLUME OF HIS POEMS, AND CONTAINING SEVERAL PIECES HITHERTO UNPUBLISHED; WITH ILLUSTRATIVE NOTES AND AN ACCOUNT OF THE LIFE OF THE AUTHOR. BY JAMES PATERSON, EDITOR OF THE POEMS OF THE SEMPILLS OF BELTREES, ETC., ETC. Thomas George Stevenson, Antiquarian and Historical Bookseller, 87 Princes Street, Edinburgh. M.DCCC.L.

In the 'Introduction' Paterson acknowledges his 'deep debt of gratitude to Mr. Laing for the use of a manuscript volume, containing not only most of the Poems and Songs of Hamilton given to the public through the medium of former editions, but several others never before printed.' This MS. volume was purchased by Laing at the sale of the library of his friend George Chalmers, author of *Caledonia*, in 1842.

While not here attributing this edition of Hamilton's poems to Laing, I do not, in a survey of his literary labours, feel justified in excluding it from view, when we know his connection with its production. There is every reason to conclude that it was with his concurrence and help, if not, indeed, at his instigation, that the work was undertaken by Paterson and carried through the press, Laing's manuscript being the basis of its issue.

It is proper here to explain that the printed *Proceedings* of the Society of Antiquaries of Scotland begin with ' Volume I. Edinburgh, 1855, containing the papers of the Sessions 1851-52, 1852-53, and 1853-54.' Consequently papers communicated by Laing prior to 1851, as noted in preceding pages, are not preserved in print unless in the pages of the *Archæologia Scotica*, issued by the Society, when so stated ; or made use of otherwise by Laing himself.

1851

94. ORIGINAL LETTERS RELATING TO THE ECCLESIASTICAL AFFAIRS OF SCOTLAND CHIEFLY WRITTEN BY, OR ADDRESSED TO HIS MAJESTY KING JAMES THE SIXTH AFTER HIS ACCESSION TO THE ENGLISH THRONE. VOL. I. M.DC.III-M.DC.XIV. VOL. II. M.DC.XIV-M.DC.XXV. Edinburgh. M.DCCC.LI.

This work, in two volumes, as above, 866 pages in all, was presented to the Bannatyne Club by Beriah Botfield ; but in the Preface, dated from Norton Hall, Northamptonshire, 28th November 1851, the following occurs :

' It may be proper to take this opportunity of stating that the publication was recommended to me by the secretary of the Club [Laing], who kindly offered his services, both in forming the collection and in conducting it through the press.'

Laing's labours in connection with it are again made

obscure by his persistent modesty in suppressing his name; but in the printed catalogue of the Club's issues (1867) it is expressly stated that the series of letters was collected and edited by him.

95. NOTE ON POMONA AS THE NAME OF THE MAINLAND OF ORKNEY.

Read to the Society of Antiquaries 8th December 1851, and printed in the Society's *Proceedings,* vol. i. p. 16.

96. NOTICE OF PETITION FROM THE INHABITANTS OF SOUTH LEITH, ADDRESSED TO GENERAL MONCK, PRAYING HIM TO RESTORE TO THEM THE USE OF THE PARISH CHURCH. (*Proceedings,* S. A. Scot., vol. i. p. 158.)

The Church of South Leith had been used by the Cromwellians as a storehouse for ammunition during nearly six years, 1651-57.

1852

97. ON THE STATE OF THE ABBEY CHURCH OF HOLYROOD SUBSEQUENTLY TO THE DEVASTATIONS COMMITTED BY THE ENGLISH FORCES IN THE YEARS 1544 AND 1547.

Read to the Society of Antiquaries 13th December 1852, and printed in their *Proceedings,* vol. i. p. 101.

98. SPECIMEN OF A PROPOSED CATALOGUE OF THE LIBRARY OF THE LATE W. H. MILLER

(of Craigentinny) AT BRITWELL HOUSE, BUCKS. 4to.

It is stated in the Laing sale catalogue that only 30 copies were printed for private circulation, and that a copy had lately been sold in Edinburgh for £9, 5s. In the Laing sale it brought £5, 10s.

1853

99. ENGRAVED PORTRAIT OF THOMAS THOMSON, ADVOCATE, PRESIDENT OF THE BANNATYNE CLUB.

It is accompanied by a biographical notice by Laing, of 12pp.

100. VARIOUS PIECES OF FUGITIVE SCOTTISH POETRY; PRINCIPALLY OF THE SEVENTEENTH CENTURY. SECOND SERIES. EDINBURGH. M.DCCC.LIII. Post 8vo.

This contains 48 pieces, up to 1707. Of the first series, published in 1825, only 70 copies were printed. The second series has a new 'Preface' without signature, as was the case with the former issue.

101. ILLUSTRATIONS OF THE LYRIC POETRY AND MUSIC OF SCOTLAND. BY THE LATE WILLIAM STENHOUSE. Originally compiled to accompany the 'Scots Musical Museum,' and now published separately, with ADDITIONAL NOTES AND ILLUSTRATIONS. WILLIAM BLACKWOOD AND SONS, EDINBURGH AND LONDON. MDCCCLIII.

LITERARY WORK 195

102. THE SCOTS MUSICAL MUSEUM; consisting of UPWARDS OF 600 SONGS, with proper Basses for the Pianoforte. ORIGINALLY PUBLISHED BY JAMES JOHNSON; and now accompanied with copious Notes and Illustrations of the Lyric Poetry and Music of Scotland. By the late WILLIAM STENHOUSE. WITH ADDITIONAL NOTES AND ILLUSTRATIONS. New Edition—in four volumes. William Blackwood and Sons, Edinburgh and London. MDCCCLIII.

This, and the 'Illustrations' immediately preceding, both carry an 'Advertisement' signed 'David Laing. Edinburgh, May 1853,' and with it the 'Preface,' signed by him, dated 'Signet Library, Edinburgh, MDCCCXXXIX,' which was prefixed to the issue of the *Scots Musical Museum* of that year, the new volumes being enlarged and amended editions of that work.

103. A DEFENCE OF POETRY, MUSIC, AND STAGE PLAYS. BY THOMAS LODGE, OF LINCOLN'S INN. TO WHICH ARE ADDED, BY THE SAME AUTHOR, AN ALARUM AGAINST USURERS; AND THE DELECTABLE HISTORY OF FORBONIUS AND PRISCERIA. WITH INTRODUCTION AND NOTES. LONDON: PRINTED FOR THE SHAKESPEARE SOCIETY, 1853.

The 'Introduction' is signed 'David Laing. Edinburgh, June 1853.' Only two copies of the tract, printed as above, are known to exist, the one in the Christie Miller Library, and the other in the Bodleian.

104. NOTICES OF THE FUNERAL OF JAMES, SECOND EARL OF MURRAY.

Read to the Society of Antiquaries, and printed in their *Proceedings*, vol. i. p. 191.

1854

105. ON THE PRESENT STATE OF THE RUINS OF IONA.

Twenty-five copies privately printed. Two of these disposed of in the Laing sale, one with an original drawing by J. Logan, and the other with vignette. The original is a paper communicated to the Society of Antiquaries, and printed in their *Proceedings*, vol. ii. p. 7.

106. ALBUM OF THE BANNATYNE CLUB. NO. III. 1854.

Containing a list of works recommended to the Club for publication.

107. CATALOGUE OF THE BOOKS PRINTED FOR THE MEMBERS OF THE BANNATYNE CLUB SINCE ITS INSTITUTION. FEBRUARY M.DCCC.LIV. (105 Books).

108. A CONTEMPORARY ACCOUNT OF THE EARL OF HERTFORD'S SECOND EXPEDITION TO SCOTLAND, AND OF THE RAVAGES COMMITTED BY THE ENGLISH FORCES IN

September 1545. From a Manuscript in Trinity College, Dublin.

Read to the Society of Antiquaries 17th April 1854, and printed in their *Proceedings,* vol. i. p. 271.

109. Suggestions for a National Exhibition of Scottish Portraits in Edinburgh in the year 1855, including a Communication on the subject from Thomas Carlyle, Esq.

Read to the Society of Antiquaries 22nd May 1854, and printed in their *Proceedings,* vol. i. p. 284.

Memoir of Thomas Thomson, Advocate, Edinburgh, mdccclivi. Presented to the Bannatyne Club by James T. Gibson-Craig and C. Innes.

The Preface is signed by Innes, who acknowledges his obligation to Lord Cockburn, then deceased, and to ' Mr. Laing, the Secretary of the Club, who has afforded me zealous assistance in this labour of love.' Few books of a historical or biographic character relating to Scotland were produced at this time without Laing's help being invoked and readily granted; but such help does not justify this book, or others similarly indebted, being ascribed to Laing, as is done by T. G. Stevenson in his list, and it is accordingly not included in the present enumeration.

110. The Works of John Knox. Collected and Edited by David Laing. Vol. III. Bannatyne Club. mdccclivi.

1855

111. A SERIES OF ETCHINGS CHIEFLY OF VIEWS IN SCOTLAND. BY JOHN CLERK OF ELDIN, ESQ. MDCCLXXIII-MDCCLXXIV. WITH ADDITIONAL ETCHINGS AND FACSIMILES FROM HIS DRAWINGS. EDINBURGH: PRINTED FOR THE BANNATYNE CLUB. M.DCCC.LV.

'Preface' signed 'David Laing, February 1855,' and 'Biographical Notices of John Clerk, Esq.' At the end, a 'Description of the Views' in copious notes. Folio.

112. BREVIARIUM ABERDONENSE. PARS ESTIVA. Londini. Apud J. Toovey. MDCCCLIV. BREVIARIUM HYEMALIS. Londini. Apud J. Toovey. MDCCCLIV.

The elaborate 'Preface,' separately printed, is signed 'David Laing, Edinburgh, September 1855.' Accompanying it is a reprint of the *Compassio Beate Marie* (the Office of Our Lady of Pity) printed about the year 1520 by John Story, Edinburgh, of whom nothing more is known. Only one copy of this original is understood to be in existence. The *Breviarium* was printed by W. Chapman, 1509-10. It was prepared under the direction of Bishop Elphinstone of Aberdeen, and only four copies of the original edition are known. The editor of the reprint was the Rev. W. J. Blew.

113. THE WORKS OF JOHN KNOX. COLLECTED AND EDITED BY DAVID LAING. VOLUME IV. BANNATYNE CLUB. MDCCCLV.

LITERARY WORK

114. SUGGESTIONS FOR THE REMOVAL OF ST. MARGARET'S WELL, NEAR RESTALRIG, IN THE VICINITY OF EDINBURGH, TO A MORE FAVOURABLE SITE.

Read to the Society of Antiquaries 10th December 1855, and printed in their *Proceedings*, vol. ii. p. 143.

115. THE BANNATYNE MISCELLANY: CONTAINING ORIGINAL PAPERS AND TRACTS, CHIEFLY RELATING TO THE HISTORY AND LITERATURE OF SCOTLAND. VOLUME III. PRINTED AT EDINBURGH: M.DCCC.LV.

The contents—

    Two Ancient Records of the Bishopric of Caithness, from the Charter Room at Dunrobin. (Cosmo Innes.)

    Extract from a Manuscript Volume of Chronicles in the possession of the Right Hon. Lord Panmure: 'De Tributariis Insulis'; 'De Orcadibus Insulis'; the 'Chronycle of Scotland' in a part; 'De Johanne Ballialo'; 'Nomina Regum Scotorum.'

    Diploma of Thomas, Bishop of Orkney and Zetland, and the Chapter of Kirkwall, addressed to Eric King of Norway, respecting the Genealogy of William Saint Clair, Earl of Orkney. With a Translation by Dean Thomas Guild, Monk of Newbattle, 1554.

    Extract from Thorm. Torfaei Orcades.

    The Testament of Alexander Sutherland of Dunbeath, at Roslin Castle, 15 November 1456.

The Testament of Sir David Synclar of Swynbrocht, Knycht, at Tyngwell, 10 July 1506.

The Diary of John Lesley, Bishop of Ross, April 11-October 16, 1571.

The Preface by Henry Charteris to his edition of Henry's *Wallace*, printed at Edinburgh, 1594.

A Catalogue of the Bishops of Orkney, 1112-1477 [by Professor Munch of Christiania].

Notes by Professor Munch on the Extracts from the Panmure Manuscript in the present volume.

The Testament of Richard Lawson, Bookseller and Merchant-Burgess of Edinburgh. 1622.

The Progress of my Lord Walden's Journey in Scotland in August 1614.

Carta Jacobi Tertii Regis Scotorum, de Tenemento Terre cum Orto murato in Burgo de Edinburgh, concess. David de Dalrympill, 15 Octobris, 1471.

Proceedings of the Commissioners of the Kirk at a Meeting held at Edinburgh, in July 1627.

An Account of the Foundation of the Leightonian Library. By Robert Douglas, Bishop of Dunblane.

Letters relating to the Leightonian Library, Dunblane, 1703-1710.

Letters of Assedation to Agnes Countess of Bothwell; and other Deeds connected with the Hepburns, Earls of Bothwell, and the Hepburns of Waughton, 1520-1564.

A Godly Exhortation, as set forth by John, Archbishop of St. Andrews, commonly styled 'The Twopenny Faith,' 1559.

A Plan of the City of St. Andrews from an Original Drawing by James Gordon, A.M., Minister of Rothiemay, 1642.

The Contract with James de Witte, Painter, for the Portraits of the Kings of Scotland in the Palace of Holyrood : and the Accompt for Portraits, by Godfrey Kneller, of King Charles II. and his brother James, Duke of York, 1684.

Extracts from ' The Richt Way to the Kingdome of Hevine,' by John Gau, printed at Malmoe, in Sweden, 1533.

An Advertisement and General Queries for the Description of Scotland, by Sir Robert Sibbald, M.D., His Majestie's Geographer for Scotland, 1682.

Proposals by Walter Gibson, Merchant in Glasgow, to Persons who wish to Transport themselves to America, 1684.

Advertisement to all Tradesmen and others, who are willing to Transport themselves into the Province of East-New-Jersey in America, 1684.

Extracts from the Acts and Proceedings of the Presbytery of Haddington, relating to Dr. Gilbert Burnet, and the Library of the Kirk of Salton, 1664-1669.

Letters of Patrick Earl of Bothwell, and Articles which he undertook to maintain at the appointment of the King of France, 1548-1549.

Additional Extracts relating to the Earls of Bothwell and the Master of Hailes.

The Retour and Royal Warrant of Taxation of the Lands in the Sheriffdom of Edinburgh, in the year 1479.

1856

116. Notice of the Death of Robert Blackader, Archbishop of Glasgow, during a

PILGRIMAGE TO THE HOLY LAND, IN THE YEAR 1508.

Read to the Society of Antiquaries 14th April 1856, and printed in their *Proceedings,* vol. ii. p. 222.

117. AN OBITUARY AND CALENDAR OF SCOTTISH SAINTS, EXTRACTED FROM THE MARTYROLOGY FOR THE USE OF THE CHURCH IN ABERDEEN, A MS. OF THE SIXTEENTH CENTURY.

Read to the Society of Antiquaries 12th May 1856, and printed in their *Proceedings,* vol. ii. p. 256.

118. A FEW REMARKS ON THE PORTRAITS OF SIR WILLIAM WALLACE.

Read to the Society of Antiquaries 15th December 1856, and printed in their *Proceedings,* vol. ii. p. 308.

119. THE WORKS OF JOHN KNOX. COLLECTED AND EDITED BY DAVID LAING. VOLUME V. BANNATYNE CLUB. MDCCCLVI.

1857

120. A PENNI WORTH OF WITTE : FLORICE AND BLANCHEFLOUR ; AND OTHER PIECES OF ANCIENT ENGLISH POETRY, SELECTED FROM THE AUCHINLECK MANUSCRIPT. PRINTED AT EDINBURGH FOR THE ABBOTSFORD CLUB. M.DCCC.LVII.

The Preface is signed 'David Laing. Edinburgh 1857.'

LITERARY WORK

121. INVENTORY OF ORIGINAL DOCUMENTS IN THE ARCHIVES OF GEORGE HERIOT'S HOSPITAL, EDINBURGH. PRINTED FOR THE GOVERNORS. MDCCCLVII.

The Preface acknowledges that they 'have been favoured with the able advice and unwearied assistance of David Laing, Esq., of the Signet Library, to whom they are thus placed under a deep debt of gratitude.' His own name is carefully withheld by himself.

122. A NOTE ON THE SUBJECT OF PROTOCOL BOOKS AS CONNECTED WITH PUBLIC RECORDS.

Read to the Society of Antiquaries 16th February 1857. *Proceedings,* vol. ii. p. 350.

123. INVENTAR OF POPISH TRINKETS GOTTEN IN MY LORD TRAQUAIR'S HOUSE, ANNO 1688; ALL SOLEMNLY BURNT AT THE CROSS OF PEEBLES. WITH SOME REMARKS.

Read to the Society of Antiquaries 8th June 1857. *Proceedings,* vol. ii. p. 454.

124. HISTORICAL DESCRIPTION OF THE ALTARPIECE PAINTED IN THE REIGN OF KING JAMES III. OF SCOTLAND, BELONGING TO HER MAJESTY, IN THE PALACE OF HOLYROOD.

Read to the Society of Antiquaries 30th November 1857. *Proceedings,* vol. iii. p. 8. Some copies were privately printed. In a note Laing takes no credit for the restoration to Scotland of this important work of art, and says that it was 'entirely due to the enthusiastic zeal of my friend, Mr. W. B. Johnstone, R.S.A.' The memorial to the sovereign was signed by the Dukes of Hamilton and Buccleuch, the Marquess of Dalhousie, and other influential personages.

125. ENCYCLOPÆDIA BRITANNICA. (Eighth Edition). ADAM AND CHARLES BLACK, EDINBURGH. MDCCCLVII. ARTICLE ON THOMAS MCCRIE, D.D., Author of the 'Life of Knox.'

It is noted in the general view of this edition that articles bearing the initial letter 'L' are by David Laing. The present article, however, bears no such, or any other, indication of its being his work. But there is preserved a letter from Adam Black to him, dated 31st March 1857, the year of publication, asking him to abridge, by at least one-half, his article on McCrie, which leaves no doubt as to the authorship. So early as in 1836 Laing had been asked to prepare an article on McCrie for the *Encyclopædia*. Dr. McCrie, his son, complained of this as taking away the ground for his own intended memoir of his father. The correspondence between him and Laing on the subject is preserved. It is probable that several other contributions by Laing in regard to Scottish worthies may be discovered in this *Encyclopædia* and other works of the same kind.

1858

126. A CATALOGUE OF THE GRADUATES IN THE FACULTIES OF ARTS, DIVINITY AND LAW, OF

THE UNIVERSITY OF EDINBURGH, SINCE ITS FOUNDATION. EDINBURGH : M.DCCC.LVIII.

This catalogue was prepared by Laing in accordance with a resolution of the Senatus; but at a meeting of the committee of the Bannatyne Club, on 30th June 1858, authority was given for a sufficient number of copies being printed on the Club paper for distribution among the members.

127. MEMOIRS OF THE INSURRECTION IN SCOTLAND IN 1715. BY JOHN, MASTER OF SINCLAIR. FROM THE ORIGINAL MANUSCRIPT IN THE POSSESSION OF THE EARL OF ROSSLYN, WITH NOTES BY SIR WALTER SCOTT, BART. PRINTED AT EDINBURGH : M.DCCC.LVIII.

Issued by the Abbotsford Club 'under the joint superintendence of Mr. James Macknight and Mr. Laing.' The Preface is signed by Macknight only.

128. ORIGINAL LETTERS OF MR. JOHN COLVILLE, 1582-1603. TO WHICH IS ADDED HIS PALINODE, 1600. WITH A MEMOIR OF THE AUTHOR. EDINBURGH. M.DCCC.LVIII. Presented to the Bannatyne Club by the Earl of Selkirk.

The 'Memoir' of 40 pp. is by Laing, bearing his initials 'D. L.'

129. NOTE ON THE BIRTHPLACE OF JOHN KNOX.

Read to the Society of Antiquaries 18th January 1858. *Proceedings,* vol. iii. p. 57.

130. HISTORICAL NOTICES OF THE FAMILY OF KING JAMES I. OF SCOTLAND, CHIEFLY FROM INFORMATION COMMUNICATED BY JOHN RIDDELL, ESQ., ADVOCATE.

Read to the Society of Antiquaries 8th March 1858. *Proceedings,* vol. iii. p. 87.

131. PROPOSALS FOR CLEANING AND LIGHTING THE CITY OF EDINBURGH (WITH ORIGINAL SIGNATURES OF A NUMBER OF THE PRINCIPAL INHABITANTS) IN THE YEAR 1735. WITH EXPLANATORY REMARKS.

Read to the Society of Antiquaries 12th December 1858, and printed in their *Proceedings,* vol. iii. p. 171.

1859

132. REGISTRUM CARTARUM ECCLESIE SANCTI EGIDII DE EDINBURGH. A SERIES OF CHARTERS AND ORIGINAL DOCUMENTS CONNECTED WITH THE CHURCH OF ST. GILES, EDINBURGH. M.CCC.XLIV-M.D.LXVII. EDINBURGH: MDCCCLIX. (Bannatyne Club.)

An Introduction, 'Historical Notices of the Collegiate Church of St. Giles, Edinburgh,' with an elaborate 'Appendix,' 113 pages in all, signed 'David Laing,' is quite a book in itself, manifesting all his usual learning and research.

133. BEN JONSON IN EDINBURGH IN THE YEAR 1618.

Read to the Society of Antiquaries 16th February 1859. *Proceedings,* vol. iii. p. 206.

134. CONTRACT BETWEEN THE CITY OF EDINBURGH AND JOHN MEIKLE FOR A CHIME OF MUSICAL BELLS, 1698. From the original, preserved in the Archives of the City of Edinburgh.

Read to the Society of Antiquaries 10th January 1859. *Proceedings,* vol. iii. p. 196.

1860

135. SOME ACCOUNT OF LIEUTENANT-COLONEL WILLIAM MERCER, AUTHOR OF 'ANGLIÆ SPECULUM; OR, ENGLAND'S LOOKING-GLASSE.' LONDON, 1646.

Read to the Society of Antiquaries 9th January 1860. *Proceedings,* vol. iii. p. 341.

136. STATEMENT RELATIVE TO THE REMOVAL OF ST. MARGARET'S WELL.

Read to the Society of Antiquaries 13th February 1860. *Proceedings,* vol. iv. p. 365.

137. CONCORDIA FACTA INTER ANGLICOS ET SCOTOS, 3 January 1322-23, COMMUNICATED BY PROFESSOR MUNCH (WITH REMARKS BY MR. LAING).

Read to the Society of Antiquaries 21st May 1860. *Proceedings,* vol. iii. p. 454.

138. TRACTS BY DAVID FERGUSON, MINISTER OF DUNFERMLINE. MDLXIII-MDLXXII.

Presented to the Bannatyne Club by the Very Rev. John Lee, D.D., LL.D., Principal of the University of Edinburgh, with a short Preface by 'David Laing. Edinburgh, October 1860,' which may be taken as implying that its preparation and carrying through the press was by him (Laing).

1861

139. REGISTRUM DOMUS DE SOLTRE, NECNON ECCLESIE COLLEGIATE S. TRINITATIS PROPE EDINBURGH, ETC. CHARTERS OF THE HOSPITAL OF SOLTRE, OF TRINITY COLLEGE, EDINBURGH, AND OTHER COLLEGIATE CHURCHES IN MIDLOTHIAN. EDINBURGH: MDCCCLXI. 4to.

Presented to the Bannatyne Club by the Duke of Buccleuch and Lord Lindsay. A long and learned Preface of 121 pages signed ' David Laing.'

140. THE HISTORY OF SCOTTISH POETRY. BY DAVID IRVING, LL.D. WITH A MEMOIR

AND GLOSSARY. EDINBURGH: EDMONSTON AND DOUGLAS. 1861.

An 'Advertisement' bears the initials 'J. A. C.' [John Aitken Carlyle], but the 'Memoir of Dr. Irving' is by his friend Laing.

141. HISTORICAL NOTICES OF THE PROVOSTRY OF KIRKHEUGH, ST. ANDREWS.

Read to the Society of Antiquaries 11th February 1861. *Proceedings*, vol. iv. p. 76.

142. NOTICE OF 'A DECLARATION AGAINST THE NATIONAL COVENANTS OF SCOTLAND,' 1685, WITH ADDITIONAL NOTICES AND REMARKS ON THE NATIONAL COVENANTS OF SCOTLAND.

Read to the Society of Antiquaries 13th May 1861. *Proceedings*, vol. iv. p. 232.

143. ANNIVERSARY ADDRESS TO THE SOCIETY OF ANTIQUARIES OF SCOTLAND ON THE STATE OF THE SOCIETY FROM 1831 TO 1860. By DAVID LAING, Vice-President, and Secretary for Foreign Correspondence, with 3 Portraits.

Printed in *Archæologia Scotica*, vol. v. part 1, pp. 1-44.

144. SPECIMEN OF THE NORSE LANGUAGE AS PRESERVED BY THE REV. GEORGE LOW

IN HIS UNPUBLISHED TOUR IN THE ORKNEY AND SHETLAND ISLANDS, 1774.

This is the Hildina ballad printed in Low's *Tour*, Edinburgh 1879, and since expounded by Professor Marius Haegstad (Christiania, 1890). The present issue is of 8 pages octavo (25 copies printed), with a Note —'The above is a literal extract from Low's original manuscript, now in my possession,' signed 'David Laing. Edinburgh, October 1861.'

1862

145. HISTORY OF THE UNIVERSITY OF EDINBURGH FROM ITS FOUNDATION. BY ANDREW DALZEL, PROFESSOR OF GREEK IN THE UNIVERSITY. WITH A MEMOIR OF THE AUTHOR. EDINBURGH: EDMONSTON AND DOUGLAS, 1862. 2 volumes.

   I. Memoir, by Cosmo Innes.
   II. History, by David Laing.

146. SIR PETER YOUNG OF SEATON. ADDITIONAL NOTICES.

Proceedings of the Society of Antiquaries, vol. iv. p. 427.

147. NOTICE RESPECTING THE CROSS OF EDINBURGH.

Read to the Society of Antiquaries 10th March 1862. *Proceedings*, vol. iv. p. 420.

148. INTRODUCTORY REMARKS TO EXTRACTS FROM THE PRESBYTERY RECORDS OF DALKEITH RELATING TO THE PARISH OF NEWBATTLE DURING THE INCUMBENCY OF MR. ROBERT LEIGHTON, 1641-1653.

Read to the Society of Antiquaries 14th April 1862. *Proceedings,* vol. iv. p. 459.

149. REMARKS ON THE CHARACTER OF MARY OF GUELDRES, CONSORT OF KING JAMES II. OF SCOTLAND, IN CONNECTION WITH AN ATTEMPT TO DETERMINE THE PLACE OF HER INTERMENT IN TRINITY COLLEGE CHURCH, EDINBURGH.

Read to the Society of Antiquaries 9th June 1862. *Proceedings,* vol. iv. p. 566.

150. NOTE RESPECTING THE ROYAL EXCHANGE, EDINBURGH, AND THE ORIGINAL LIST OF SUBSCRIBERS IN 1752.

Read to the Society of Antiquaries 9th June 1862. *Proceedings,* vol. iv. p. 593.

151. EDINBURGH IN EARLY TIMES, WITH ILLUSTRATIONS.

Read to the Society of Antiquaries 8th December 1862. *Proceedings,* vol. v. p. 7.

1863

152. The Diary of Alexander Brodie of Brodie, MDCLII-MDCLXXX, and of his son James Brodie of Brodie, MDCLXXX-MDCLXXXV. Extracts from the existing Manuscripts and a Republication of the Volume printed at Edinburgh in the year 1740. Aberdeen: Printed for the Spalding Club, MDCCCLXIII.

The 'Preface' is by Laing, and bears his signature, 'David Laing. Edinburgh, 1862.'

153. Note on the supposed Cranium of Robert Logan of Restalrig.

Read to the Society of Antiquaries 13th April 1863. *Proceedings,* vol. v. p. 105.

154. Memorandum respecting the Smellie Correspondence, presented to the Society of Antiquaries by the Trustees of the late John Smellie, Esq., F.S.A.Scot.

Read to the Society 11th May 1863, and printed in *Proceedings,* vol. v. p. 120.

155. Biographical Notice of Professor Peter Andreas Munch [of Christiania, Norway].

Read to the Society of Antiquaries 30th November 1863. *Proceedings,* vol. v. p. 173.

156. **Svmmaire de l'Origine Description et Merveilles d'Escosse. Par Jehan Desmontiers.** Imprimé à Paris en 1588. Réimprimé en 1863 par G. Gounouilhou, rue Guiraude, 11, à Bordeaux. (80 copies, one on vellum.)

Laing, in a brief Preface, signed by him at Edinburgh, November 1862, tells what he knows of this small book, mostly an abridgment from Hector Boece's *History*. A vellum copy was in the British Museum, and only one other, imperfect, known to him in this country. The superintendence of the reprint was entrusted to his friend Monsieur Francisque Michel of Paris.

1864

157. **The Works of John Knox. Collected and Edited by David Laing. Volume VI. Parts I. and II. (Bannatyne Club.)** MDCCCLXIV.

158. **Notes relating to the Interment of King James III. of Scotland and his Queen, Margaret of Denmark, in the Abbey Church of Cambuskenneth.**

Read to the Society of Antiquaries 12th December 1864. *Proceedings*, vol. vi. p. 26.

1865

159. **The Poems and Fables of Robert Henryson, now first collected, With**

Notes, and a Memoir of his Life. By David Laing. Edinburgh. mdccclxv. William Paterson, Princes Street.

The Preface, Memoir, and Appendix by Laing occupy 60 pages; the 'Notes and Various Readings' extend to 80 pages.

160. Stephen Hawes. The Conversyon of Swerers: A joyfull Medytacyon to all Englonde of the Coronacyon of Kynge Henry the Eyght. Edinburgh: Reprinted for the Abbotsford Club. m.dccc.lxv.

Two poems, printed in black-letter. An inset gives the original title, *The Conuercyon of Swerers*. The Preface is signed 'David Laing. Edinburgh, 1865.'

161. The Poems of William Dunbar: First Collected and Published in the year m.dccc.xxxiv. Supplement. Edinburgh: William Paterson. m.dccc.lxv.

A brief Preface, signed 'David Laing. Edinburgh, September 1865.'

162. Notice respecting the Monument of the Regent Earl of Murray, now restored, within the Church of St. Giles, Edinburgh.

Read to the Society of Antiquaries 31st January 1865. *Proceedings*, vol. vi. p. 49.

LITERARY WORK

163. NOTES RELATING TO MRS. ESTHER (LANGLOIS OR) INGLIS, THE CELEBRATED CALIGRAPHIST, WITH AN ENUMERATION OF MANUSCRIPT VOLUMES WRITTEN BY HER BETWEEN THE YEARS 1586 AND 1624.

Read to the Society of Antiquaries 11th December 1865. *Proceedings,* vol. vi. p. 284.

164. A FACSIMILE OF GORDON OF ROTHIEMAY'S BIRD'S EYE VIEW OF EDINBURGH, 1647. WITH AN HISTORICAL NOTICE. EDINBURGH, W. & A. K. JOHNSTON, 1865. 4to.

The 'Historical Notice' is by Laing, bearing his signature.

1866

165. ABBOTSFORD CLUB. A LIST OF THE MEMBERS; THE RULES; AND A CATALOGUE OF BOOKS PRINTED FOR THE CLUB SINCE ITS INSTITUTION IN 1833. EDINBURGH: M.DCCC.LXVI.

Preface, with the initials 'D. L.' and the date 'January 1866.'

166. NOTES ON THE RESTORATION OF THE SHAFT OF THE OLD CITY CROSS, EDINBURGH.

Read to the Society of Antiquaries 12th March 1866. *Proceedings,* vol. vi. p. 375.

1867

167. THE EPITAPHS AND MONUMENTAL INSCRIPTIONS IN GREYFRIARS CHURCHYARD, EDINBURGH. Collected by JAMES BROWN, KEEPER OF THE GROUNDS, AND AUTHOR OF THE 'DEESIDE GUIDE.' WITH AN INTRODUCTION AND NOTES. EDINBURGH: J. MOODIE MILLER. MDCCCLXVII.

In his Preface the author acknowledges his indebtedness to 'above all, David Laing, Esq., LL.D., who has contributed the valuable historical Introduction, and has kindly and readily given his assistance or advice during the whole time the sheets have been passing through the press.' The 'Introduction' of 72 pages bears the modest initial ' L.'

168. ADVERSARIA. NOTICES ILLUSTRATIVE OF SOME OF THE EARLIER WORKS PRINTED FOR THE BANNATYNE CLUB. EDINBURGH. MDCCCLXVII.

The Preface is signed 'David Laing, Secretary,' June 1867. Fourteen works issued by the Club are described; and the whole ends with an Appendix in reference to the testimonial presented to him by the Club in 1861, with his address in reply, and a lithographed plate of the testimonial.

169. ROYAL LETTERS, CHARTERS, AND TRACTS, RELATING TO THE COLONIZATION OF NEW SCOTLAND, AND THE INSTITUTION OF THE ORDER OF KNIGHT-BARONETS OF

Nova Scotia. 1621-1638. Edinburgh. m.dccc.lxvii. Completed and presented to the Members of the Bannatyne Club by the Editor.

The Preface of 127 pages in reference to the documents, and to Sir William Alexander of Menstrie, Sir Robert Gordon of Lochinvar, and the other personages named, is signed 'David Laing,' with the date 'April 30, 1867.'

170. List of Members and the Rules, with a Catalogue of the Books printed for the Bannatyne Club since its Institution in 1823. Edinburgh: m.dccc.lxvii. (Contains 116 works.)

The Preface is signed by David Laing. Edinburgh, 1867.

171. A Contemporary Account of the Battle of Flodden. From a MS. in the possession of the Author.

Read to the Society of Antiquaries 11th March 1867. *Proceedings,* vol. vii. p. 141.

1868

172. A Compendious Book of Psalms and Spiritual Songs, commonly known as 'The Gude and Godlie Ballates.' Edin-

BURGH: REPRINTED FROM THE EDITION OF 1578. M.DCCC.LXVIII.

A Preface of 56 pages, signed by Laing, with the date 1867. The original title is given in facsimile:

> 'Ane Compendious Buik of godlie Psalmes and Spirituall Sangis collectit furthe of sindrie partis of the Scripture, with diveris utheris Ballatis changeit out of prophane Sangis in godlie sangis, for avoyding of sin and harlatrie. With augmentation of sindrie gude and godlie Ballatis not contenit in the first editioun. Imprintit at Edinburgh be Johne Ros for Hendrie Charteris. M.D.LXXVIII. Cum privilegio Regali.'

Altogether a rare and curious volume.

173. NOTE ON A PAINTED CEILING IN A HOUSE AT LINLITHGOW.

Read to the Society of Antiquaries 9th March 1868. *Proceedings,* vol. vii. p. 412.

174. AN ACCOUNT OF THE SCOTTISH PSALTER OF A.D. 1566, CONTAINING THE PSALMS, CANTICLES AND HYMNS, SET TO MUSIC, IN FOUR PARTS, IN THE MANUSCRIPTS OF THOMAS WODE OR WOOD, VICAR OF SANCTANDROUS. (With facsimile plates.)

Read to the Society of Antiquaries 13th April 1868. *Proceedings,* vol. vii. p. 445. It seems to have been afterwards separately printed. A copy of date 1871 appeared in the Laing sale catalogue, part i. p. 138, and is also in the British Museum. Another, of date 1876, was in the third portion of the library, p. 71.

175. HISTORY, ETC., OF THE NEW PAINTED WINDOW IN THE PARLIAMENT HOUSE, EDINBURGH. Only a few copies, privately printed. 1868.

So described in the Laing sale catalogue. I have not seen a copy.

1869

176. ETCHINGS BY CHARLES KIRKPATRICK SHARPE WITH PHOTOGRAPHS FROM ORIGINAL DRAWINGS POETICAL AND PROSE FRAGMENTS AND A PREFATORY MEMOIR. WILLIAM BLACKWOOD AND SONS. MDCCCLXIX.

The 'Memoir' of Sharpe of 58 pages is by Laing, unsigned. They were on intimate terms, as shown by correspondence between them.

177. ON THE SUPPOSED 'MISSING SCHOOL OF DESIGN' IN THE UNIVERSITY OF EDINBURGH. 1784.

Read to the Society of Antiquaries 11th January 1869. *Proceedings,* vol. viii. p. 36.

178. INTRODUCTORY NOTE TO AN ACCOUNT OF ST. COLUMBA'S ABBEY, INCHCOLM, BY THOMAS ARNOLD.

Read to Society of Antiquaries 11th January 1869. *Proceedings,* vol. viii. p. 46.

179. A BRIEF NOTICE OF AN ANCIENT MS. OF THE FOUR GOSPELS, BROUGHT FROM

ABYSSINIA AND PRESENTED TO THE SOCIETY (WITH OTHER MSS.), BY CAPTAIN CHARLES MCINROY, STAFF SERVICE, MADRAS.

Read to the Society of Antiquaries 11th February 1869. *Proceedings,* vol. viii. p. 52. The MS. of the Gospels is preserved in the library of the Society of Antiquaries.

1870

180. BIOGRAPHICAL NOTICES OF THOMAS YOUNG, S.T.D., VICAR OF STOWMARKET, SUFFOLK. [Died 1655.] BY THE EDITOR OF PRINCIPAL BAILLIE'S 'LETTERS AND JOURNALS.' EDINBURGH: MDCCCLXX.

An introductory Note, explaining the circumstances of the issue of the book, is signed 'David Laing. Edinburgh, July 1869.' There is also a 'Postscript and Appendix' with the initials 'D. L.,' and the date 'Edinburgh. November 1870.' Privately printed.

1871

181. THE POETICAL WORKS OF SIR DAVID LYNDSAY OF THE MOUNT, LORD LYON KING OF ARMS. A NEW EDITION CAREFULLY REVISED. IN TWO VOLUMES. EDINBURGH: WILLIAM PATERSON. MDCCCLXXI.

Laing had in view a complete edition of Lyndsay's works, but the coarseness of the phraseology in some parts made him reluctant to proceed with it, and the project was for the time abandoned. The above expurgated edition, however, made its appearance at the date it bears, and was not favourably received. It contains a 'Preface' signed by Laing, and a 'Memoir' of Lyndsay of 46 pages. A second edition, in three volumes, was published in 1879, after Laing's decease.

182. CATALOGUE OF THE PRINTED BOOKS IN THE LIBRARY OF THE SOCIETY OF WRITERS TO H.M. SIGNET IN SCOTLAND. PART FIRST — A-L. EDINBURGH : PRINTED FOR THE SOCIETY BY NEILL AND COMPANY. MDCCCLXXI.

'Advertisement,' signed 'David Laing, Librarian. Edinburgh, October 2, 1871.' The catalogue was completed by Dr. Thomas Graves Law, his successor in office.

183. SCOTT EXHIBITION. 1871. Catalogue of the Exhibition HELD AT EDINBURGH, IN JULY AND AUGUST 1871, ON OCCASION OF THE COMMEMORATION OF THE CENTENARY OF THE BIRTH OF SIR WALTER SCOTT. (Jointly with James Drummond, R.S.A.) 4to.

184. EDINBURGH IN EARLY TIMES, WITH ILLUSTRATIONS. THE EARLY VIEWS BOTH NORTH AND SOUTH OF THE CITY.

Read to the Society of Antiquaries 8th May 1871. Noticed in the *Proceedings* of the Society, vol. ix. p. 223.

1872

185. THE ORYGYNALE CRONYKIL OF SCOTLAND. BY ANDRO OF WYNTOUN. EDITED BY DAVID LAING. IN THREE VOLUMES. EDINBURGH : EDMONSTON AND DOUGLAS. 1872.

Volumes i. and ii. appeared in 1872 in the series of 'The Historians of Scotland,' with an 'Introductory Notice' by Laing dated Edinburgh, November 1872. Volume iii. was issued by William Paterson in 1879 (after Laing's decease) with a short Preface by Laing, of date November 1876; but no notice regarding him, or of the completion of the work by other hands, is given.

186. NOTICE OF AN ORIGINAL PRIVY SEAL DOCUMENT RELATING TO THE INVASION OF SCOTLAND BY KING HENRY VII. IN THE YEAR 1497.

Read to the Society of Antiquaries 10th June 1872. *Proceedings,* vol. ix. p. 540.

1873

187. ODE TO THE CUCKOO : EDINBURGH, 1770. WITH REMARKS ON ITS AUTHORSHIP. IN A LETTER TO JOHN CAMPBELL SHAIRP, ESQ., LL.D., PRINCIPAL OF THE UNITED COLLEGE, UNIVERSITY OF ST. ANDREWS. EDINBURGH : MDCCCLXXIII. Sixty copies

printed. Second impression one hundred copies.

This is an earnest vindication by Laing of the Rev. John Logan, one of the ministers of Leith, against the aspersions of those who accused him of having appropriated from young Michael Bruce, the poet, the credit of being the author of the *Ode*.

188. THE POETICAL WORKS OF ALEXANDER CRAIG OF ROSE-CRAIG, 1604-1631, NOW FIRST COLLECTED. PRINTED FOR THE HUNTERIAN CLUB. MDCCCLXXIII.

Introductory Notice of sixteen leaves, signed 'David Laing. Edinburgh.' Two hundred copies printed exclusively for members of the Club, with ten additional for presentation by the Council.

189. ON PROCESSIONS AND OTHER PUBLIC CEREMONIALS IN SCOTLAND prior to the Union, A.D. 1707. With Illustrations.

Read to the Society of Antiquaries of Scotland 12th May 1873. Reserved for subsequent publication, but never printed.

190. AN ACCOUNT OF THE FUNERAL OF GEORGE, FIRST MARQUESS OF HUNTLY, IN JUNE 1636.

Read to the Society of Antiquaries 9th June 1873. Reserved for subsequent publication, but never printed.

191. INTRODUCTORY NOTE TO A 'NOTICE SUR LA VIE DE JEAN RAMSAY DE SAINT

Andrew en Ecosse, Professeur à l'Universite de Turin, et Medecin de Charles III., Duc de Savoie, par M. Alexandre de Meana, Turin.'

Read to the Society of Antiquaries 9th June 1873. *Proceedings*, vol. x. p. 294.

192. Historical Description of the Altarpiece painted in the reign of King James III. of Scotland, belonging to Her Majesty, in the Palace of Holyrood. A Supplemental Notice.

Read to the Society of Antiquaries 9th June 1873. *Proceedings*, vol. x. p. 310. Printed separately, 1875, and a copy disposed of in the Laing sale.

193. Additional Notes concerning Alexander Gordon, A.M., Author of the 'Itinerarium Septentrionale,' 1726.

Read to the Society of Antiquaries 8th December 1873. Supplementary to a paper by Dr. Daniel Wilson, printed in *Proceedings*, vol. x. p. 369.

1874

194. Mrs. Erskine, Lady Grange, in the Island of St. Kilda.

Read to the Society of Antiquaries 8th June 1874. *Proceedings*, vol. x. p. 722.

1875

195. ETCHINGS BY SIR DAVID WILKIE, R.A., LIMNER TO H.M. FOR SCOTLAND, AND BY ANDREW GEDDES, A.R.A., WITH BIOGRAPHICAL SKETCHES.

Containing, according to the Laing sale catalogue, 'portraits and choice proofs of Etchings.' It was sold for £13, 10s. Mr. James T. Gibson-Craig was interested, with Laing, in the production of this work, and there is preserved a lengthened correspondence with the widow of Geddes in regard to the material for it.

196. THE POETICAL WORKS OF PATRICK HANNAY, M.A., MDCXXII. PRIVATELY PRINTED MDCCCLXXV. Presented to the Members of the Hunterian Club by Thomas Russell.

The 'Memoir' by David Laing, F.S.A. Scot., 40 pp., bears the initials 'D. L.' with the date 'Edinburgh, 1875.'

197. CORRESPONDENCE OF SIR ROBERT KERR FIRST EARL OF ANCRAM AND HIS SON WILLIAM THIRD EARL OF LOTHIAN. EDINBURGH. MDCCCLXXV.

The Bannatyne Club had been wound up in 1871, but it was thought desirable that this book should be issued from the important manuscript material at Newbattle Abbey. Lord Lothian wished that Dr. Laing should undertake the work, and he consented, though, as he explained in the Preface, he had actually on his hands more work of a like kind than he could ever expect to accomplish. It was accordingly undertaken and completed in two large quarto volumes, 563 pp., the 'Preface' and the 'Memoirs' of the two earls occupying 108 pages. The completed work was presented 'to the Surviving Members' of the Club by the then Marquess of Lothian, a very cordial friend of Laing, as is disclosed in the correspondence which passed between them.

1876

198. THE FORRESTER MONUMENTS IN THE CHURCH OF CORSTORPHINE. With Drawings by W. P. Burton.

Read to the Society of Antiquaries 10th January 1876. *Proceedings*, vol. xi. p. 353.

199. A NOTICE OF THE MONUMENT OF WILLIAM CARSTARES, PRINCIPAL OF THE UNIVERSITY OF EDINBURGH, ERECTED IN 1727, AND RESTORED IN 1876, WITH A COPY OF THE ORIGINAL CONTRACT.

Read to the Antiquaries on 8th May 1876. Printed in *Proceedings*, vol. xi. p. 525.

200. AN ORIGINAL LETTER TO THE LAIRD OF WISHAW RELATING TO THE PROCEEDINGS AGAINST JAMES AIKENHEAD, 'THE ATHEIST,' AND THE TRIAL OF WITCHES AT PAISLEY IN 1696.

Communicated to the Society of Antiquaries, with remarks and explanations, 14th February 1876. *Proceedings*, vol. xi. p. 438. The case of Aikenhead is that of the poor youth who was hanged in Edinburgh for his doubts and difficulties about the doctrine of the Trinity. The tendency of Laing's remarks is towards exoneration of the ministry and of others who urged the prosecution of Aikenhead and of the so-called ' witches.'

201. AN EPISODE IN THE LIFE OF MRS. RACHEL ERSKINE (LADY GRANGE), DETAILED BY HERSELF IN A LETTER FROM ST. KILDA, JANUARY 20, 1738, AND OTHER ORIGINAL PAPERS. (Supplementary to previous notice of 8th June 1874.)

Reprinted in a revised form in the *Proceedings* of the Society of Antiquaries, vol. xi. p. 595; with 36 separate copies for private circulation. (November 1876.)

1877

202. NOTICE OF TWO ORIGINAL DOCUMENTS DEPOSITED IN THE MUSEUM BY THE TRUSTEES OF THE LATE MISS AGNES BLACK, PERTH.

Read to the Society of Antiquaries 8th January 1877. *Proceedings,* vol. xii. p. 63.

203. INQUIRIES RESPECTING SOME OF THE EARLY HISTORICAL WRITERS OF SCOTLAND. (Supplementary to previous communications, 1846, etc.)

Read to the Society of Antiquaries 8th January 1877. *Proceedings,* vol. xii. p. 72.

204. NOTICE OF TWO ORIGINAL DOCUMENTS, WITH SIGNATURES EXHIBITED TO THE MEETING. I.—THE NATIONAL COVENANT, November 1638; II.—THE COMMON OR GODLY BAND, December 1557.

Read to the Society of Antiquaries 14th May 1877. *Proceedings,* vol. xii. p. 216.

205. JOHN, EARL OF GOWRIE, AND THE ALLEGED CONSPIRACY AT PERTH, 5 August 1600. AN HISTORICAL ENQUIRY, IN TWO PARTS. PART I. THE KING'S MANIFESTO; OR, 'A DISCOURSE OF THE UNNATURAL AND VILE CONSPIRACIE, ETC.' EDINBURGH, 1600.

Read to the Society of Antiquaries 11th June 1877. Printed in the Society's *Proceedings,* vol. xii. p. 311, where it is stated that ' This first portion of the *Historical Enquiry* is reserved for the *Archæologia Scotica,* vol. v. part ii., now in the press, the author expecting that he will be able to complete the *Enquiry* and to lay it before the Society during the present session,'—an expectation which he was not permitted to carry out.

206. LADY GRANGE IN EDINBURGH, 1730 : Forming a Supplementary Notice to that in the *Proceedings* (vol. xi.), with a copy of the Original Letter of Separation and Aliment addressed by Lady Grange to her husband, now presented to the Society by Mr. Spowart of Broomhead.

Read to the Society of Antiquaries 11th June 1877, and printed in the Society's *Proceedings,* vol. xii. p. 312.

1878

207. NOTICES OF JOHN, DUKE OF LAUDERDALE, AND THE DISPERSION OF HIS LIBRARY AND CORRESPONDENCE.

Read to the Society of Antiquaries 13th May 1878 (not printed).

208. ON THE EARLY HISTORICAL WRITERS OF SCOTLAND. 1878.

According to the Laing sale catalogue only 32 copies were printed. The one then offered realised £1. 1s. (It is an article contributed to the Society of Antiquaries.)

209. A THEATRE OF SCOTTISH WORTHIES; AND THE LYF DOINGS AND DEATHE OF WILLIAM ELPHINSTONE, BISHOP OF ABERDEEN. BY ALEXANDER GARDEN, ADVOCATE, ABERDEEN. PRIVATELY PRINTED MDCCCLXXVIII.

Presented to the members of the Hunterian Club by Alexander B. Stewart. The 'Introductory Notice of Alexander Garden and his Poetical Works,' 10 pp., is signed 'David Laing. Edinburgh, July 1878.'

210. FACSIMILES OF DESIGNS FROM ENGRAVED COPPERPLATES ILLUSTRATING *le liure de la Ruyne des Nobles Hommes et Femmes par Jehan Bocace de Certald: Imprimé à Bruges par Colard Mansion, Anno* **M.CCCC.LXXVI. WITH A PRELIMINARY**

Notice, By David Laing, Foreign Secretary Society of Antiquaries of Scotland. Edinburgh: M.DCCC.LXXVIII.

Minor title, 'Illustrations to the volume of Boccace printed at Bruges in 1476: 45 copies printed for the various recipients named, H.M. Queen Victoria heading the list.' The Dedication is:

> 'To the Most Honourable the Marquess of Lothian, K.T., this description of a rare volume in his Lordship's library at Newbattle Abbey is respectfully inscribed by the Editor.'

A frontispiece is given, headed:

> 'Here begynneth the boke of Johan Bochas discryving the fall of princes princesses and other nobles: Translated into Englysche by John Lydgate monke of Bury begynnyng at Adam and Eve and endying with Kyng Johan of Fraunce taken prisoner at Poyters by Prince Edwarde.'

Lord Lothian got 3 copies, the editor 2, other recipients 18, and 25 to libraries as a parting acknowledgment of aid received from them. A copy in the Laing sale brought £7.

According to Small, in the Bibliographical Memoir prefixed to the edition of the *Select Remains of the Ancient Popular and Romance Poetry of Scotland*, which he issued in 1885, this book of the 'Engraved Copperplates' was Laing's last publication. This may be so; but in the immediately preceding volume, *A Theatre* of *Scottish Worthies*, the Introductory Notice is signed by Laing with the date 'July 1878,' only three months before his death. This, at least, leaves it open to question which of the two volumes was the last to leave his hands.

In addition to the works quoted above, which were issued during Laing's lifetime, he was at the time of his death engaged upon the following, viz.:

211. THE ORYGYNALE CRONYKIL OF SCOTLAND. VOLUME III. BY ANDRO OF WYNTOUN.

This is the work to which Laing referred when recovering consciousness after the stroke which finally carried him off, as already related under the heading of his Personal History, in the month of October 1878. It was published by William Paterson, Edinburgh, in the following year. Two manuscripts of the *Cronykil* had been borrowed from the Advocates' Library, and were returned by Laing's trustees after his death.

212. FACSIMILE OF AN ANCIENT HERALDIC MANUSCRIPT EMBLAZONED BY SIR DAVID LYNDSAY OF THE MOUNT, LYON KING OF ARMS, 1542.

Second edition 'Edited by David Laing, LL.D.,' published by William Paterson, Edinburgh, 1878. Laing had agreed to supply a new 'Introduction,' and also, on loan, the several copperplates used in the printing of the first edition. While the plates were supplied, nothing by way of Introduction had been furnished; and the new edition was issued with 'The original Advertisement prefixed to the first edition' of 1822.

213. A BALLAD BOOK BY CHARLES KIRKPATRICK SHARPE, ESQ., M.DCCC.XXIII. Reprinted with Notes and Ballads from the Unpublished MSS. of CHARLES KIRKPATRICK SHARPE, Esq., and SIR WALTER SCOTT, Bart. Edited by the late DAVID LAING, LL.D. WILLIAM BLACKWOOD AND SONS, Edinburgh and London, 1880.

Frontispiece a picture of Sharpe, walking. 'The task of arranging the present book was originally entrusted . . . to the late David Laing, and he was engaged upon this task at the time of his lamented death. . . . Whatever value it may possess is due to David Laing's experience and taste. . . . Mr. Laing only lived to see the reprint through the press, but the Introduction has been written, and the selections have been made, in accordance with the views expressed by him a few weeks before his death.' (*Prefatory Note.*)

214. THE POETICAL WORKS OF SIR DAVID LYNDSAY WITH MEMOIR, NOTES, AND GLOSSARY. BY DAVID LAING, LL.D. EDINBURGH: WILLIAM PATERSON. MDCCCLXXIX.

In three volumes. 485 copies printed.

'ADVERTISEMENT

'The Publisher much regrets that Mr. Laing has not been spared to witness the publication of this work. It was begun by him so far back as the year 1869, and during the passing of the sheets through the press he added everything that could illustrate the writings of Sir David Lyndsay. In particular the valuable facsimiles from the numerous old editions of Lyndsay's works, and the accurate biographical details so characteristic of the lamented Editor, will always attest his skill in that department of literature.' The Publisher hoped that the Glossary prepared by John Small, M.A., would be 'a suitable conclusion to this work on which the late Editor spent so much labour.' The copyright of the edition of 1822, with Introduction, belonged to Laing's executors, but was not insisted on.

In making up the preceding lists I have been tempted once and again to linger over the precious items in course of being recorded—to glance at their literary or historical import, and their bearing upon the mental attitude, at the time, of the indefatigable and loving editor who had rescued so many of them from oblivion, and, by their republication, had imbued them with new life, and set them out on a fresh career of usefulness and delight for students and booklovers in all time. But the limits of the present undertaking forbade enlargement in this way; and the mass of rare and curious *morceaux* of Scottish literature, history, and antiquities, so laboriously brought together from the times of old, must be left to speak for themselves and tell their own tale. To attempt anything like a critical survey of the whole field of Laing's literary achievements would require a volume of itself; but, however much one might desire such a work, its execution must be left to other hands.

It may be worth while noting that of the foregoing books and other literary productions for which we are indebted to Laing—

39	were issued by the		Bannatyne Club.
1	..	,,	Maitland Club.
6		,,	Abbotsford Club.
4		,,	Wodrow Society.
3		,,	Hunterian Club.
2		,,	Shakespeare Club.
1		,,	Spalding Club.

56

107 { were communicated to the Society of Antiquaries of Scotland.

163

The remainder, 51 in number, were therefore issued by Laing himself, or printed by private arrangement otherwise.

It would not be proper to conclude this account of Laing's work in the domain of letters without referring to his DONATIONS to the Museum of the Society of Antiquaries of Scotland, though these are only a part of the invaluable services rendered

LITERARY WORK 235

to that body during the greater part of his lifetime:

LITERARY AND OTHER DONATIONS TO THE NATIONAL MUSEUM OF ANTIQUITIES

Stukeley's *Antiquities of Stonehenge and Abury*, folio.
Genealogy of the House of Drummond, 4to.
Rapin, *Histoire d'Angleterre.*
Æn. Vici Imagines Cæsarum.
Portrait of Sir Ewen Cameron of Locheil.
Standard yard-measure of Edinburgh.
Two pamphlets on cleaning the streets of Edinburgh.
Maitland's *History of Edinburgh.*
Memoirs of the Life, Writings, etc., of William Smellie, 2 vols.
Tabular View of the Genealogy of the Family of Hay in Scotland.
Diary of Alexander Brodie of Brodie, 1652-80.
Powder-horn found at Sheriffmuir.
Selection of Scots Airs for the Violin.
Six Solos for the Violin.
Xenophon, in Greek and Latin, 10 vols. ⎱ Published by W. Laing,
Thucydides, 6 vols. ⎰ David's father.
Poems and Fables of Robert Henryson. ⎱ David Laing, Editor.
Poems of William Dunbar, 2 vols. ⎰

Portraits of Charles I. and II.
Commemoration medal in bronze (Dec. 4, 1875)
  of Thomas Carlyle.

In addition to the above there was bequeathed to the Society of Antiquaries a valuable collection of PORTRAITS, chiefly in oil colours, and a collection of engraved GEMS, thirty-nine in number, all as already described under the head of Testamentary Bequests. Nor must the citizens of Edinburgh forget that, among his other public-spirited efforts, it is mainly to his initiative, his persistent efforts, and in several instances his own purse, that they are indebted for the following permanent memorials in the city, viz. :

St. Margaret's Well, removed from its old squalid quarters near Restalrig, and re-erected in the King's Park.
Monument to the Regent Murray, in the Church of St. Giles, restored.
Altar-Piece of Trinity College Church, restored to Scotland, and now preserved in Edinburgh.
Monument to George Buchanan, in Greyfriars Churchyard.
Monument of Principal Carstares, in Greyfriars, restored.
Plate, with initials 'I. K.,' to mark the supposed resting-place of John Knox in St. Giles Churchyard, now Parliament Square.

Monument in Greyfriars Churchyard to the Rev. Alexander Murray, D.D., Professor of Oriental Languages in the University of Edinburgh, author of *The History of European Languages*, etc., ' the Shepherd Boy who rose to be the most eminent linguist and oriental Scholar of his day.' Dr. Murray died in 1813, and the monument was erected in 1877.

VI

CORRESPONDENTS

LAING seems to have preserved most of the letters addressed to him, and these are now assorted in a number of bundles with a rough approach to classification, alphabetical and otherwise. The gross number I estimate at about 7500, with a bundle of replies, in draft, say 350, making a total of nearly 8000. Through all the letters I have laboriously waded, making a list of the names of the principal writers, and noting items of special interest contained in a few of them. The limits of the present work render necessary a severe condensation of any excerpts that may be made. There is further a bundle of at least 1000 'Family Letters' which I have not examined.

Of the correspondents about sixty are Peers of the realm, or members of noble families. Seven are Lords of Session; and the remainder are antiquaries, scholars in this country and abroad, and a miscellaneous array of inquirers in matters of literature, history, art and antiquities, extending over a period of about sixty years, the whole involving an amount of labour in investigating and replying that is almost inconceivable. Every application seems to have been met with courteous attention and ungrudging help, and the acknowledgments are replete with expressions of gratitude and reverential esteem. Only on two occasions are there indications of departure from the normal suavity in which the correspondence with his wide circle is couched. The first case is that of a somewhat importunate correspondent, from whom no less than fifty-eight letters remain, and who, at one time, provoked from Laing a sharp remonstrance for ' parading ' his (Laing's) name in connection with one of his own intended publications. The other occasion was when it was intimated to him that, by a decision of the Edinburgh University Court, ' persons whose right to membership rests upon their holding certain offices in the University, cease to be members of the General Council when they cease to hold the office which conferred the membership.' This apparently reasonable regulation did not meet Laing's approval, and he promptly replied, on 18th November 1870, as follows, after some introductory explanations of his position : ' As it appears I am now a special exception, it is no great sacrifice on my part to ask you (and you might even throw Doctor [his honorary degree of

LL.D.] into the bargain) to withdraw my name from your Register of Voters.'

But this incident did not lead to the alienation of his affections from ' Oure Tounis College,' for four years later, on 4th April 1874, he writes to Sir Alexander Grant, the Principal, offering to subscribe £50 for the University Buildings Extension Scheme. And the munificent bequest of his manuscript collection to the University authorities has already been described.

Dealing with the correspondence in detail it may be remarked, in regard to letters from men of rank and title, that they are mostly in reference to membership of the Bannatyne Club, with which they thought it an honour to be associated, and the Club's publications. The letters, therefore, usually possess a merely passing interest, and only a limited number call for notice.

The clever but eccentric EARL OF BUCHAN wrote as follows:

'DRYBURGH ABBEY. *September* 12, 1820.

'DEAR SIR,—I received a mass of papers from Bp. Abernethy Drummond relating to Drummond of Hawthornden, and observed among others some of the *primæ curæ* of his works, and a few letters from Drayton and others of his correspondents. The whole I deposited with James Cummyng, the then Secretary of the Society of Antiquaries, which I had the honour to found in Scotland, but of which I was not otherwise a member. Scotland seems only to have a decided genius for antiquarian poetry and metaphysics, yet Robertson, Dalrymple of Hailes, not to

CORRESPONDENTS

speak of MacLaurin, Gregory, Smith, Black and Watt, who are equal to every encomium, have shewn that my countrymen have heads capable of very different attainments than the *Galimatias* of the Waverley press.—I am, dr. Sir, yrs. with regard, BUCHAN.'

Again :

'DRYBURGH ABBEY. *October* 15, 1822.

'DEAR SIR,—It gave me pleasure to shew attention to Mr. Falborg, and I regret that, having altogether withdrawn from giving my name to literary publications, I cannot subscribe to that concerning Denmark.

'With kind regards to yr. family, I remain, dear Sir, yrs. etc., BUCHAN.'

'*To* Mr. David Laing.'

LADY GWYDYR, writing from Drummond (*i.e.* Drummond Castle) on 22nd October 1823, about books, adds in friendly fashion :

'Lord Gwydyr desires to join me in best regards to you, Mr. and Miss Laing.'

LORD HOUGHTON (the well-known Richard Monckton Milnes of an earlier date) writes to Laing, in a very friendly way, about books, from ' Keir, Friday.' A previous address is 26 Pall Mall.

LORD LINDSAY has a continuous correspondence (forty letters) from 1834 to 1860, some from Echt, Aberdeenshire, afterwards written ' Dunecht ' (the scene of the body-snatching tragedy at a later date); some from Haigh Hall,

Wigan, and the others from Balcarres, and from residences in London. From 1870 to 1878 there are several further letters from him when Earl of Crawford and Balcarres. He had sent to Laing a copy of his book *The Lives of the Lindsays*, in regard to which he writes from Echt House on 10th July 1849:

> 'MY DEAR SIR,—You could not have done me a greater kindness than by pointing out the error into which I had fallen respecting the authorship of the *Golden Treasury* by David Lindsay, and which, on the assertion of I forget what writer, I attributed to the Bishop of Ross. [Explanations follow.]
>
> 'I have little doubt there are very many errors throughout the *Lives*, and which I must hope, through the aid of my friends, and my own subsequent researches, to rectify hereafter.—Believe me always, very sincerely yrs.,
> 'LINDSAY.'

This is an instance of Laing's candid criticism, and of the weight attached to it by a distinguished author.

The MARQUESS OF LOTHIAN was a frequent and very friendly correspondent up to within a month of Laing's decease.

The EARL OF ROSEBERY, at an early stage of his career, on 24th October 1871, from Dalmeny Park, wrote an eloquent acknowledgment of Laing's learning and helpfulness.

From the EARL OF MORTON and the Dowager LADY MORTON there are several letters, mostly without date. On 20th October 1856 his Lordship wrote from Dalmahoy:

> 'I have to thank you very much for your recommendation as to my picture of the Regent Morton, which I am persuaded is the best and safest course that can be taken for its preservation.'

LORD PLAYFAIR, then Professor Lyon Playfair, in view of a parliamentary candidature, addressed Laing as follows:

> '*Private.*   14 ABERCROMBY PLACE,
> EDINBURGH. 8 *June* 1867.
>
> 'DEAR SIR,—In the event of the Scotch Reform Bill becoming law, I propose to become a candidate for the Universities of Edinburgh and St Andrews.
>
> 'I do not know whether you know sufficient of my habits of business and tastes to justify you in so soon making up your mind whether you can support me. . . It would be very agreeable to me if, after you have made up your mind, I should be fortunate enough to receive your support, that you would permit me to add your name to my General Committee.—Yours sincerely,
>
> 'LYON PLAYFAIR'

The **MARQUESS OF RIPON** writes as follows:

> '1 CARLTON GARDENS, S.W. 11 *July* 1874.
>
> 'Lord Ripon presents his compliments to Mr Laing, and having heard that there is reason to hope that Mr. Laing will be present at the approaching meeting of the Royal Archæological Institute at Ripon, Lord Ripon trusts that Mr. Laing will do him and Lady Ripon the honour of staying with them at Studley Royal on that occasion.
>
> 'As the meeting is to begin on the 21st inst., Lord Ripon hopes that Mr. Laing will come to Studley on the 20th.'

Laing did not accept the invitation. From a draft reply he appears to have said:

> '... I trust, however, your Lordship will accept in good part an apology for my not availing myself of this unexpected honour. I find it prudent, at an advanced period of life, to live very quiet and retired, and for ten years past have found the advantage of declining all invitations.
>
> 'Nevertheless, I hope to be able to attend the meetings,' etc., etc.

Of Lords of Session the principal correspondent is LORD COCKBURN. Fifteen letters.

> From 1828 to 1841 he dates from 14 Charlotte Square; in 1852 from 2 Manor Place, and in 1853-54 from Bonaly, all short notes, mostly about Bannatyne Club matters, and none of them specially suggestive of his own personality, so lovably known to us still.

From others of the Scottish judges we may note the following, viz.:

LORD MURRAY (John Archibald Murray of Henderland).

> A big parcel of letters about Bannatyne Club and other matters—the preservation of the Cathedral of Iona, and the building of the embankment in front of his house, Ramsay Lodge, on the Mound, which the seniors of the present generation can remember some years afterwards giving way at the foundation, and tumbling down. It was not replaced. The following letter in regard to Iona, marked 'Confidential,' penned nearly sixty years ago, deserves reproduction as showing his Lordship's view of a certain phase of the cataclysm of the Reformation period, Laing having apparently been reflecting severely on the rapacity of the nobles at that time.

'11 GREAT STUART STREET, EDINBURGH.
'25 *December* 1854.

'DEAR MR. LAING,—I return you the proof of the letter which you have done me the honour of addressing to me. Both the letter itself and the correction are so judicious that I have nothing to suggest, unless perhaps that you might reconsider the sentence at the top of page 12. I admit to the fullest extent the grasping disposition of the Scotch nobility and gentry, but although that may account for their laying hold of the lands, it will hardly do so for destroying the buildings, which [it] appears to me can be more easily attributed to fanatical zeal and neglect, and perhaps a little pilfering of a strange description to get second-hand tombstones.

'There is a tradition at Strachur that there are some boat-loads of stones which were brought from Iona, and there are some in the churchyard which resemble the tombstones at Iona very much. I hope you will come and examine them. The fishermen assert that one of the boats being pursued, they were obliged to throw the tombstones into the loch, at a place which they point out. A friend wished me to dredge for them, which I was no way inclined to do. But you may consider whether it is *safe* to assert anything very positively on the subject. Admitting which, I think you may assume, that the nobility were grasping, and the clergy and people sufficiently fanatical and roguish to take and destroy anything, but I do not know whether Scotch people like to be reminded of the bad qualities of their predecessors. Perhaps it may do them good, however.—Believe me, dear Mr. Laing, very truly yours, JOHN A. MURRAY.'

LORD JEFFREY. Two letters.

'CRAIGCROOK. *Monday*, 18 *August* 1844.

'MY DEAR SIR,—On my return here on Saturday evening I had the honour of receiving your obliging letter of the 5th together with the copy of your very handsome edition of Dunbar, with which you have been kind enough to present me.

'That I take such an interest in the subject as to make me not altogether unworthy of the gift, you will perhaps be disposed to allow, when I tell you that I have already read all your Memoir, more than half of your Notes, and better than a hundred pages of the most difficult part of the text, and that I am delighted with the way in which the publication is got up, as well as with the general appearance of the book. To show you that I do not flatter, I must add that 1 am not so well satisfied with the *Glossary* as with the other parts of the work.

'I feel, however, that you have conferred a great favour not only on the lovers of antiquity, but on the admirers of poetry, by this publication; and beg to return you my grateful thanks for the honour you have been pleased to do me by the flattering way in which you have offered it to my notice.—I have the honour to be, dear Sir, your obliged and very faithful servant,

'F. Jeffrey.'

The above is quite a characteristic letter from the great *Edinburgh* reviewer.

Lord Neaves. Forty-one letters, many of them informal notes, mostly from 19 Charlotte Square.

'1 *July* 1870.

'My dear Mr. Laing,—I have been thinking a good deal of late about Scotch literature, in which your labours will for ever remain a valuable and memorable monument of accurate criticism.

'But what do you say to a small *popular* volume with a *selection* from the various works of our very best authors—Barbour, Wintown, Henryson, Montgomerie, etc.—something, in short, in the style of Sibbald's *Chronicle*, but in a compressed shape?

'This, I feel assured, would not depreciate the regular standard editions of the authors, but, on the contrary, would introduce and recommend them to notice.

'I should be very glad to co-operate with you about a 5s. volume of this kind, so as to preserve among our countrymen a love and knowledge of our excellent vernacular, which I fear there is some danger of their losing.

'I daresay you will think I have too many irons in the fire already; but I suggest the thing as it occurs to me — Ever yours truly,   CHARLES NEAVES.'

To this there is a reply, in draft, by Laing, in which he says:

'For myself I am content to go on quietly in my old course, without caring one jot for popularity. Unluckily my time is so occupied and wasted that I can hardly get anything done. Yet, old as I am, I hope still to be spared to finish one or more schemes which I have been dreaming about longer than I can almost believe. One is, not a popular, but a cheap, series of the old Scottish Poets, in the shape of Pickering's Aldine Poets,' etc., etc.

It is clear from the above suggestion of a popular reprint of Scottish poets, even if there were no other evidence, that the brilliant and versatile Lord Neaves could address himself to more serious poetical literature than the original compositions usually attributed to him.

Lastly, LORD GLENCORSE. Five letters.

'EDINBURGH. *Jany*. 26, '78·

'MY DEAR MR. LAING,—Can you tell me whether there was in the 17th Century a general commission for managing the affairs of the Universities of Scotland, which held its meetings in Edinr. ?

'Dr. Lyon Playfair insists that there was, and that its first meetings were held in 1647-48. But the only traces I can find of such an institution are (1) an overture by the General Assembly to Parliament recommending something of the kind (Acts of Assembly 1641, Sect. ix.), and (2) a record of the overture having been laid before Parliament (Acts of Parlt., vol. v. p. 367).

'I cannot find that any Act or appointment of a Commission followed on this. If you have information on the subject I shall feel very much obliged by your giving me the benefit of it.—Yours most faithfully, JOHN INGLIS.'

Such a letter from such an accomplished lawyer and antiquary is another instance of the fact that Laing was the literary and historical referee of his day more than any man in Scotland.

Among the MISCELLANEOUS CORRESPONDENTS, foreigners as well as British, are men and women of all types, not a few of them deserving to be classed as 'Celebrities.' With some the correspondence is extensive and long-continued. For example, the numbers of letters received from the following are as stated :

W. H. Miller and S. Christy Miller, both of Craigentinny, and John Miller of Lincoln's Inn, K.C.	294
Beriah Botfield, M.P.	137
Francisque Michel, the French littérateur	116

Robert Pitcairn, of the *Criminal Trials*	114
John Lee, D.D., Principal of Edinburgh University	113
Rev. A. B. Grosart, LL.D.	75
W. B. D. D. Turnbull, Advocate, Antiquary	75

with many more of fewer, but still large, individual numbers. While many of the letters are naturally of a business, or formal, character, there is still a large proportion evincing the personalities of the writers, and sometimes possessing touches, directly or incidentally introduced, of an interesting kind. Of these only a limited number can be glanced at here.

Rev. W. Lindsay Alexander, D.D.

'17 Brown Square. 30 *May* 1868.

'My dear Sir,—Accept my best thanks for your kind present of a copy of your edition of the *Gude and Godlie Ballates*. It is a publication of very much interest; and edited by you it will be esteemed by all students of Church History as a valuable addition to existing and get-at-able stores of imformation regarding the Reformation literature.—Believe me, yours very faithfully,

'W. Lindsay Alexander.'

Dr. Alexander here dates from the then manse of the St. Augustine Church, formerly the mansion of Sir William Miller, Lord Glenlee.

George R. Ainslie, 34 Howe Street.

'. . . I have possession *for a few days* of the only well-authenticated portrait of Queen Mary, which was given by her to the Scots College of Paris after the death of her husband, and probably on the eve of her departure for Scotland. This you will probably be desirous of seeing' (22nd April 1836).

At first sight this would suggest that the picture in question was the one now at Blairs College. But, as Dr. Hay Fleming points out to me, that picture was bequeathed by Elizabeth Curle, in her will of 24th April 1620, to the Scots College at Douai, and was brought to Scotland in 1830 or 1831. Several *copies* of portraits of Mary from French originals were shown in the Glasgow Exhibitions of 1901 and 1911. The Blairs College picture is, besides, of a late period of Mary's life.

Sir James E. Alexander, Westerton, Bridge of Allan.

Twelve letters, 1860 to 1873. About an alleged *skull* of Lord Darnley; a two-handled *sword*, said to be of Wallace, in the possession of the Countess of Loudoun; and other matters.

Miss Margaret Susan Anderson, Windmill Street, Edinburgh.

The curators of the Advocates' Library having declined to purchase from her the correspondence of the Earl of Buchan and other manuscript papers belonging to her father, the late Dr. Robert Anderson, Laing buys the whole on his own account, and she acknowledges the receipt of £100 therefor (22nd January 1838).

James Ballantyne, Edinburgh.

The following, from Sir Walter Scott, was sent by Ballantyne to Laing, and is quoted here as further illustration of Ballantyne's position as not merely printer but also the trusted critic of Scott's productions. The subject is apparently 'Rokeby,' Canto First:

'Dear James,—I send you the whole of the canto. I wish Erskine and you would look it over together and consider whether upon the whole matter it is likely to make an impression. If it does really come to good, I think there are no limits to the interest of that style of composition, for the varieties of life and character are boundless.—Yours truly, W. S.'

'I don't know whether to give Matilda a mother or not. Decency requires she could [sic] have one, but she is as likely to be in my way as the gudeman's mother according to the proverb is always in that of the good wife' (n.d. Postmark 'Melrose').

Another (n.d.) in regard to 'The Lord of the Isles'—

'DEAR SIR,—You have now the whole affair excepting two or three concluding stanzas. As your taste for bride's cake may incline you to desire to know more of the wedding, I will save you some criticism by saying I have settled to stop short as above. Witness my hand, W. S.'

There is also a letter from John Ballantyne, James's brother (the 'Rigdumfunnidos' of Scott), without date, from 'Trinity,' *i.e.* Trinity Grove, his place of residence in the time of prosperity, and another from John Ballantyne, James's son, without date, in which he says:

'I believe I am the only individual now alive who dined with him [Scott] the last time he ever sat at his own table in Abbotsford. I remember well every incident of the occasion, tho' it is 40 [years] sin syne noo.' He adds that he is 'as poor as a rat.'

Professor John Stuart Blackie, LL.D.

Five letters, 1864 to 1876, mostly undated, and almost illegible. One from '24 Hill Street,' 26th March [1864], is as follows:

'MY DEAR SIR,—It gives me great pleasure to intimate to you that the Senatus Academicus this day conferred on you the degree of LL D., the ceremonial to take place on the 20th.

'Public announcement will be made. This is only private. Burton and Robertson are to be dubbed along with you.—Sincerely yours, JOHN S. BLACKIE.'

This recognition by the Senatus came after he had been carrying on his great work for about fifty years under their eyes. In another letter Blackie addresses Laing as 'My dear Historian.'

WILLIAM BLADES, Printer and Bibliographer, 1861-77.

The letters are mostly about the Caxton celebration in 1877, for which Laing informed him of several Caxtonian examples—

'another of the many good deeds which have laid the whole world of bibliophiles under obligation to you.'

Laing offered to guarantee for £300 the safety of certain volumes if entrusted to his care.

WILLIAM BLACKWOOD, Publisher.

Several letters in 1814 and later, usually from 'Princes Street.'

'DEAR DAVID,—I am very anxious to see you as soon as possible. . . . It is something of considerable consequence to us both which I wish to show you *in confidence,* and to have your advice about.'

On 21st June 1814—

'It is reported that the Crafty[1] and his partner in the *Encyclopædia* have quarrelled. I have not heard anything certain about it, but it is extremely likely to have happened —indeed it is a wonder it has not happened ere now.'

---

[1] The 'Crafty' was Constable, Blackwood's great rival, Scott's friend and publisher. The term was applied in the famous 'Chaldean Manuscript,' attributed to 'Christopher North,' which at the time created such a sensation and bitterness of feeling in Edinburgh.

The following is an amusing PS. to another letter:

'An old lady of my acquaintance informs me that her servant heard a Mr. Laing, Bookseller in Edinburgh, proclaimed last Sunday in the West Church. If this should be you, you have managed matters very quietly.'

Sir David Brewster.

Letters from 1827 to 1864. One, of special interest, is dated from 10 Coates Crescent, March 26, 1827.

'I think you have just reason to take offence on this occasion—not that five black balls were put in against you [at the Royal Society meeting], for nothing is more common than to see many black balls at our elections, and every person is entitled to exercise his privilege—but at the absence of so many of your friends on that occasion, as the presence of even one more would have carried your election.'

In another letter he asks Laing to deliver a small packet to Mons. Biot, the scientist, in Paris; and also to procure for him there certain books which he requires for his article on Hydrodynamics for the *Encyclopædia* [*Britannica?*].

John Brown, 23 Rutland Street, the 'beloved Physician.'

The only dated letter is of 14th July 1873, in reference to the still unsettled question of the authorship of the *Ode to the Cuckoo,* in which he gives preference to Michael Bruce, while Laing strongly supported Logan.

'Dear Mr. Laing,—You gave me a great pleasure when you gave me your letter. Such a piece of thorough work is not common, and it is pleasant to think one man lives who knows so much. I don't know that your proofs have greatly changed my tendency to believe in Bruce as against Logan. It is not a question easy to get out of the region of doubtful disputation, but I think the preponderance is still in favour of Bruce—the local evidence and that letter of Davidson seem to me very strong.

'The letters in the Appendix are very interesting, and that list of the poems with the names appended curious, but not conclusive, to my mind — a U.P. mind you must remember! It is Grosart, not my cousin, who made the 'subsequently' blunder. The said Grosart writes me that he is to answer you. I hope he will imitate your style.—Yours ever truly, J. BROWN.'

Brown's claim of possessing a 'U.P. mind' is perhaps a little whimsical for the moment. It was not a very rigid one of that type, as all who knew him can testify.

J. J. BROWN, Dunfermline.

'MY DEAR SIR,—Allow me to introduce Mr. Joseph Paton, a very promising young artist of this place, who spent last winter in London and is anxious to get a look at Froissart, and perhaps one or two other things you can show him. He is a grandson of the author of the little work in which you were interested' (1st November 1843).

This is Sir Joseph Noel Paton of later times, Queen Victoria's Limner for Scotland.

GILBERT BURNS, brother of the poet.

The following letter addressed not to Laing but to Mr. Alex. Cunningham, Edinburgh, deserves a place here:

'DEAR SIR,—I herewith send you a small punch-bowl of Inveraray Marble. To present you with so paltry a vessel of base materials requires some explanation.

'Mrs. Burns has for some time expressed a wish to present you with some small testimony of the sense she has of your friendly attachment to her children as well as to their father. I have advised her that as this Bowl has acquired some celebrity from Dr. Currie's having connected it with his description of the social powers as well as habits of its former owner, it will be an agreeable present to you, and I hope it will reach you while Mr. Syme is with you, that in his company the melancholy luxury of the recollection of joys that are past may be produced in your mind, so susceptible of tender impressions.—I am, my dear Sir, yours most truly, GILBERT BURNS.'

> ' Ye whom social pleasure charms,
> Whose hearts the tide of kindness warms,
> Who hold your being on the terms
> "Each and the others";
> Come to my Bowl, come to my arms,
> My friends and brothers.'—BURNS.

J. F. CAMPBELL.

Two letters, 1872.

This must be John Frederick Campbell 'of Islay,' in reference to his Highland book, for which he 'courted the approval of the best of living Editors' (*Popular Tales of the West Highlands, orally collected*).

GEORGE CHALMERS, London, author of *Caledonia*.

Letters of a very friendly type—'Dear David.' He shows in one letter that the *Dragon* was the emblem of the Scots for many ages before the *Red Lion* was thought of. Letters of 1818 and 1822 are much about Zachary Boyd.

ALEXANDER CHISHOLM, Painter, London.

A letter of 3rd April 1844 is about his picture, 'Taking the Oath of the Covenant,' which had been coldly received at Glasgow, but which he himself declared to be 'in the opinion of the first men in the country—the finest picture in point of design and composition that has ever been painted in this country.' He died in 1847, leaving his family in embarrassed circumstances.

DR. JOHN AITKEN CARLYLE. Brother of the Sage of Chelsea.

Seventeen letters, 1861 to 1877. The following are samples:

'62 Hanover Street. 12 *May* 1865.

'My dear Mr. Laing,—To-day I have received a letter from my brother Thomas, dated yesterday, in which there is a message for you; and, as I cannot call to-day, I copy it here:

'" Our weather is rainy these two days, large floods of soft rain; everything beauty itself when the sun gets out. I have been reading in Laing's *Knox* since Froude ended: thank Laing again from me; his faithful, solid, accurate ways are worthy of all honour.'—Yours very sincerely,

'J. A. Carlyle.'

'The Hill, Dumfries. 1 *July* 1865.

'My dear Mr. Laing,—Many thanks for the copy of your new edition of Henryson, which I received by post two days ago. I have already read the most of it, and find you have done everything possible to make it faithful and complete. It forms a very nice volume, and I have set it up beside Lord Hailes, Sir Tristram, etc. I have not yet finally decided in regard to my journey to Christiania, my brother Thomas being still in Dumfriesshire, and undecided too, but I will tell you in good time if I resolve to go, and need any letters of introduction. —I am, very sincerely yours, J. A. Carlyle.'

'The Hill, Dumfries. 15 *October* 1866.

'... My brother Thomas has always taken great interest in everything connected with St. Columba and the early ecclesiastical history of Scotland, and is already as well acquainted with the subject as any one I know, but he expects something more from Reeves.' [The volumes accordingly sent to him].

Allan Cunningham, London. Poet and miscellaneous writer, the 'honest Allan' of Scott.

Thirty-seven letters, 1822 to 1841. A large and interesting confidential correspondence, at first from Eccleston Street, Pimlico, afterwards from 27 Belgrave

Place. There are references to Scott, Byron, Shelley, George Chalmers, Joanna Baillie, and others.

'3 *May* 1822.

'The pressure of many things not so congenial to my heart as books and ballads has hindered me from acknowledging your letter sooner. Your kindness takes a shape very dear to my heart in offering so frankly the use of your collections for my projected publication. [He then describes the works of a lyrical nature which he has gathered, and proceeds]—

'I perfectly agree with you in your wish to preserve the familiar simplicity—which some men have called coarseness—of our ancient songs. I am no fastidious person and rather a fearless one, and I shall assuredly treat the old ballads—their infirmities of expression—with mildness and lenity. To prune and starch and lander them up to the present taste for exterior decorum and capricious delicacy will be injurious and unjust, and will show me to the world as a vain and a conceited and a cowardly person. What I wish to do is this. Some songs are so decidedly gross as to leave no option between omission and amendment—these I must render purer; and some are fragments and require to be completed—these I must make whole. The Jolly Beggars, a cantata, contains some of Burns's best songs—few of them are in collections, and all of them deserve to be there. I can think that a chastening hand might be advantageously laid on that wild work, The Merry Muses. When you come to London I shall be most happy to see you in my little lonely home, where you will find such cheer as a muse-maker can command, and a hearty, warm welcome'

Thus Cunningham on the literary ethics of earlier poetry, a difficulty and discouragement to Laing in his dealing with Sir David Lindsay of the Mount and others of our old singers.

Reverting to the same subject at a later date (14th January 1824), Cunningham resumes his moralising to his friend as follows:

'Oh David, my sedate and excellent friend, beware of the company of the young and fair critics who are sitting in judgment on the transgressions of the lyric muse, and are laying their white hands on the naked and forbidden parts of song. Keep out from among them when they discuss, with the freedom of innocence and modesty, the failings and lapses of the high-kilted muse of Caledonia. And let those gentle dames beware lest they become infected with the very spirit they are seeking to abate. I'll tell you a story, a *perfectly true* story.

'There was a lady, young and fair and plump and rosy, a sincere pray-er and much of a saint, who, armed in the panoply of holiness, marched away to the conversion of a lascivious girl who had cast away favours among mankind and had much to repent. The saint drew such a charming picture of the joys of virtue and devotion, and the sinner such a glowing portrait of the pleasures and enjoyments of sin, that they mutually converted each other—the sinner grew a saint and the saint a sinner.

'Let our ladies therefore beware, lest in removing the lasciviousness of songs they grow not themselves defiled. I think the songs which pleased their grandmothers may well please them—we talk, indeed, more about virtue, but is it practised more?'

'*July* 22, 1822.

'DEAR DAVID,—I have worked carefully through the Lights and Shadows since I saw you—they are very eloquent and dreamy, full of lofty emotions, with too little of real positive life. They are poured out with great vehemence and great sweetness, and, had the author imagined less and trusted observation more, his work would have been what few could mend. Nothing can be more apart from the Lights and Shadows than the Parish Annals class which, excellent in their own limited way, are facsimiles from real life, warts and ferntickles and all, and, though full of curious things and dry Scottish humour, fail to make anything like a strong impression. Of the want of morality in Adam Blair, much may, and much has been said—but the man who has dreed hard weird and punishment for his wickedness and repented, as the hero of that impressive tale has done, may surely return to his rank in society and his place in men's hearts, since we find that repentance finds favour before a tribunal as strict as that of man. I also think it a little too dreamy and tasting of the German school—faults which will amend as years ripen judgment in the author.

'I had a call from Wilkie yesterday; he has recd. his final commission for John Knox's picture from Lord Liverpool. He carried M'Crie's history in his hand and read some of the more graphic passages to his lordship, who was much pleased, and took a note of the book. . . . —With every wish for your welfare, I remain, my dear David, your very sincere friend,

'ALLAN CUNNINGHAM.'

'*To* David Laing, Esq.'

Cunningham's letters being so numerous and excellent, full of interesting thought and feeling, there is some difficulty in making selections, but a few further specimens must be given.

'*5 August* 1823.

'Some good-natured friend sent me the other day the last number of your new review, in which my tales are noticed. The reviewers can endure no other man's works save those of the author of *Waverley*. I think he is quite right in his admiration, and no one can admire them more than I do. But we must not quarrel with the stars because the moon is brighter, nor tread the daisy underfoot because in beauty and in perfume it is excelled by the rose,' etc.

'*November* 29, 1822.

'I have not formed any acquaintance with Joanna Baillie If I should meet her, which is more than probable, I shall introduce your name, and mention your wish. She has knowledge enough of the world and enthusiasm enough to know that to comply with such a request is in itself honourable. . . .

'We have endured of late a literary visitation from Italy—the *Liberal*—the production of Byron, Hunt, and poor ill-fated Shelley. The bird over which they so long brooded has come forth with wings of lead—much was expected—perhaps too much, and the disappointment is grievous. I am sorry at this wilful degradation of Byron's fine genius, and I have something of the hope of his salvation which Burns had for the redemption of Satan. I am wae to think upon the den into which he has made this voluntary tumble—a man when he scorns his country is ready for anything. . . . How is Mr. Hogg, and what is he doing?'

'*November* 18, 1823.

'I have been infamously disappointed in my wished-for journey to Scotland—but there is a gude time coming. There is a time for me to write a glorious romance in prose or in rhime—there is a time for me to write you a noble Cameronian lyric—there is a time for me to edite my four volumes of Scottish songs—and there is a time when we too shall meet and be merry, and knock the dust out of our throats and out of some old-world matters at the same time. Do write me a letter, a long letter.'

'*October* 5, 1825.

'My faithful David,—What are you about?—what bright and buried worthy are you dragging from oblivion into day? I live in the hope that some future Laing will find my prose and verse skulking among dull bodies of divinity in some rich man's library, who made the bargain for the books and signed it with his mark—and thus arresting descent into oblivion by a hundred years'

On 10th January 1825 he writes buoyantly as follows:

'I assure you, my dear friend, my heart is light and my spirit is up at the thought of emerging from the purgatory of magazines to breathe upper air. Escaped from the reign of Chaos and old Night, I may wing my own way unmolested into sunshine and have a chance of shining among the stars of the morning.'

But this hopefulness was not lasting. Within three years from the last date it had given way to despair:

'27 BELGRAVE PLACE. 23 *April* 1828.

'Alas, my dear David, I have too many excuses for this seeming neglect [in answering a letter of Laing's]. Fortune, who formerly looked quietly on my struggles, has now taken the field against me, and success follows none of my undertakings. If I lend a man twopence he repays me with a penny; if I bargain for ten pounds I am paid with five—the wind which blows good to others blows mischief to me, and nothing which I set my mind on prospers. To add to all this, for these last eight weeks the measles have been with us, or the poison they infuse; and I think I merit the prayers of the General Assembly, if the prayers of the righteous would avail one whose case is so desperate. I have lost on an average £150 within these fifteen months,' etc

'18 *October* 1832.

'Alas, we have lost our illustrious friend Scott; there is no star in the north now. I wrote a little hasty notice of his life and works for the *Athenæum* which has not been unwelcome here. I have had many more compliments than what were merited about it.'

'6 *July* 1836.

'I am not sure that I shall write any more books: a nightmare has come upon the publishing trade, and an author such as I cannot obtain a sum at all equal to his labours.'

This letter winds up with an interesting account of the talents and success of his two sons in India.

'27 Belgrave Place. 10 *Sept.* 1841.

'My dear David,—My heart warmed and my cheek reddened when I read your kind letter. You will oblige me by collecting some memoranda respecting Wilkie: do you know his Scotch Fair, Pitlessie? I should have said he thought much of it himself, rather as a composition and full of matter than as a well-painted picture. . . . God bless you.—Yours with esteem,   Allan Cunningham.'

Chantrey, the sculptor, with whom Cunningham had long worked, had a great regard for him, and left him an annuity of £100, with reversion to his widow, but he lived only to receive a single payment, for he died in the following year, 1842, highly esteemed by all. His *Life of Sir David Wilkie* was published after his death.

Peter Cunningham, 27 Lower Belgrave Place, London. [1834.]

'. . . Our friend Tom Campbell is off to Algiers, flying from Paris to avoid the bitter but unjust sarcasms of the *Quarterly Review.* When he is here again I will remember your wish to have "Ye Mariners of England" in his handwriting.'

The writer is a son of Allan Cunningham.

Rev. Alexander Dyce, Rosebank, Aberdeen and London.

Forty-two letters, 1820 to 1867.

'*Nov.* 24, 1820.

'My dear Sir,—For a considerable time past I have been preparing for the press a translation from the Greek of *The Supplement to the Iliad*, by Quintus Calaber, a poem which has never been rendered into English, while versions have been made of Greek poetical works in every respect its inferior. As it is that sort of book which can have but a limited sale, I have determined, after much consideration, to print by subscription a

certain number of copies in a handsome shape, and have reason to expect many subscriptions in Oxford and London. [Inquiries for technical and professional advice as to the issue follow.] It will be printed in London and published by a bookseller there—by Parker at Oxford—and have you any objections to become my publisher at Edinburgh, and to receive subscribers' names, though I confess I do not expect many in your city?—Yours truly,
'ALEX. DYCE.'

REV. T. F. DIBDIN, D.D., Rector of St. Mary's, Bryanston Square, and Chaplain in Ordinary to Queen Victoria, author of *The Bibliographical Decameron*, and other works.

There are twenty-eight letters, from 1821 to 1842, all full of friendliness and humour, about his books, his travels and proceedings generally, with cravings for Laing's help, pecuniary and otherwise, from time to time. The signature is frequently by a curiously devised monogram of T. F. D. One or two samples of his style may be sufficient:

'EXMING VICARAGE,
'NEWMARKET. *Sep.* 19, '35.

'MY DEAR SIR,—It is an age since we met, and *almost* an age since we saw each other.

'Can you help me with a name or two for the enclosed?[1] I have recently got yours from Longmans, but I want some of your *Viri Illustrissimi*, Bannatyners, etc. etc. I have very lately "fallen upon evil days," and want my friends, right and left, north and south, to aid me with their £1, 5s. for as honest and rich a pennyworth as they shall receive at the hands of any veteran scribe; and you know that, in my time, I have deserved well of the fraternity, in all its ramifications.

---

[1] This seems to refer to his *Reminiscences of a Literary Life*, published in 1836.

'I hope the impression will be exhausted on delivery in November. Can you get me Professor Napier and T. Thomson?—remembering always that I am a good old Whig of the genuine constitutional school.

'I know you will do a good stroke for me if you can. *Vale et nostrum sis memor.*—Most truly yours,

'T. F. DIBDIN.'

On 10th November he thanked Laing for the 'cohort of subscribers' received through him:

'You have been very kind, very active, and very *successful*; for your men are "men of war," giants in their several departments, not of the dwarfish or pigmy growth of the ordinary run of men. In regard to the "Root of all Evil"—the insane root, if you please, pray allow my publisher, John Major (a good man and true, tho' albeit a bit of a Tory) to send the copies at once to Black's; and do you, I beseech you, seize the *golden opportunities* of pouching the said mammon for me. . . . I am much edified by the last *blue* and *buff* exhibition [*i.e.* the *Edinburgh Review*]. . . . Farewell, and may you prosper ever more, both in your public and private capacity. Will Caddell disclose the number of copies printed of *his* edition of Scott's works? I should much like to know, and soon. How many, on the whole, did Constable print?

'Write *smack*—at once. I want to *hit* Lord Moncreiff. —Yours very truly, T. F. DIBDIN.'

On 13th November he wrote that he had spent Friday and Saturday with the Duke and Duchess of Northumberland at Alnwick Castle, and was passing on to Newcastle.

'35 MORAY PLACE [EDINBURGH].
'*Saturday.*

'DEAR MR. LAING,—Expect me within an hour or so. I arrived last night—full of glory, etc. etc. My machinery must be instantly put into motion. T. F. D.'

'*Nov.* 12.

'Do pray, my dearly beloved Boke-Man, answer my Boke Questions. You make my carriage "stop the way" cruelly in the streets of Edinburgh. I can't get on. 1000 thanks to W B D D T' [Turnbull].

On 10th August 1842. 'You will be pained to hear that my health is sinking.' He was born in 1776, and died in 1847.

F. J. FURNIVALL, London. Dr. Furnivall, the famous scholar and philologist, who died in 1910.

Eighty-one letters, 1864 to 1878.

'5 ST. GEORGE'S SQUARE, PRIMROSE HILL, N.W.
'4 *Nov.* 1869.

'MY DEAR SIR,—The attack on Mr. Chappell and myself in the new edition of Watson's *Poems*, pp. xxv.-vii., renders it necessary for me to appeal to you for copies of the two volumes in your Pinkerton MS., so that we may have the whole of the text before us, and be able to argue the question from internal evidence.—Always truly yours,
'F. J. FURNIVALL.'

'7 *April* 1873.

'... Yesterday I was with your old acquaintance, Dr. C. Mackay,[1] at his pretty little place at Boxhill. He said you had ten years' work in hand, which is a fair share.'

'1 *May* 1876.

'... I was with Bradshaw at Cambridge, and in the library all Sunday correcting my *Chaucer* proofs. We were talking of you and your power of work, and what an example you set us all.'

JAMES T. GIBSON-CRAIG, W.S,. Edinburgh.

A large correspondence. Some letters from the family seat of Riccarton, but mainly from [12] 'Picardy Place,' and latterly 'York Place' [24]. One as early as 27th March

---

[1] Dr. Charles Mackay, author of 'Cheer, Boys, Cheer,' etc. etc.

1827. Laing is usually addressed as 'My dear Sir,' but at least seven are to 'Dear Sir David.' In one he asks Laing to dine with him at Riccarton at six o'clock, when he 'would not be troubled with woman-kind.' In another he says, 'Mr. Toovey tells me that he *yesterday* purchased at Dowell's sale of the Belhaven books a copy of Caxton's *Golden Legend*, wanting only the last leaf, for £60, and that he has already sold it for £200.' His own library (1888) realised £15,509, over 9000 lots.

Rev. A. B. Grosart, LL.D., Blackburn, Lancashire. Formerly well known as resident at Kinross.

Seventy-five letters, 1846 to 1877. The earlier ones are full of pathetic interest in reference to his literary beginnings; the later, in his more experienced days, are more formal and reserved. Laing took a great amount of trouble in helping him.

J. O. Halliwell, 11 Tregunter Road, West Brompton, London (afterwards known as J. O. Halliwell-Phillipps).

Thirty-one letters, 1864 to 1872. Of great interest, mainly about early editions of Shakespeare, and the bequest of his Shakespeare Library to the University of Edinburgh.

H. Kerr, 39 Upper Brunswick Place, Brighton and Huntlyburn, Melrose.

In reference to Abbotsford papers. He would wish to see Laing at Edinburgh or Abbotsford, to consider as to the preservation, or partial destruction, of these papers.

John Lee, D.D., LL.D., Principal of the University of Edinburgh.

CORRESPONDENTS

One hundred and thirteen letters, from 1816 to no one knows when, for most of them are without date, *e.g.* 'Saturday.' About the latest of any certainty is one headed 'January 11, 1856.' The earlier ones are from St. Andrews, the later ones from the 'College, Edinburgh.' A charming correspondence, about special books and literature generally. Many of the letters extend to four pages, large quarto.

'ST. ANDREWS. 27 *January* 1818.

'MY DEAR SIR,—I received yours per Mr. William Cowper, a tall well-dressed person of a prelatical aspect but with a Presbyterian tongue in his head. I am proof against his arts, but I am not sure whether I shall always retain him as an inmate in this house, lest in process of time he should corrupt my boys. . . .

'I am sorry you think so lightly of my three volumes of tracts. Keep them carefully till I come. If I were to part with them in the lump, I would not let them go under nine guineas. If I take out about one-tenth of the whole, I would give the remainder for seven guineas.—I remain, my dear Sir, yours faithfully, JOHN LEE.'

'ST. ANDREWS. 20*th April* 1818.

'As to the tracts and other books which you meant to send by last week's carrier, I will be much obliged to you to send them by the very first coach after you receive this, I mean by the Fife Union Coach which starts from Scott's in Princes Street on Wednesday morning at half-past seven o'clock. They would require to be booked on Tuesday evening, and to have a direction to forward the parcel from Cupar by the St. Andrews runner. . . .

'I do know some little thing about Ninian Winzet, but it is not at my finger ends. Of the Scottish Psalms I am as ignorant as the child unborn.'

'ST. ANDREWS. 19*th October* 1820.

'I have not time to write to you at any length, as I am obliged to go to Aberdeen in a few days, and I have many previous arrangements to make. The situation to which

I am going is one for which I felt no anxiety, but as it was obtained without any influence, and as in some respects it promises to be more advantageous than my present appointment, I consented to undertake it after being so advised by those who have my interest most at heart. I enter on the office with great inconvenience, and under circumstances very far from cheering, as the state of my family compels me to leave them behind me, and the only circumstance which I can expect to keep me from thinking too much of them will be the necessity of constant hard labour. For five months I shall have to meet three hours every day with my students—but only one hour every day is spent in lecturing The other two are employed in examinations, and in College exercises performed by the students. This kind of occupation is in some measure new to me. But I can reconcile my mind to anything which I conceive to be useful, and I never shrink from active exertion.'

He is in the habit of confidentially acquainting Laing with his personal and family affairs in this way.

'12 CHARLOTTE SQUARE. *July* 11, 1835.

'MY DEAR SIR,—I find I have just one spare copy of the little narrative which was printed six years ago on the subject of the Buik of the Universal Kirk of Scotland. The circumstances are now greatly altered, as the Governors of the College [1] are quite willing to surrender the volumes on receiving such authority as will secure them against any future charge of breach of trust. The conditions on which they hold this deposit are now well known. I read the indenture last year, when I inspected the books for the second time. The precise words I do not recollect— but the English of them is something to this purpose, that the President and Fellows bound themselves and their successors never to deliver up the books, nor to allow

---

[1] The 'College' is Sion College, London, where these records of the Church of Scotland were detained.

any copy or extract to be taken from them, so long as Episcopalian Church government shall not be restored in Scotland—a condition which, as I humbly conceive, was not consistent with the law of the land, inasmuch as by the Treaty of Union and the Act securing the Protestant religion and Presbyterian Church government, the King and Parliament had solemnly bound themselves that the government of the Church, not by Bishops, but by Kirk-Sessions, Presbyteries, Synods, and General Assemblies, should be effectually and unalterably secured to all succeeding generations as the only government of the Church within the kingdom of Scotland. But we need not now contend about the propriety or impropriety of the terms of a covenant which the lapse of a century has convinced one of the high contracting parties may be at last renounced—the more especially as the other contracting party is not in a condition to enforce compliance—having long ago been removed to that middle state on which he wrote a huge folio volume, and which, whether subject to Episcopalian or Presbyterian rule, is at least beyond the jurisdiction of the Court of Chancery, as well as of the Town Council of Edinburgh, from the Records of which it appears that Mr. Archibald,[1] grandson of the Marquess of Argyll as he was, and Bishop of a persecuted Church as he afterwards became, was prosecuted by the Procurator Fiscal for a riot committed on a Sunday evening in the house of Widow Allan, Vintner, and afterwards boxing the ears of George Young, merchant-burgess, one of the Constables of the City, and attempting to draw his sword on him—the said Mr. Archibald having at the same time on his back a scarlet coat, emblematical of his truculent and belligerent disposition.

'But this is an episode not very obviously relevant to

---

[1] The 'Mr Archibald' here referred to as an inmate of purgatory was the Reverend Archibald Campbell, D.D , son of Lord Neil Campbell, and grandson of the first Marquess of Argyll. He was an Episcopalian clergyman, and afterwards Bishop of Aberdeen (1721). He removed to London and joined the Non-jurors.

the case, for the bloody assault on the Constable occurred in 1703, whereas the rape of the records was not perpetrated till 1733—the gentleman by this time having changed colours, not from black to red, like a lobster boiled, but from red to black, like the writer hereof, who in 1803 sometimes wore scarlet, but now in 1835 wears nothing but black, and is sufficiently disposed to use as much violence in taking back the Church property as the arch-spoliator employed in giving it away.

'But as my paper is exhausted, and your patience also, I now relieve you from purgatory, where I am sure Mr. Archd. must be as long as the ill-gotten gear is not restored.—I remain, yours very faithfully, J. LEE.'

JOHN MILLER of Lincoln's Inn, London.
W. H. MILLER of Craigentinny, Edinburgh.
S. CHRISTY MILLER of Craigentinny, Edinburgh.

Two hundred and ninety-four letters, 1816 to 1877. A very intimate and confidential correspondence, generally about ancient literature, and their great family library at Britwell House, Buckinghamshire.

'Pray turn your attention to *Scottish History*, and don't throw away your time upon its *antiquities*. If you do not, I am certain you will repent it when it is too late' (John Miller, 13th January 1823)

'Pinkerton is, without exception, the most conceited and inelegant coxcomb I ever met with, and hardly think my house can hold him' (John Miller, 10th February 1820).

In reference to the illness of George IV.:

'... The very thought of becoming a King is said to have already made the Duke of Clarence [William IV.] so mad that he has little chance of ever filling that character' (John Miller, 22nd September 1830).

WILLIAM MILLER, 23 Walcot Square, Lambeth, London.

He writes in 1871 saying that he is one of those, about fifty in number, who helped to rear the Scott Monument in Edinburgh. He is now foreman to a firm of contractors in London, and is very desirous to get a good picture of the monument as a touching memorial of other days.'

MARK NAPIER, Advocate, 6 Ainslie Place, Edinburgh. Historical writer, well known in connection with the disputed story of the Wigtown Martyrs.

'If you "Mr. Sheriff" me I shall "Doctor Laing" you. We are both men of genius, and utterly independent of such minor and vulgar dignity as appertains to a Scotch Sheriff or a Scotch "Doctor"' (15th December 1877).

'I believe there is no great historian whatever, especially historians of the Church, who are thoroughly accurate and faithful. Nor are historians of the State much better. Hume, Hallam, Malcolm Laing, Brodie, Macaulay, etc., etc., are all inaccurate and unfaithful. There is more lying in history than in romance' (no date).

PATRICK NEILL, M.A., Canonmills Cottage, Edinburgh. The learned Printer—(Neill & Co.).

Three letters, 1837 to 1847. One letter relates to his pamphlet on the new Edinburgh railways, especially the Scotland Street tunnel, against which he bitterly protests.

GABRIEL NICOL, Bookseller, Pall Mall, London.

Writing to 'Mr Laing, jun., Bookseller, Edinburgh,' about some books little known in this country, he says that of them 'I know nobody a better judge than yourself.' This was in 1814, when David was only twenty-one years old.

THOMAS ORR, 3 Ronaldson's Buildings, Leith Walk, Edinburgh.

> He writes on 20th June 1867 that he has discovered a method of 'analysing and tracing the derivation of words,' the names of cities and persons, and the origin and rise of their 'heraldry.' But he is very poor, etc. etc.

JOHN RICHARDSON, 5 Fludyer Street, Westminster.

> Eleven letters, 1819 to 1860. He describes himself as a descendant of Covenanting 'rebels,' and is anxious to make out his family genealogy as such.

DAVID D. SCOTT, Briery Yards, Hawick.

> Twenty-two letters, 1856 to 1874. Subjects—Scottish History, Bannockburn, and Flodden, the latter a Scottish *victory*; a high admiration of King James IV., whom he declares to be 'our greatest monarch,' etc., etc. Laing is 'the *facile princeps* of Scottish archæologists.'

REV. HEW SCOTT, D.D., Anstruther.

> Thirty-five letters, 1851 to 1871. Mostly small informal scraps. On 18th December 1867 he bewails the poor result, financially, of his great work, the *Fasti Ecclesiæ Scoticanæ*, the 1st part showing an actual loss. 'I find myself disheartened and tremble at proceeding further. No gin-horse has worked harder than I have done for years, and here is the result, only making business for printers and booksellers. The 2nd part is now ready, with an Index surpassing for names any book that has ever come through my hands.'

MRS. THOMAS SLIDELL, Newport, Rhode Island, U.S.A. She is a great-granddaughter of Dr. Witherspoon, and thinks herself a descendant of John Knox, 'through his daughter Elizabeth Welsh.' She desires from Laing 'an unbroken chain.'

Thomas Stevenson, Engineer, 17 Heriot Row.

On 6th May 1874 he introduces 'my son Robert Louis Stevenson. He is anxious to get some information about John Knox.'

David Stewart, Annan, and Gretna Hall.

Seven letters, 1816 to 1823. About books and prints for sale. 'I have a Livy's head, now 2000 years old or thereby. It was brought to this country by the famous Earl of Bute,' and was said to have cost him about £100.

Rev. John Struthers, Minister of Prestonpans.

Seven letters, 1867 to 1878. Reference is made to John Aitchison, chaplain of the Scots Guards in Paris, 1558. Alexander Aitchison, under a charter of James v., built Aitchison's Haven, now known as 'Morrison's Haven,' near Musselburgh.

John Sobieski Stuart.

Nearly a score of letters, dated from Kames Castle, 1 Castle Street, and Eilean Agais, Beauly, all craving literary aid. One or two are in the third person—'The Chevalier Stuart,' etc. etc.

John Swinburne, Capheaton, Newcastle-on-Tyne.

Old family deeds sent to him by Laing, taken by the housemaid to light the fires, to his horror (1867).

W. B. D. D. Turnbull, Advocate, Edinburgh, 67, and afterwards 25 Great King Street. In Lincoln's Inn from 1853.

Seventy-five letters, 1836 to 1861. An intimate and confidential correspondence with many touches of humour. In 1852 he intimated (to another correspondent) that he had then had 'his first brief' (*i.e.* in London). The library in Edinburgh of 'Alphabet' Turnbull, as he was called, was reckoned one of the finest private collections. He was an ally of Laing in Bannatyne Club publications.

PATRICK FRASER TYTLER, the historian.

Twenty letters. In 1838, when in London finishing his *History of Scotland*, he, for pecuniary reasons, resigned his membership of the Bannatyne and Maitland Clubs and the Society of Antiquaries of Scotland. But in 1843 he, 'being a very little richer,' asks to be reinstated in the Bannatyne Club, which was done. The correspondence is of a fine tone and character.

WILLIAM UPCOTT, London Institution.

He introduces to Laing 'Baron Friedel, a friend of the late Lord Byron, who is engaged in publishing a series of portraits of Greek chiefs and other eminent characters engaged in their cause' (30th March 1826).

J. H. WIFFEN, Librarian to the Duke of Bedford, Woburn Abbey.

'6 *month* 18*th*, 1835.

'ESTEEMED FRIEND,—Thy favour of the 5th inst. I have only received just now from the Duke of Bedford. I am very happy to learn that HIS Grace has enriched his library here by a complete set of the publications of the Bannatyne Club. . . .—Thine very truly,

'J. H. WIFFEN, *Librarian.*'

SIR DANIEL WILSON, University College, Toronto.

Sixteen letters. In 1845 from 25 Hanover Street, in 1851 from 17 Archibald Place, in 1852 from 12

Graham Street, and from Toronto from 1855 to 1877. A fervent lover of Edinburgh, and perhaps the best authority on her history and antiquities. He is in these letters always bewailing his exile in the New World, and the gradual disappearance of his Edinburgh friends. A touchingly interesting correspondence; the Quigrich of St. Fillan, and its recovery for the Scottish National Museum, perhaps the most important of the matters dealt with.

J. P. Wood, W.S., Edinburgh.

He had a list of the early Writers to the Signet, and Laing was now (4th November 1869) thinking of preparing a chronological list of the members.

This selection of notes from a few of the large army of Laing's correspondents will serve in some degree to illustrate the variety of their characters and of the subjects in which their interests lay. It is impossible to deal with further names in detail in this way, but it would yield a wholly inadequate impression of the extent of correspondence, literary and friendly, to which Laing was subjected were we to end here. A simple further list, selected from among the better-known names, therefore follows :

Adam, William, of Blair Adam.   1832-75.
Aiton, Rev. John, D.D., minister of Dolphinton. 1835.

Baillie, James Kennedy, D.D., County Tyrone, Ireland.
Bain, Joseph, Record Searcher, Senr. and Junr., 1828-78.
Baird, George Husband, Principal, University of Edinburgh. 1818-36.
Balfour, David, of Balfour and Trenabie. 1857-67.
Bannatyne, Sir William Macleod. From Whitefoord House, Canongate. n.d.
Barclay, Thomas, Principal of Glasgow University.
Begg, James, D.D., Edinburgh. 1850-66.
Bell, M. Montgomerie, Edinburgh. 1876.
Billings, R. W., London, Architect.
Bliss, Philip, Oxford. 1829-42.
Blood, Bindon, Ireland. Famous Book-collector.
Botfield, Beriah, M.P. One hundred and thirty-seven letters.
Brisbane, Sir Thomas Makdougall, Bart. 1832-55.
Brodie, George, 20 Northumberland Street, Historiographer Royal for Scotland.
Brodie, John Clerk, of Idvies, W.S. 1871-77.
Bruce, O. Tyndall, of Falkland. n.d.
Brunton, Professor Alexander, D.D., Edinburgh.
Burnett, George, Lyon King of Arms. 1866.
Burton, John Hill, LL.D. 1847-75.

Carruthers, Robert, LL.D., Inverness.

Chalmers, Patrick, of Aldbar.
Chambers, Robert, LL.D., Edinburgh. 1821-67.
Chambers, William, LL.D., Edinburgh. 1873-75.
Clerk, Rev. Archibald, LL.D., Kilmallie. 1870-76.
Clerk, John (Lord Eldin). 1867.
Clerk, Sir George, of Penicuik, Bart. 1855-62.
Collier, J. Payne, London (Music). 1832-67.
Constable, Archibald, Sir Walter Scott's publisher. 1807-25. Constable's letters are dated from High Street in 1820, from Ealing in 1821, from Polton House in 1824, and from Princes Street in 1825.
Constable, David, son of Archibald. 1828.
Constable, Thomas, son of Archibald. 1842-67.
Conway, Moncure D., London.
Cotton, Henry, Archdeacon of Cashel. 1851.

Dalzell, Sir John Graham, Bart., of Binns, 54 Hanover Street. 1838.
Dryden, Sir Henry E. L., Bart., Canons Ashby, Northamptonshire. Distinguished Antiquary.

Ferguson, and Munro-Ferguson of Raith. 1815-75.
Ferrier, Professor J. F., 12 York Place. 1837.
Forbes, Alexander Penrose, Bishop of Brechin. Nine letters. n.d.
Forbes, Rev. G. H., Burntisland. 1865-74.
Forbes, Professor Patrick, Aberdeen. 1826-30.

Froude, J. A., Historian. 1864.

Gordon, Rev. Thomas, minister of Newbattle. Fifty-three letters. 1861-76.

Hamilton, Professor Sir William, Bart. Sixteen letters, mostly n.d.
Harvie-Brown, J. A., of Dunipace. 1878.
Hazlitt, W. C., London. 1865.
Henderson, E., LL.D., Inverkeithing. Forty-six letters. 1852-78.
Hibbert-Ware, Samuel, M.D., a very large lot, of much interest.

Innes, Cosmo, Advocate, Professor of History. Forty-one letters.

Kelland, Professor Philip, Edinburgh. 1865.

Laing, Alexander, LL.D., Newburgh, Fife.
Laing, Samuel (*Heimskringla*), 1 Moray Place.
Lyell, Sir Charles, of Kinnordy. Eighteen letters. 1832-45.

Madden, Sir Frederic, British Museum. Forty-seven letters. 1831-59.
Maidment, James, Advocate, Edinburgh. Thirty-one letters. 1825-72.

Maitland, S. R., Librarian and Keeper of the MSS. at Lambeth Palace.
Marwick, Sir J. D., Edinburgh and Glasgow. 1861-78.
Masson, Professor David, LL.D. 1870-71.
Maxwell, Sir Herbert, Bart. 1866.
Mercer, Græme R., Glen Talchon, Perthshire. Twenty-four letters. 1859-78.
Mitchell, Professor A. F., St. Andrews. Thirty letters. 1866-78.
Mitchell, Sir Arthur, K.C.B. (Recommending a candidate for the Chair of Anatomy.) 1867.
Mure, William, of Caldwell. 1831-32.
Murray, John, Albemarle Street. Seven letters. From 1828.
Murray, Thomas Graham, of Stenton, W.S. 1876.
Mylne, R. W., London (King's 'Master Masons' family). Twenty-five letters. 1850-76.

Mackenzie, W. Forbes, from Stobo Castle. 1838.
Mackenzie, John Whitefoord, W.S., Royal Circus. 1832-72.
Maconochie, Alexander, of Meadowbank. 1848-61.
McLauchlan, Rev. Thomas, D.D., Viewforth, Edinburgh. 1858.

Napier, Macvey, Professor, Edinburgh.

Nichols, John Gough, learned Editor, etc. Fifteen letters. 1862-70.
Nott, David D., Briery Yards, Hawick (with a pen-and-ink likeness of Scott). 1871-73.

Omond, Rev. J. R., D.D., Monzie. 1876.
O'Reilly, Edward, Dublin, *re* Ossian. 1818-29.

Parker, J. H., Oxford and Rome. 1870.
Patrick, R. W. Cochran-, of Woodside. 1874-77.
Petrie, George, Sheriff-Clerk of Orkney. 1848-58.
Pinkerton, John, from Paris. 1824.

Ramsay, Very Revd. E. B., Dean of Edinburgh. 1859-70.
Ross, Rev. William, D.D., Aberdour. 1858-62.

Sandford, Bishop, Edinburgh. 1823.
Scott, James R. Hope-, Abbotsford. 1871.
Scott, William, of Raeburn, a cousin of Sir Walter.
Shairp, J. C., Principal of the United College, St. Andrews. 1871.
Simpson, Sir James Y., Bart., 52 Queen Street, n.d.
Sinclair, Sir John, of Ulbster, Bart., 133 George Street. 1820.
Sinclair, Alexander, 133 George Street. Thirteen letters.

Skeat, W. W., Cambridge. 1869-78.
Skelton, (Sir) John, 20 Alva Street. 1864.
Skene, William Forbes, LL.D. 1860-78.
Smith, Rev. Sydney, Divine and Wit, from 'Grosvenor Street.' 1836.
Smith, Dr. John Alexander, 7 West Maitland Street.
Smith, R. A., Musician. 1823.
Stanley, Arthur Penrhyn, Dean of Westminster. 1866-77.
Steven, Rev. William, Scots Kirk, Rotterdam. 1827-39.
Stevenson, Rev. Joseph, Antiquary, London. Thirty-one letters. 1830-64.
Stewart, Sir M. R. Shaw, Ardgowan. 1847.
Stirling, William, of Keir. 1825-27.
Story, Rev. R. Herbert, D.D. Seven letters. 1872-76.

Thomson, Thomas, Antiquary. Ninety-one letters. 1824-76.
Todd, Dr. John H., Trinity College, Dublin. Twenty-seven letters. 1840-60.
Trevelyan, Sir W. C., Bart. Fifteen letters. 1852-78.

> Urgent invitations (*inter alia*) for Laing to come to Wallington. Letters mostly omit the year.

Trotter, Henry, of Mortonhall. 1827.

Utterson, Edward V., London. Thirty-nine letters. 1822-50.

Walker, Sir Patrick, of Coates. From 'Drumseugh.' 1827.
Way, Albert, Wenham Manor, Reigate. Thirty-seven letters. 1856-74.
Wemyss, Mrs., of Wemyss. Four letters.

Among the FOREIGN CORRESPONDENTS are the following:

Anatole de Barthélemy, of the Imperial Society of the Antiquaries of France, from the 'Palais du Louvre.' 31st May 1867, three years before the overthrow of Imperialism there.
F. Bólling, Secretary to the Royal Library, Copenhagen. 1824-58.
Chr. Bruun, Principal Librarian to the Royal Library, Copenhagen. 1863-69.
Kristian de Bure frères, Paris. 1815.

M. J. S. S. Campbell, Deputy Librarian, Royal Library, The Hague, Holland. 1857.
Antonio Ceriani, Ambrosian Library, Milan. In Italian—'Carissimo Signore.' 1867.
Sebastian Coleti, Venice. 1818.
Zach. Collin, from Sweden, Philologist. He was thinking of going to the Orkneys for making researches into the nature of the language there. Letter from Paris. 1862.

Dr. Merle D'Aubigné of Geneva. His parting thanks in leaving Edinburgh. 1845.

S. Maurice Dietrichstein, Imperial Library, Vienna. 1841.

Professor Ernest Dubois, Nancy. 1872.

> Inquiring about 'William Barclay, Ecossais, né à Aberdeen, c. 1560.'

T. B. Georgères, Public Library, Bordeaux. 1866.

F. D. Gerlaon (place uncertain—in Latin). n.d.

Georg Joachim Goeschen, Leipzig. 1814-15. Addressed to Laing's father.

Professor T. Goel, University of Leyden (in French). 1841.

Svend Grundtvig, Copenhagen. 1859.

> Inquiring about the Norse ballad 'Hildina,' of Foula, Shetland, which he proposes to render in Danish and English verse.

Charles Halm, Munich. 1861.

F. Herbst, Numismatist, Copenhagen. 1867.

Baron de Harschedal, Rue des Beaux-Arts, No. 17, Paris.

> He says he is the author of several 'estimated works,' and asks Laing (6th December 1839) to be editor in English of another of his, which he declined.

J. J. L. Jacob, Rotterdam. 1838.

Dr. Ferdinand Keller, Zürich (of *Lake Dwellings* fame). 1860.

G. L. Klemming, Stockholm. Books exchanged. 1858.

Prince Alexander Jakovlévitch Labanoff de Rostoff, Russian Prince. Born 1788.

Four letters, three in 1839 and one in 1843. One is from Heidelberg, two from Paris, and the last from London. All are in French, in reference to his 'Projet de publication d'un Recueil complet des Lettres de Marie Stuart,' for which purpose he solicits aid from Laing and from any other sources of information in Scotland. The letters are in the usually formal French style, and do not call for transcription here. Prince Labanoff had a large collection of portraits of Queen Mary, of which a Notice and Catalogue was published in St. Petersburg in 1860.

George Livermore, Boston, U.S., of Harvard University.

Francisque Michel, distinguished French Antiquary and man of letters, author of many publications.

One hundred and sixteen letters of very friendly type about literature and personal affairs—from Paris, Bordeaux, and Lyons in France, and from London, Oxford, Edinburgh, Glasgow, and elsewhere in Great Britain. Laing is addressed variously as 'Mon cher Monsieur David,' 'My dear Sir,' 'Dear Mr. Laing,' 'My dear Mr. Laing,' 'Monsieur et cher Maître,' 'My dear Friend,' 'Dear Mr. David,' and very frequently as 'Mon cher David.' The dates are from 1837 to 1878. From London on 9th September 1862 he writes to 'the patriarch of Scottish literature. May he live long and happy.' His book, *Les Écossais en France— les Français en Écosse*, is naturally a subject of frequent reference. He was well received in Scotland, visiting Lord Lindsay at Dunecht in Aberdeenshire, Dr. Laing at Portobello, and other prominent men.

Of the letters, eighty are in French and thirty-six in English. In view of paying a visit to Edinburgh, he writes from Lyons on 19th September 1855:

'Mon cher David,—. . . Maintenant, mon cher ami, je n'ai plus qu'une chose à vous demander. Où dois-je loger à Edinburgh ? Tout en faisant les choses convenablement à mon rang je ne dois point oublier que je suis un homme de lettres, par conséquent peu riche, et dans l'obligation d'acheter des livres, etc., etc. Indiquez-moi donc l'hôtel ou la maison où nous pourrons descendre et nous loger. . . .

'Adieu, mon cher ami ; mille amitiés et compliments,
'Francisque Michel.'

The hotel or house of lodgment here led up to turned out, there is little doubt, to be Laing's house in Portobello. Writing from Oxford in 1859 he states that he has been received there 'avec une cordialité qui m'a rappelé la vôtre.'

In a letter of 1862 he writes :

'I am truly delighted to understand that you intend to come to London, intending myself to stay here till next November. Did I not see you I would have come to Edinburgh, which is always so full of attractions for me. Moreover, I have not yet done with Scottish literature and antiquities ; but to carry on my schemes in that respect, I want to be encouraged by the nobility and the gentry of the country, otherwise I do not ask for more than a sale paying the printing expenses, having written my book merely for love.

'If I told you what Lord Lindsay did for its diffusion you would not believe it. Although I entertain high opinion of your Scotch peers, I would never have imagined such a liberality.

'My wife, who never forgot you, dear Mr. David, nor your sweetness, sends you her best regards, as well as to your most amiable sister, whose marmalade is still spoken of at Bordeaux. I hope before we die you will come to take her hither, to enable us to give you as much diversion as we can.

'Remind me, pray, to our common friends, as Messrs. J. Whitefoord Mackenzie, James Gibson-Craig, *e tutti quanti.*—And believe me, dear Mr. Laing, yours very sincerely,
'FRANCISQUE MICHEL.'

Maulde & Renou, Printers, Paris. 1840.

A. de Meana, Turin—writing from the mansion of His Royal Highness the Duke of Genoa. 1874.

Dr. Joh. Moldenhawer, Royal Librarian, Copenhagen. 1824-58.

F. Molter, Library of the Grand Duke of Baden, Carlsruhe. 1841.

Niebuhr, B. G., Bonn. 1829.

J. T. F. Noordrick, The Hague. In French. 1849.

Rosalie Olivecrona, Upsala, Sweden. 1859.

Ch. Petersen, Hamburg. 1860.

'Royal' Library, Paris. (At varying times 'Impériale' and 'Nationale.') 1838-39.

Professor Frederick Schiern, Copenhagen. 1870-73.

P. Schmid, Copenhagen, Councillor, Chevalier of several orders. He has made a 'rare et complète' collection of antiquities, and offers the same for 1000 francs, 'un prix extrêmement modéré.' 1870.

Count Steenbock, Secrétaire de la Légation de

Suède et Norvège. From London. A manuscript to be sent to Laing from the University of Lund. 1860.

J. Techener, Bookseller, Paris. 1859.

A. Teulet, Paris. A large parcel of letters in French; historical connection of Scotland with France, books, printing, etc. 1839-60.

Charles Trummer, LL.D., Hamburg. 1845-47.

Auguste Vallet, Paris. Early English and Scottish students at the University of Paris. The names given. 1838.

Baron Van Westreene de Tiellandt, The Hague, Holland. To Laing—' My dear Sir and friend.' 1849.

J. J. A. Worsaae, Danish Antiquary and Historian, afterwards Minister of Public Instruction, Copenhagen.
Professor Charles C. Rafn, Copenhagen.
Thorlak Gudmundson Repp, Copenhagen.
Professor P. A. Munch, Christiania.
} 1840-1855.

These Danish, Norwegian, and Icelandic scholars were desirous that a collation of the manuscripts, and a translation into English, of the *Orkneyinga Saga* should be produced, and for a number of years the proposal was urged in correspondence with Laing and others in this country. For the literary work Repp demanded £270, but Professor Jón Sigurdsson was disposed to undertake it for £100. It was found impossible to raise in Denmark and Norway the necessary funds for this and for the cost of publication of the work. The Bannatyne Club was appealed to through Laing, but without result, and no more was heard of the proposal.[1]

Regret has already been expressed that amid a correspondence so extensive there is so little preserved of letters from Laing's own pen, the numerous imperfect replies, in draft, with deletions and uncertain amendments, not being admissible as wholly accurate examples. By the kindness of Mr. Archibald Constable, whose grandfather, Archibald Constable, Scott's publisher, was on terms of intimate acquaintance with Laing, I am permitted to make use of the following letters from William Laing and David, his son, to Constable, and to his son David Constable, at that time in London. The letters are not without character and flavour. Their dates range from 1809 to 1824.

I

William Laing to Archibald Constable. It bears no date, but is backed up 'Wm. Laing. March 1809.'

---

[1] This entry has a peculiar interest for the writer of the present memoir. Unaware of the proposal referred to and its failure, he resolved, more than forty years ago, that the *Saga* should be made available in English; and having secured the co-operation of learned friends, the late Mr. Jón A. Hjaltalin, Icelander, and Dr. Joseph Anderson, he had the translation set on foot, and published the work on his own responsibility—*The Orkneyinga Saga, translated from the Icelandic by Jón A. Hjaltalin and Gilbert Goudie, edited, with Notes and Introduction, by Joseph Anderson. Edinburgh: Edmonston and Douglas, 1873.* It is now out of print.

'DEAR SIR,—You seem to have taken offence where none was in the most remote degree intended.

'When your clerk called I was troubled about a trifling business, and besides am ill with a confounded headach. I had also to run down to Leith, from whence I am but just arrived. A gentleman of your acquaintance forced me to lend him, against my inclination, every farthing I could muster this morning, just before I got your card. I scarcely knew what I was doing. I don't know that you have or ever had any occasion to think I have acted unfriendly. I knew he was a confidential clerk, and it did not strike me at all about the impropriety of a verbal message instead of a card, as he seemed to know the business. I wish to be on good terms with all, and not you especially.—I am, dear Sir, yours truly, WILLM. LAING.'

'Saturday.'

II

David Laing to David Constable, 63 Fleet Street, London.

'*February* 10, 1815.

'DEAR SIR,—Herewith you will receive two copies of the catalogue of Drummond's books, which you wrote for about three weeks ago. They would have been sent sooner had they been finished, but being very busy with our own catalogue (which was of rather more importance than the other), I had not time to look at the first sheet of it, and which was all that I had anything to do with, the rest being done by Mr. Gillies, Sir Egerton's friend

'You have been scored down as a subscriber for the others you desired, and when any others are determined upon, which will likely be soon, I shall let you know concerning them in good time.

'The 8vo. copy of Drummond came safe, and for which I heartily thank you, it answering my purpose sufficiently, and saves the disagreeable necessity of borrowing.

'The new edition of *Roger Ascham* is just arrived. I am much pleased with it, except in one point, which I wish from my soul had been followed—that is, the orthography—no doubt it would have given the editor more trouble, and perhaps been a little more expense to the publisher, but I should suppose neither worth thinking of. I hate any book that is not given in the original state that it first appeared in. Tho' I have some idea who the editor is [1]—pray tell me. The general style of the execution of the typography pleases, although from a few minutes' glance it appears not to be quite *immaculate*. It is more reasonable in the price than many republications that now come out.

'Be so good as let me hear from you often, when you have leisure, and give me any news. This I beg as a favour. I have no more to add at present, and remain,—Yours sincerely,

'DAVID LAING.'

'*P.S.*—As you frequently see Mr. Chalmers [of *Caledonia*], in order that you may receive these catalogues the sooner, I enclose them, with a copy going to him, by the post. It was only finished three days since.   .   D. L.'

'Mr. D. Constable.'

To WILLIAM LAING.

1815.	To 2 Drummond's Catalogue, sells 9s.
Feb. 10.	4to bds. (only 50 printed) . . 7s.—14s.

III
William Laing to Archibald Constable.

'EDINR. *Thursday morning.*
[Backed up '1818.']

'DEAR SIR,—You would greatly oblige me could you but spare a few minutes to conclude the Old Book business with John Ballantyne. They are quite in my way, and are receiving injury by exposure. On the other side I have marked from my last catalogue the prices (of a few which I have added from my stock, being mostly duplicates), at which they shd. have sold for, but this does not enter into the valuation which I know you will fairly put on them.

[1] [John George Cochrane, 1781-1852.]

'I received last night the quire list, which is certainly the largest I have yet seen here. I most sincerely hope it will succeed to your satisfaction. I was much amused with one lot, *Kerr's Voyages.* Now, where the devil has this collection come from ? Had all the shops from Johnny Groat's House to the Land's End been sweeped, I should have thought not one-fourth could, at any price, have been found, Princes Street excepted. I shall certainly bid for this precious work, but not higher than 3d. per lib.—I am, my dear Sir, yours faithfully as a friend, but not as a tool. WILLM. LAING.'

[Among the prices quoted are : Johnson's *Dictionary,* £5, 5s. ; Gordon's *Itinerary,* £3, 10s. ; Pennant's *Scotland,* 3 vols., £5, 5s. ; *Antiquities of Herculaneum,* 14 vols., £29 ; Buffon, 32 vols., £25].

IV

William Laing to Archibald Constable.

'DEAR SIR,—Many thanks for the trouble you have taken with Mr. Ballantyne. . . . His own proposal originally was to allow a reasonable credit as an inducement to attend his sales, and many a hundred [pounds] he has got by such attendance. This you know was reasonable, as it is generally done so in London. I deny that he has had any trouble, as he alleges, in getting a settlement. Sometimes we differed about a month, which was nothing, and sometimes in getting a long account examined, the ships having fallen aside he might have sent more than once ; but what is that in so many transactions ? In short, I was so much hurt by his very absurd conduct, that I refused to attend Dr. Miller's sale, and the sale will tell this to the hurt of the family. I shd. not have sent any more had you not spoken to me at Wm Martin's funeral. He has lost more by his conduct than he is aware of. I meant to have given him Dr. Rutherford's and Commissioner Philip's sales, but would not, and he may yet find more reason for repenting of his conduct, which I do regard as any [thing] else than that of one who depends on all his friends for help, or at all attentive to his own interest. I can assure him that neither he, nor any of his connections, shall have any trouble with me in future, and they may all—— [?]—I remain, dear Sir, yours very truly,   'WILLM. LAING.'

'Archibald Constable, Esq.'

'EDINR. 27 *April* 1820.'

V

David Laing to Archibald Constable.

'EDINR. *Decr.* 12, 1821.

'MY DEAR SIR,—I send you a little volume of old Scotish [*sic*] poetry,[1] in the hopes it may amuse you during some idle hour. If it has no other recommendation for you to add it to your collection, it will have that of scarcity—and all the copies, I may say, are now out of my hands.

'May I take this opportunity to remind you of what you once promised me—Ritson's unfinished volume, which you was to have published—as I wish very much to have a copy of it.

'We hear frequent accounts of your convalescent state, and we all hope you will soon be able to return amongst us as usual.—With best wishes, I remain, very truly yours,

'DAVID LAING.'

'Archd. Constable, Esq., London.'

VI

David Laing to Archibald Constable.

[n.d., but backed '*Feb.* 1823.']

'DEAR SIR,—I meant to have called to have said that Thursday, 27th Febry., is fixed for holding the first Anniversary Meeting of the Bannatyne Club in Barry's Hotel, No. 8 Princes Street,[2] at 5 o'clock.

---

[1] This volume was probably the *Poems* by Alexander Scott, from a manuscript written in the year 1568, issued by Laing in this year, 1821.

[2] Barry's Hotel was afterwards removed to the west end of Queen Street, the premises now occupied by the Edinburgh Ladies' College.

'Dinner on the table at half-past five precisely (Sir Walter Scott in the Chair), when I hope you will find yourself able to venture out.—I remain, yours very truly, DAVID LAING.'
'Archibald Constable, Esq.
    'Park Place.'

VII
David Laing to Archibald Constable.

'*Thursday* [n.d —1824.]

'MY DEAR SIR,—Some time ago you said you had some articles to communicate for the *Bannatyne Miscellany*. As the first part is now commenced, and it is hoped will be finished in time for the Novr. meeting—should you be able to lay your hands on anything curious I shall be glad to have them as soon as convenient.

'You were likewise so kind as say you would favour me with a sight of David Herd's MS. collection—which, if you could let me have for a few days, I should esteem greatly.

'By the way, I find you have my copy of Young's *Breviary of the Later Persecutions*, which, as it is two or three years since you had it to compare with the edition you have, it may be as well to let me have it again. My copy is the black-letter edition, 1669 (I think), bound in dark-coloured calf, with gilt leaves. You will easily know it.—I remain always, yours faithfully, DAVID LAING.'
'Archibald Constable, Esq.'

VIII
David Laing to Archibald Constable.

[n.d.—1824.]

'MY DEAR SIR,—I should have returned this curious manuscript[1] long since, but always deferred in the hope of doing

---

[1] This refers to a MS. containing the tunes of the Reformation Psalm-book, written by Thomas Wood of St. Andrews in 1566. The subject is dealt with in a paper by Laing read to the Society of Antiquaries in 1868—No. 174 in the preceding list of his works.

so in person, and offering you my best thanks for the loan of it. Mr. Stenhouse, to whom (with your permission) I showed it, tells me that it is a *duplicate* copy of the *part* which Mr. Blackwood has—and which is the *Bassus*. Indeed, on comparing this MS. with the music in the 1635 edition, it is clear that this is the same.—I remain always, yours very truly,

'DAVID LAING.'

'Archibald Constable, Esq.'
[With a book.]

For the next two letters I am indebted to Mr. Alexander G. Forman, W.S., to whose grand-uncle, Mr. James Nairne, W.S.,[1] they were addressed by Laing at a turning-point in his career—his election as Chief Librarian of the Society of Writers to H.M. Signet in 1837.

'*Monday*, 19 *June*.

'DEAR SIR,—Sir Jas. [Gibson-] Craig is to propose, and Mr. Tytler to second, my nomination as a candidate. As I am sending round the enclosed Circular to such of the Members as are likely to support me on Wednesday, I should be glad to know if you have secured me some additional votes, as I should regret omitting to send Circulars to such Gentlemen.—Yours always, D. LAING.'

'*To* James Nairne, Esq.'

II

'EDINR. *June* 22*d*, 1837.

'MY DEAR SIR,—In reply to your most kind congratulatory note, I called this forenoon to say that my brother and myself

---

[1] Nairne in 1830 presented to the Bannatyne Club *A Relation of Proceedings concerning the Affairs of the Kirk of Scotland*, 1637-38, by John, Earl of Rothes, which Laing edited for him—No. 24 in the preceding list of his works.

would have the greatest pleasure in accepting your invitation for Thursday first.

'But I also intended writing you a few lines to say how much I feel indebted for the warm and friendly part you took *from the first* in promoting my success.

'Now in reference to this I have a favour to ask. Some time ago you were looking about for a copy of Wood's *Peerage,* for common use. I hope you will accept the copy herewith sent, not as payment *in kind* for your exertions on my behalf, but simply as an acknowledgment of gratitude.—Being ever very sincerely, yours, D. LAING.'

'*To* James Nairne, Esq.'

[Etc. Etc Etc.]

VII

FAMILY CONNECTIONS

WE have seen, under the head of 'Ancestry,' that Dr. Laing was unable to trace his family beyond his grandfather—

WILLIAM LAING, Merchant-Tailor in the Canongate. His wife was —— Straiton, who died in 1795. Their son was—

WILLIAM LAING, Bookseller and Publisher, Edinburgh, David's father. Born in 1764, he married Helen Kirk, and died in 1832. Their large family consisted of the following, besides some who died in infancy:

1. WILLIAM. Became minister of Crieff, and died in the manse there on 16th March 1845, his wife having predeceased him by ten years. He had three sons:
    John William } who went to New
    Francis Gregory } Zealand.
    David, died in Edinburgh in 1879.
   and four daughters:
    Jane, married D. A. Eisdale.
    Helen, married Archibald Stirling Irving.
    Joanna Gregory, married the Rev. William

FAMILY CONNECTIONS 297

Murray, M.A., and died without issue on 20th January 1892.

Wilhelmina Margaret, married Frederick Martin Alston, who then resided at 50 North Castle Street, Edinburgh, and died without issue.

Mary Melville, married William Reid, Farmer, Pittentian, Perthshire. Died in 1892, leaving a son, William David Melville Reid, who now resides in Edinburgh.

2. DAVID, the subject of this memoir, died unmarried.

3. GILBERT. Born in 1801. Was a licentiate of the Church of Scotland, but joined the Free Church after the disruption of 1843. He resided at Langley Bank, Perth, and died there on 9th January 1877, not apparently having had a fixed charge. He was unmarried. He was in the habit of coming to Edinburgh from time to time, and I well remember his pleasant calls on the relative with whom I, a schoolboy from the remote isles of the North Sea, then resided, and his saluting me, with lively patting on the head, as his 'namesake.' Little did either of us then surmise that the small boy was destined to become the biographer of the family—at all events of David, its most distinguished member.

4. JAMES. He was originally intended for the Church, but in 1831 he joined in partnership with Charles Forbes, under the firm name of Laing & Forbes, Booksellers. Owing to the state of his health it became necessary for him to go abroad, and the firm (at 92 Princes Street) was dissolved on 1st February 1845. He obtained the position of Deputy Postmaster-General of the Central Province of Ceylon, and died at Kandy on 9th September 1846. He had been for some time proprietor and editor of the *Ceylon Herald*. He left some coffee estates, which were the subject of correspondence with David Laing in later years. He was unmarried.
5. MARY. Married James Sanson, Melville Lodge, Ontario, Canada. She died in 1871, leaving the Reverend Alexander Sanson, Trinity Parsonage, Toronto, and David Laing Sanson, of the same address.
6. JESSIE MILLER. Born in 1798, and died at St. Asaph, North Wales. She was buried from the house of her brother David, at Portobello, on 15th July 1866.
7. AGNES. Born 1802, died 21st September 1865. The inventory of her personal estate, recorded 21st March 1866, amounted to £4284.
8. MARGARET. Married Alexander Sanson, Solicitor of Customs, Dublin. Born in 1804, died 4th April 1892. She was, like her

brother, fond of art, curios, and antiquities; and of all these her house, Hawthorn Brae, Duddingston, contained a large collection which she was at all times ready to exhibit and explain. She was greatly attached to the ancient parish church of Duddingston, and presented to it a handsome small organ, fitted up in the apse behind the fine Norman arch. Her house she bequeathed for a charitable purpose.

9. EUPHEMIA, the last survivor of William Laing's family, remained beside her brother David in the house, East Villa, James Street, Portobello, for the long period of fifty-three years, from its purchase in 1843 till her death on 4th March 1896, she having survived him for eighteen years. A quaint Scottish lady of the old school, and very deaf for many years, she yet had a pleasure in maintaining the traditions of the house, and many were the pleasant gatherings, in the way of lectures and entertainments of an interesting and instructive character, in the library, then still beautiful, though depleted of most of its original treasures and adornments. Miss Laing's inventory amounted to £24,661.

In 1817, on the erection of the Waterloo (or 'Regent') Bridge and Calton Jail, and the construction of the Regent Road, skirting the side of the Calton Hill, by which many of the interments in the old burying-ground in that quarter were disturbed and displaced, William Laing had another place of sepulture provided for his family in the New Calton Burying-Ground further east. In this tomb William Laing himself, David, and other members of the family, rest. It consists of the back and two side walls, and is closed in front by an iron railing and gate. The inscriptions are as follows :

1. *On a tripartite mural monument at the back—*

(*centre*)

1817

THE BURYING PLACE OF

WILLIAM LAING

SACRED TO THE MEMORY OF

WILLIAM LAING

BOOKSELLER IN EDINBURGH

WHO WAS BORN XX JULY MDCCLXIV

AND DIED X APRIL MDCCCXXXII

IN THE 68TH YEAR OF HIS AGE

AND OF

HELEN KIRK

HIS WIFE, THE ONLY CHILD OF

DAVID KIRK AND HELEN MELVIN

WHO WAS BORN XXVII JULY MDCCLXVII

AND DIED XVIII JANUARY MDCCCXXXVII

IN HER LXXTH YEAR

ALSO OF

DAVID LAING, LL.D.

THEIR SON

BORN XX APRIL MDCCXCIII

DIED XVIII OCTOBER MDCCCLXXVIII

(*On the left*)

To the Memory
of
Three Children of
William Laing
Helen, Francis
and Helen
and of
Other Relatives
whose remains
Removed
from the Old
Burying Ground
of Calton, were
here deposited
in the month of
March MDCCCXVII

(*On the right*)

To the Memory
of
the following Children
of William Laing

Jessie Miller
born 1798
died 15 july 1866

Gilbert
born 1801, died 1877

Agnes
born 1802
died 21 septr. 1865

Euphemia
born 1808
died 4th march 1896

2. *On a monument attached to the east wall—*

SACRED
TO THE MEMORY OF
ALEXANDER SANSON
LATE OF H.M. INLAND REVENUE, DUBLIN
WHO DEPARTED THIS LIFE ON 5TH SEPTR. 1863
IN THE 64TH YEAR OF HIS AGE
OF AMIABLE DISPOSITION, UPRIGHT CONDUCT
AND SINCERE PIETY

MARGARET LAING
HIS WIDOW
BORN 1804, DIED 4TH APRIL 1892
I AM THE RESURRECTION AND THE LIFE
JOHN XI CHAP. 25TH VERSE

3. *On a slab inserted in the west wall—*

HERE LYS DAVID KIRK, SMITH IN
CALTON, WHO, AT THE AGE OF 74
ENTERED INTO REST JUNE 26, 1784

ALSO

MARGRAT CUNNINGHAM
SPOUSE TO DAVID KIRK, SMITH
IN CALTON, WHO DIED FEBR. 28TH
1765, AGED 75 YEARS
ALSO HELLEN MELLVIN
HIS SPOUSE, WHO DIED
JULY 29TH 1767, AGED 35
YEARS.
MEMENTO—MORI

N.B.—This slab has evidently been transferred to this place from the Old Calton Burying-Ground.

It has been seen that David Laing's sister Mary (No. 5 in the family list) was married to James Sanson, of Ontario, Canada. They left two sons,

FAMILY CONNECTIONS

the Rev. Alexander Sanson and David Laing Sanson, both of the city of Toronto. A note of their respective families has been supplied to me.

1. CANON SANSON'S FAMILY:
    Robert Sanson, M.D., Calgary, Alberta.
    Norman Sanson, Government Museum, Banff, Alberta.
    John Sanson.

2. DAVID LAING SANSON'S FAMILY:
    Mary Melville Sanson, 49 Princes Square, Hyde Park, London.
    Mrs. Ward, wife of Rev. George B. Ward, M.D., Essex, Ontario.
    Mrs. Thomas J. White, Collingwood, Ontario.
    Mrs. Joseph B. Sheridan, c/o Rev. George B. Ward, Essex, Ontario.
    Mrs. Spencer Over, 55 South Angel Street, Providence, R.I., U.S.A.
    David Melville Sanson, The Canadian Bank of Commerce, Toronto.
    J. St. Clair Sanson, Nanton, Box 136, Alberta.
    William N. Sanson, c/o D. M. Sanson, The Canadian Bank of Commerce, Toronto.

FINIS

INDEX

ABBOTSFORD, 182, 185, 251.
—— Club, 63, 76, 120, 134, 173, 185, 189, 202, 205, 214, 215, 234.
Abel, Friar Adam, 183.
Aberdeen, William Elphinstone, Bishop of, 198, 229.
—— Martyrology for Church of, 202.
Abyssinia, MS. of Gospels from, 219.
Adair, John, F.R.S , 170.
Adam, Right Hon. William, of Blair Adam, 69 89, 275.
Adcock, Gilbert, waste-paper merchant, xxxviii, 128, 129, 130.
Advocates' Library, 26, 50, 51, 78, 79, 152.
Aikenhead, James, 'Atheist,' 226.
Ainslie, George R., 249.
Aitcheson's Haven, 188.
Aiton, Rev. John, D D., Dolphinton, 275.
Albany, Duke of, 154, 175, 176.
Aldis, Harry G , 150.
Alesius, Alexander, Scotus, 162.
Alexander the Great, 165.
—— Prince of Scotland, 173, 184.
—— Sir James E., of Westerton, 250.
—— Sir William of Menstrie, 217.
—— Rev. William Lindsay, D.D., 249.
Alloway Kirk, 106.
Alston, Frederick Martin, 297.
Altar-piece in Holyrood Palace, 203, 224, 236.
America, 201.
Amsterdam, 31, 34, 86.

Ancram, Earl of, 110, 225.
Anderson, David, architect, Aberdeen, 135.
—— Miss Margaret Susan, 250.
—— Rev. James, 183.
—— Rev. John, 127.
—— Joseph, LL.D (*Orkneyinga Saga*), 288.
Annandale Peerage Case, 111, 120.
Antiquaries of Scotland, Society of, *passim*.
Antwerp, 36, 37, 87.
Arbuthnot, Sir William, Bart., 31
Archbishops in Church of Scotland, Consecration form, 179
Argyle Square, Edinburgh, 5, 17.
Armada, Spanish, 163.
Arnold, Thomas, architect, 219.
Atholl Family, Jacobite Correspondence of, 173
Asloan Manuscript, 111, 120.
Atkinson, Stephen, *Gold Mines in Scotland*, 134, 158
Auchinleck MS. and *Chronicle*, 111, 120, 171, 202
—— James, poet, 170.
Augustin, St., *Cité de Dieu*, 86.
Aylmer, — Writer in Edinburgh, 175.
Ayton, Sir Robert, poet, 162.

BAILLIE, JAMES KENNEDY, D.D., 276.
—— Joanna, 257, 259.
—— Robert, A.M. Principal, University of Glasgow, 96, 174, 177.
Bain, Joseph, 276.

U

Baird, George Husband, Principal, University of Edinburgh, 276.
Balfour, David, of Balfour and Trenabie, 276.
Balliol, John, King of Scotland, 199.
Ballantyne, James, 58, 250.
Balmerino, Lord, 181.
Bancroft, Dr., 179.
Bannatyne Club, *passim*.
—— George, poet, 158, 163, 164.
—— Sir William Macleod, 276.
Barbour's *Bruce*, 140, 246.
Barclay, J. M. (R S.A.), 116.
—— Thomas, Principal, University of Glasgow, 276.
—— William, Ecossais, 283.
Barthélemy, Anatole de, 282.
Bassandyne, Thomas, 170.
Beaton, Cardinal, 162.
—— James, Archbishop of Glasgow, 178.
Bedford, Fred. W. (LL.D.), 116
Begg, Rev. James, D.D., 116, 276.
Bell & Bradfute, 10.
—— M. Montgomerie, W.S., 116, 276.
Bennet, L., bookseller, Rotterdam, 10.
Bergen-op-Zoom, 35
Betoun, Sibilla, attendant of Mary Queen of Scots, 176.
Beza, Theodore, 145, 179.
Billings, R. W., architect, London, 276.
Bishops in Church of Scotland, Consecration form, 179.
Black, Adam, publisher, Edinburgh, 24, 28, 31, 35, 38, 39, 204.
—— Miss Agnes, Perth, 227.
Blackader, Robert, Archbishop of Glasgow, 201.
Blackie, Professor John Stuart, 125, 251.
Blackwood, William, publisher, Edinburgh, 10, 24, 28, 252.
Blades, William, bibliographer, 252

Blew, Rev. W., 198.
Blind Harry's *Wallace*, 146, 200.
Bliss, Rev. Philip, D.C.L. Oxford, 70, 276.
Blood, Bindon, 276.
Bocace, Jehan, de Certald, 229.
Boece, Hector, 142.
Bólling, F., Copenhagen, 282.
Booksellers in Edinburgh (1577-1687), wills of, 170.
Borthwick, Sir John, 162.
Botfield, Beriah, M.P., 185, 192, 248, 276.
Bothwell, Agnes, Countess of, 200.
—— Earls of, 200, 201.
Boyd, Rev. Robert, of Trochrig, 162, 179.
Breviarium Aberdonense, 198.
Brewster, Sir David, 25 *note*, 94, 253.
Brisbane, Sir Thomas Makdougall, Bart., 276.
Britwell House, Bucks, 81, 194, 270.
Brodie, Alexander, of Brodie, 212.
—— George, Historiographer Royal, 276.
—— James, of Brodie, 212.
—— John Clerk, of Idvies, 276.
—— William, R.S.A., 116.
Brown, David, 24, 31, 35, 38.
—— James, 216.
—— J. J., Dunfermline, 254.
—— John, M.D. (*Rab and his Friends*), 253.
—— W. Beattie, R.S.A., 116.
Brougham, Lord, 28.
Bruce, Michael, poet, 223, 253.
—— O. Tyndall, of Falkland, 276.
—— Robert, minister of Edinburgh, 162.
—— William, of Symbister, 187.
Bruges, 229, 230.
Brunton, Professor Alexander, D.D., 69, 276.
Brussels, 31, 37, 38, 43, 75.
Bruun, Chr., Copenhagen, 282.
Buccleuch, Duke of, 204, 208.
Buchan, Earl of, 190, 240.

INDEX 307

Buchanan, David, 170.
—— George, 49, 110, 170, 236.
Burnet, Rev. Gilbert, D.D., Bishop of Salisbury, 135, 201.
Burnett, George, Lyon King of Arms, 276.
Burns, Gilbert, brother of the poet, 254.
—— Robert, Kilmarnock edition of his poems, 141.
Burton, John Hill, LL.D., 116, 173, 276.
Byron, Lord, 257, 260.

CAITHNESS, BISHOPRIC OF, 199
Calderwood, Rev. David, M.A, historian, 189.
Callander, John, of Craigforth, 159, 160.
Calvin, John, 144.
Cambridge, 98.
Cambuskenneth Abbey, 213.
Campbell, Rev. Archibald, D.D., 269.
—— John, of Kinyeancleuch, 178.
—— John, Executioner of Strathearn, 190.
—— John Francis ('of Islay'), 255.
—— M. J. S. S., The Hague, 282.
—— Thomas, poet, 262.
Canongate, Edinburgh, 14, 17, 18, 19, 20, 21.
Canterbury, 40, 100.
Carlyle, Dr. John Aitken, 255.
—— Thomas, 76, 97, 121, 174, 197, 236.
Carmichael, James, minister of Haddington, 179.
Carruthers, Robert, LL.D., Inverness, 276.
Carstares, William, Principal, University of Edinburgh, 226, 236.
Cathkin, James, bookseller, 162.
Caw, James L., Director of National Galleries of Scotland, 136.
Ceriani, Antonio, Milan, 282.

Chalmers' Close, Netherbow, 5, 18.
Chalmers, George (*Caledonia*), 23, 62, 67, 130, 154, 191, 255, 257.
—— James, London, 70.
—— P., of Aldbar, 277.
Chambers, Robert, LL.D., Edinburgh, 277.
—— William, LL.D., Edinburgh, 277.
—— Sir W., architect, 135.
Chantrey, Sir Francis, sculptor, 262.
Charles II., portrait of, 201.
Charteris, Henry, 200, 218.
Cheltenham, 82.
Chepman (or Chapman), W., printer, 160, 198.
Chepstow, 82.
Chetham Society, 180.
Chisholm, Alexander, painter, London, 255.
Christiania, 82, 256.
Christiansand, 87.
Church of Scotland:—
Minute of General Assembly *re* Laing, 122.
Relation concerning its Affairs, by the Earl of Rothes, 164.
Register of Ministers and Readers, 178.
Supplication of General Assembly to the Regent Morton, 178.
Vindication of, in reply to Dr. Bancroft, 179.
Matters to be used in the Eldership, 179.
Ministers, Bishops and Archbishops—Ordination and Consecration forms, 179.
Admonition to the Ministry of Scotland, 179.
Memoir of, by Daniel De Foe, 179.
Its State and Government, by Rev. W. Scott, 182.
Meeting of Commissioners at Edinburgh, 200.
History of. *See* John Knox.
—— —— *See* David Calderwood.
—— —— *See* John Row.

Clarke, Peter, 180.
Clerk, Rev. Archibald, LL.D., Kilmaillie, 277
—— Sir George, Bart., of Penicuik, 277.
—— John (Lord Eldin), 159, 198, 277.
Clerke, John Elder, 'a Redshanke,' 161.
Cochran-Patrick, R. W., 280.
Cockburn, Hon Lord, 29, 89, 197, 244.
Coleti, Sebastian, Venice, 282.
Collier, J. Payne, London, 277.
Collin, Zach., from Sweden, 282.
Colville, John, 161, 185, 205.
Comedians, English, in Scotland, 164.
Constable, Archibald, publisher, 7, 9, 28, 45, 53, 62, 252, 277, 288, 290, 291, 292, 293.
—— Archibald, LL.D., 9 note, 288.
—— David, London, 277, 289.
—— Thomas, Edinburgh, 277.
Conway, Moncure D., 277.
Conyngham, Hon. Denis, 22.
Cook, John, W.S., 116
Cooper, Richard, engraver, 17.
Copenhagen, 8, 25, 42, 54, 78, 82.
Corstorphine Church, 111, 226.
Cotton, Henry, Archdeacon of Cashel, 277.
Covenants of Scotland, 186, 209, 228, 255.
Craig, Alexander, of Rosecraig, poet, 223.
—— Sir Thomas, of Riccarton, 59, 154.
—— See Gibson-Craig.
Craigcrook Castle, 245.
Crawford and Balcarres, Earl of, 242. See Lord Lindsay.
Crichton, the Admirable, 49.
Crowland Abbey, 94.
Cumming, James, rector, Canongate School, 20.
—— James, secretary, Society of Antiquaries, 240.
Cunningham, Allan, London, 70, 256.

Cunningham, Peter, London, 262.
Curle, Elizabeth, attendant on Mary Queen of Scots, 37, 250.

DALKEITH, PRESBYTERY RECORDS OF, 211.
Dalrympill, David de, 200.
Dalrymple, Sir David, Bart. (Lord Hailes), 167.
Dalzel, Andrew, professor of Greek, 21, 210.
Dalyell, Sir John Graham, Bart., 277.
Darnley, Henry, Lord, 59, 136, 154, 250.
D'Aubigné, Dr. Merle, Geneva, 283.
Davidson, John, 179.
Davidsone, Johne, Maister of the Paedagog of Glasgow, 178.
De Foe, Daniel, 143, 179.
De Witte, James, painter, 201.
Delft, in Holland, 32.
Denholm, 102, 104.
Desmontiers, Jehan, 213.
Dibdin, Rev. T. F., bibliographer, 67, 263.
Dickson, Thomas, LL.D., 116
Dieppe, 71.
Dietrichstein, S. Maurice, Vienna, 283.
Donatus of Laurence Koster, 33.
Douglas, David, publisher, xxix, 113, 116.
—— Gawin, poet, 146.
—— James, Lord of Dalkeith, 170.
—— Robert, Bishop of Dunblane, 200.
—— Sir William Fettes, president R.S.A., 92, 115, 136.
Dresden, 82.
Drummond Castle, 241.
—— House of, 164.
—— James, R.S A., 20 note, 221.
—— Rev. Dr. Thomas, 135.
—— William of Hawthornden, 10, 50, 142, 153, 163, 166, 177, 240.
Dryden, Sir Henry E. L., 277.

INDEX

Dublin, 15, 22, 30, 52.
Dubois, Professor Ernest, Nancy, 283.
Dunbar, Professor, 21.
—— William, poet ('Makkar'), 55, 95, 168, 214, 246.
Dundrennan, Hon. Lord, 69, 89.
Dunecht, Aberdeenshire, 241, 284.
Dunian, 102, 103.
Dunrobin Charter Room, 199.
Dunstaffnage Castle, 167.
Durham, 100, 101.
Dyce, Rev. Alexander, Aberdeen, 262.
Dymock, James, 116.

EDINBURGH :—
Sheep and Cattle Market, 77.
Civic Insignia, 86.
Netherbow, ancient Sculptures at, 165.
Survey of the Castle and Town (1573), 170.
Urbis Edinburgi Descriptio (1648), 170.
Wills of Edinburgh Printers and Booksellers (1577-1687), 170.
Tumult on Anniversary of St. Giles (1588), 184.
St. Margaret's Well, 199, 207, 236.
Charter of a Tenement by King James III., 200.
Portraits of Kings in Holyrood Palace, 201.
Altar-piece of Trinity College Church, 203, 224, 236.
Sheriffdom of, 201.
Proposals for Cleaning and Lighting the City (1735), 206.
Contract for Chime of Musical Bells (1698), 207.
The City Cross, 210, 215.
The Royal Exchange (1752), 211.
Regent Murray's Monument, 214, 236.

EDINBURGH :—
Edinburgh in Early Times, 211, 221.
Gordon of Rothiemay's view of, 134, 215.
Painted Window in the Parliament House, 219.
Monument to Principal Carstares, 226, 236.
—— George Buchanan, 110, 236.
—— See Greyfriars Churchyard.
—— See St. Giles Church.
—— See Trinity College Church.
—— See University of Edinburgh.
Edmondston, Samuel, 116.
Edward I., King of England, 162.
Eldership, 179.
Elliot, Andrew, xxix.
Ellis, Adam Gib, W.S., 2.
—— Sir Henry, British Museum, 67.
—— Robert, W.S., 2.
Elmsley, Rev. Peter, 9.
Elphinstone, William, Bishop of Aberdeen, 198, 229.
Erskine, James, of Aberdona, 173.
—— Mrs. (Lady Grange), 224, 227, 228.

FALKIRK, 179.
Falkland Palace, 188.
Fenelon, Sieur de la Mothe, 161.
Ferguson, and Munro-Ferguson, of Raith, 277.
—— David, minister of Dunfermline, 208.
Ferrier, Professor J. F., 277.
Fettes, Sir William, Bart., 21.
Findlay, John Ritchie, of Aberlour, 134.
Fleming, D. Hay, LL.D., 250.
Flodden, battle of, 217.
Florence, 74, 75.
Forbes, Alexander P., Bishop of Brechin, 277.
—— Rev. G. H., Burntisland, 277.

Forbes, John, minister of Alford, 183
—— Professor Patrick, Aberdeen, 277.
Forman, Alexander G., W.S., 294.
Forresters of Corstorphine, 111, 226.
Fotheringay, 94.
Fotheringham, W. H., Kirkwall, 186
Foulder, Joe, bookseller, 23.
Foulis, Andrew, printer, 11.
Fountains Abbey, 83.
France, King of, 175, 201.
Fraser, Captain Thomas, R.A., 187.
Freemasonry, 188.
Froude, J. A., 278.
Furnivall, F. J., LL.D., 265.

GALLOWAY, PATRICK, minister of Perth, 161.
Garden, Alexander, advocate, Aberdeen, 229.
Gau, John, 201.
Geddes, Andrew, artist, 135, 225.
Geneva, 70, 73.
Georgeres, T. B., Bordeaux, 283.
Gib, Rev. Adam, Edinburgh, 2.
Gibson, Walter, merchant, Glasgow, 201.
Gibson-Craig, Sir James, Bart., 63, 294.
—— —— James T., W.S., 115, 197, 225, 265, 286.
Glasgow Archæological Society, 86.
Glencorse, Hon. Lord, 247.
Gloucester, 82.
Goel, Professor T., Leyden, 283.
Goeschen, G. Joachim, Leipzig, 283.
Gordon, Alexander (*Itinerarium Septentrionale*), 144, 224.
—— James A. M., minister of Rothiemay, 134, 200, 215.
—— Sir Robert, of Lochinvar, 217.

Gordon, Rev. Thomas, minister of Newbattle, 278.
Gouda, in Holland, 35.
Goudie, Gilbert (*Orkneyinga Saga*), 288
Gowry, Earl of, 161, 162, 228.
Grange, Lady, 224, 227, 228.
Grant, Sir Alexander, Bart., 240.
Gray, Master of, 161.
Great Malvern, 82.
Greyfriars Churchyard, Edinburgh, 110, 111, 216, 226, 236, 237.
Grosart, Rev. A. B., LL.D., 249, 254, 266.
Grundtvig, Svend, Copenhagen, 283.
Gude and Godlie Ballates, 217, 249.
Guild, Thomas, monk of Newbattle, 182, 199.
Guthrie, Hon. Lord, 125.
Gwydyr, Lady, 241.

HADDINGTON, PRESBYTERY OF, 178, 201.
Haegstad, Professor Marius, Christiania, 210.
Haerlem, 33, 34.
Hague, The, 32, 84.
Halkett, Samuel, librarian, 80.
Halliwell, J. O., 266, 314.
Halm, Charles, Munich, 283.
Hamburg, 25, 31, 41, 82.
Hamilton, John, Archbishop of St. Andrews, 143, 200.
—— Duke of, 204.
—— Professor Sir William, Bart., 64, 278.
—— William, of Bangour, 191.
Hannay, Patrick, poet, 110, 225.
Harrogate, 83, 98
Harry, Blind, 146, 200.
Harschedal, Baron de, 283.
Hart, Andrew, printer, 153, 163.
Harvie-Brown, J. A., 278.
Hawes, Stephen, 214.
Hawick, 103.
Hay, George, R.S.A., 116.
—— Sir Gilbert, 185.
Hazlitt, W. C., 156, 278.
Helvoetsluys, 83.

INDEX 311

Henderson, E., LL.D., 278.
Henry, Rev. Dr., 135.
—— III., King of France, 161.
—— VII., King of England, 222.
—— VIII., Do., 161, 214.
Henryson, Robert, poet, 213, 246, 256.
Hepburns of Waughton, 200.
Herbst, F., Copenhagen, 283.
Herdman, Robert, R.S.A., 99, 116.
Heriot's Hospital, Edinburgh, 203.
Hertford, Earl of, 196.
Hibbert-Ware, Dr. Samuel, 66, 76, 157, 180, 278.
Hildina Ballad in Shetland, 210, 283
Historical Manuscripts Commission, 128.
Hjaltalin, Jón A. (*Orkneyinga Saga*), 288.
Hogg, James, 'The Ettrick Shepherd,' 260.
Holland, Sir Richard, [62, 143], 157.
Holyrood—Abbey, Palace, Park and Church, 169, 175, 179, 188, 193, 201, 203, 224.
Hope, James, D.K.S., 115.
Horne, William [Robert?], advocate, 116.
Horner, Leonard, 28.
Houghton, Lord, 241.
Howlat, Buke of the, 62, 143, 157.
Huddersfield, 98.
Hume, Alexander, minister of Logie, 179
Hunsdon, Lord, 161.
Hunter, A. G, of Blackness, 53.
—— D., of Blackness, 116.
Hunterian Club, 120, 150, 223, 225, 229, 234.
Huntly, Marquess of, 223
Hutchison, John, R.S A., 116.

ILKLEY, 83.
Inchcolm Abbey, 219.
Inglis, Mrs. Esther Langlois or, 215.
Innes, Cosmo, LL D., 94, 197, 210, 278.

Iona, 190, 196, 245.
Irving, Archibald Stirling, 296.
—— David, LL.D., 51, 69, 78, 154, 155, 208, 209.
Isle of Man, 98.

JACOB, J. J. L., Rotterdam, 283.
James I, King of Scotland, 206.
—— II., King of Scotland, 189, 211.
—— III, King of Scotland, 200, 213, 224.
—— IV., King of Scotland, 183.
—— V., King of Scotland, 133, 169, 184
—— VI., King of Scotland, 136, 145, 161, 162, 164, 185, 192, [228].
—— VII., King of Scotland, 188.
Jamieson, Rev. John, D D., 64, 67.
Jedburgh, 102, 103, 107, 108.
Jeffrey, Hon. Lord, 28, 89, 245.
Jenner, Charles, Edinburgh, 116.
Johnson, James, 195.
Johnston, Sir Frederick, Bart., 111.
—— Thomas B., 116.
Johnstone, W. B., R S.A., 204.
Jonson, Ben, 166, 177, 207.

KAY, JOHN, miniature painter, 134, 144.
Kelland, Professor Philip, 278
Keller, Dr. Ferdinand, Zurich, 283.
Kello, John, minister of Spott, 145
Kenilworth, 98
Kennedy, Quintin, Abbot of Crossraguell, 178.
Kerr, H., Huntlyburn, 266.
Kiel, 25, 31, 41, 82.
Kirk, David, 6, 300, 302
—— Helen, 6, 17, 296, 300.
Kirkbank, 107.
Kirkheugh, St. Andrews, 209
Kirkwall, in Orkney, 181, 186, 199.
Klemming, G. L., Stockholm, 284.
Kneller, Sir Godfrey, 201.

DAVID LAING

Knight-Baronets of Nova Scotia, 216
Knox, John, 71, 95, 99, 110, 113, 144, 179, 182, 187, 197, 198, 202, 206, 213, 236, 259, 272.
Kongelige Oldskrift Selskab, Copenhagen, 78.

LABANOFF, PRINCE ALEXANDER JAKOVLÉVITCH, 284.
Laing Charters, 127
—— Alexander, LL.D., Newburgh, 278.
—— Agnes, 7, 298, 301.
—— Euphemia, 7, 124, 299, 301.
—— Francis Gregory, 296.
—— Gilbert, merchant, Edinburgh, 7.
—— Rev. Gilbert, Perth, 7, 73, 297, 301.
—— Helen, 296.
—— James, merchant, Luckenbooths, 2.
—— James, Ceylon, 7, 77, 298.
—— Jane, 296.
—— Jessie Miller, 7, 298, 301.
—— John William, 296.
—— Margaret (Mrs. Sanson), 7, 124, 298, 302.
—— Mary, 7, 298.
—— Mary Melville, 297.
—— Wilhelmina Margaret, 297.
—— William, 'Merchant Taylor,' 1, 2, 296.
—— William, bookseller and publisher, 3, 12, 17, 288, 290, 291, 296, 300, 301.
—— Rev. William, minister of Crieff, 7, 296.
—— Henry, 132.
—— Samuel (*Heimskringla*), 278.
Langlois (or Inglis), Mrs. Esther, caligraphist, 215.
Lauder, Sir John, of Fountainhall, Bart., 172, 186.
Lauderdale, John, Duke of, 112, 170, 229.
Laurie, Professor S. S., 116.
Law, John, Canon of St. Andrews, 183.

Law, Thomas Graves, LL.D., 221.
Lawson, James, minister of Edinburgh, 179.
—— Richard, bookseller, Edinburgh, 200.
Lee, Rev. John, D.D., Principal of Edinburgh University, 65, 208, 249, 266.
Leeds, 98.
Leghorn, 55.
Leighton, Robert, Bishop of Dunblane, 211.
Leightonian Library, Dunblane, 200.
Leith, South, parish church of, 193.
Lely, Sir P, 135.
Lesley, John, Bishop of Ross, 200.
Leslie, Lady, 134.
Leyden, 32, 33, 35, 85, 86.
—— Dr. John, 102.
Lindsay, Lord, 161, 208, 241, 284, 285.
Linlithgow, 218.
Livermore, George, U.S.A., 284.
Liverpool, 98.
—— Lord, 259.
Lizars, W. H., engraver, 133.
Lockhart, John Gibson, 43, 45, 68
Lodge, Thomas, of Lincoln's Inn, 54, 195.
Logan, of Restalrig, 212.
—— J., engraver, 196.
—— Rev John, minister of Leith, 223, 253.
Lothian, third Earl of, 225.
—— Marquess of, 109, 114, 225, 230, 242.
Lovat, Lord, 176.
Low, Rev. George, 209.
—— William, portrait painter, 134.
Lubeck, 82.
Lydgate, John, monk of Bury, 230.
Lyell, Sir Charles, 278.
Lyndsay, Sir David, Lyon King of Arms, 60, 133, 145, 157, 220, 231, 232.

INDEX 313

Madden, Sir Frederic, 68, 86, 278.
Maidment, James, advocate, 278.
Maitland Club, 168, 234.
—— S. R., Lambeth Palace, 279.
—— Thomas (Lord Dundrennan), 69, 89.
Malmoe, in Sweden, 201.
Malvern Hills, 82.
Man, Isle of, 98.
Manchester, 98.
Manners & Miller, booksellers, 47.
Marchmont, Earl of, 135.
Margaret of Denmark, Queen of Scotland, 213.
—— widow of Prince Alexander of Scotland, 173, 184.
Marwick, Sir James D., 116, 279
Mary of Gueldres, Queen of Scotland, 188, 189, 211.
—— of Guise, Queen, 133.
—— Queen of Scots, 37, 59, 133, 145, 154, 162, 176, 249, 284
Masson, Professor David, LL.D., 116, 166, 279.
Maxwell, Sir Herbert, Bart., 279.
Mechlin, 37.
Meerman, 32, 84, 85.
Melville, James, 178.
Melvin, Helen, 300, 302.
Menzies, J., 116.
Mercer, Lieut.-Colonel William, 207.
—— Græme R., 279.
Michel, Francisque, 72, 213, 248, 284.
Miles, Owain, 171.
Miller, John, K.C., 70, 248, 270.
—— S. Christie, 196, 248, 270.
—— William, London, 270.
—— W. H, of Craigentinny, 81, 165, 189, 193, 248, 270.
Milligan, John, W.S., 116.
Milnes, Richard Monckton (Lord Houghton), 241.
Milton, John (*Paradise Lost*), 145, 159, 160.
Minto, Earl of, 58.
Mitchell, Sir Arthur, K.C.B., 99, 125, 136, 137, 167, 279.

Mitchell, Professor A. F., St. Andrews, 279.
Moffat, Henry, of Eldin, 116.
Moldenhawer, Dr. Joh., Copenhagen, 8, 25, 286.
Molter, F., Carlsruhe, 286.
Monck, General, 193.
Moncreiff, Hon. Lord, 264.
Montgomery, Alexander, poet, 59, 145, 154, 246.
Montrose, kirk of, 178.
Morton, Earl of, 242.
—— the Regent, 178.
Munch, Professor P. A., Christiania, 200, 208, 212, 287.
Munich, 75.
Mure, William, of Caldwell, 279.
Murray, second Earl of, 196.
—— the Regent, 161, 175, 214, 236.
—— Hon. A., 135.
—— Rev. Alexander, D.D., 237.
—— Sir Andrew of Arngask, 175.
—— Sir David, 135.
—— John, publisher, 279.
—— Thomas Graham, of Stenton, 279.
—— Hon. Lord, 244.
—— Rev. William, 296.
Myll, G., St. Andrews, 170.
—— Friar, martyr, 54.
Myllar, A., printer, 160.
Mylne, R W., London, 279.
Macadam, Dr. Stevenson, 116.
M'Crie, Thomas, D.D., 204, 259.
Macdonald, James, W.S., 116.
Mackay, Professor Aeneas J. G., 116, 135, 136.
—— Dr. Charles, poet, 265.
M'Inroy, Captain Charles, 220.
Mackenzie, Kincaid, Lord Provost of Edinburgh, 41.
—— John Whitefoord, W.S., 279, 286.
—— William Forbes, 279.
Macknight, James, W.S., 205.
Makellar, Rev. W., 115, 116.
M'Laren, Duncan, Lord Provost of Edinburgh, 81.
M'Lauchlan, Rev. Thomas, D.D., 279.

Macnee, Sir Daniel, P.R.S.A., 115.
Maconochie, Alexander, of Meadowbank, 279.
Macpherson, Rev. Ranald, 123.

NAIRNE, JAMES, W.S., 164, 294.
Napier, John (*Logarithms*), 146.
—— Professor Macvey, 69, 279.
—— Mark, advocate, 271.
National Gallery of Scotland, 92, 131, 136.
—— Portrait Gallery of Scotland, 93, 99, 131, 134.
Neaves, Hon. Lord, 88, 102, 246, 247.
Neill, Patrick, M.A., 271.
Netherbow, Edinburgh, ancient sculptures, 165.
Newbattle, 182, 211, 225, 230.
Newcastle-on-Tyne, Society of Antiquaries of, 63.
New England Historic Genealogical Society, 98.
—— Greyfriars Church, Edinburgh, 115, 123.
Nichols, John Gough, London, 280.
Nicol, Gabriel, London, 271.
—— George, London, 23.
Nicoll, John ('Diary'), 171.
Niebuhr, Barthold Georg, Bonn, historian, 286.
Nisbet of Dirleton, 134.
Noordrick, J. T. F., The Hague, 286.
Norse language in Shetland, 209.
Northampton, 94.
Northern Antiquaries, Royal Society of, Copenhagen, 78.
Northumberland, Duke of, 264.
Norway, King of, 181, 199.
Nott, David D., 280.
Nottingham, 169.
Nova Scotia, Knight-Baronets of, 216.

ODE TO THE CUCKOO, 222, 253.
Olivecrona, Rosalie, Upsala, 286.
Omond, Rev. J. R., D.D., 280.
O'Reilly, Edward, Dublin, 280.

Orkney, 76, 186, 193, 199, 200, 210, 282.
—— Bishops of, 181, 199, 200.
—— Earl of, 181, 187.
Orkneyinga Saga, 287, 288.
Orr, Thomas, Edinburgh, 272.
Over, Mrs. Spencer, 303.
Oxford, 80, 81, 83, 284, 285.

PAISLEY WITCHES, 226.
Panizzi, Sir Anthony, 71.
Panmure, Lord, 165, 199, 200.
Paris, 8, 31, 38, 39, 70, 72, 284.
Parker, J. H., 280.
Parliament House, Edinburgh, 219.
Paterson, James, 191.
—— William, publisher, 116, 140, 231, 232.
Paton, Sir Joseph Noel, 254.
—— Rev. Henry, M.A., 128.
Peebles, 203.
Pencaitland church, 191.
Perth, Earl of, 190.
Peterborough, 94, 98.
Petersen, Ch , Hamburg, 286.
Petrie, George, 280.
Phillips, J. O. Halliwell-, 266, 314.
Pinkerton, John, 10, 270, 280.
Pitcairn, Robert, 249.
Playfair, Professor John, 135.
—— Lord, 243, 248.
Pont, Robert (*Parvus Catechismus*), 178.
Pomona, 193.
Pope, the, 181.
Porson's Library Sale, 22.
Portraits, Scottish, proposed exhibition of, 197.
Prague, 82.
Preston Tower, 191.
Pretender, the Young, 180
Printers and Booksellers of Edinburgh, Wills of (1577-1687), 170.
Processions, etc., in Scotland prior to 1707, 223.
Prophecies, ancient Scottish, 167.
Psalter, the Scottish, 218.

QUARITCH, B., bookseller, 139, 143.

INDEX 315

RAFN, CHARLES C., Copenhagen, 287.
Ramsay, Allan, artist, 135.
—— Very Rev. E. B., 280.
—— Jean, de Saint Andrew en Ecosse, 223.
Reid, William, Pittentian, Perthshire, 115, 297.
—— William David Melville, 297.
Renwick, James, Covenanter, 55.
Repp, Thorlak Gudmundson, 287.
Restalrig, 199, 212, 236.
Richard III., King of England, 170.
Richardson, John, Westminster, 272.
Riddell, John, advocate, 69, 206.
Ripon, 83, 98.
—— Marquess of, 243.
Robert of Dunhelm, 162.
Robertson, Rev. William, D.D., 115, 116.
Rolland, John, of Dalkeith, 171.
Rome, 74, 75, 180.
Ros, John, printer, 218
Rosebery, Earl of, 242.
Roslin Castle, 199.
Ross, Rev William, D.D., 280
Rosslyn, Earl of, 205.
Rosswall and Lillian, History of, 59, 156.
Rothes, Earl of, 164, 294.
Rotterdam, 9, 24, 31, 32, 35, 73, 82, 83, 84.
Rouen, 72.
Row, John, minister of Carnock, 176.
—— —— Principal of King's College, Aberdeen, 176.
Roxburgh, 108.
Roxburghe Library Sale, 15, 22, 29.
—— Earl of, 162
Roxburghshire, 101.
Royal Archæological Institute, 243.
—— Library, Paris, 176, 286
—— Scottish Academy, 87, 95, 123, 131, 136.
—— Society of Edinburgh, 25, 30, 253.
Ruberslaw, 102.

Runciman, John, artist, 135, 136.
Russell, Lord John, 87.
—— Thomas, 225.
Rutherfurd, Hon. Lord, 89.

SALTOUN KIRK—Bishop Burnet's Library, 201.
Sandford, Bishop, 280.
Sanson, Alexander, Dublin, 298, 302.
—— Rev. Alexander, Toronto, 298, 303.
—— David Laing, 298, 303.
—— David Melville, 303.
—— James, Ontario, 298, 302.
—— J. St. Clair, 303.
—— John, 303.
—— Mrs. Margaret Laing or, 7, 124, 298, 302
—— Mary Melville, 303.
—— Norman, 303.
—— Robert, 303.
—— William N , 303.
Scheveningen, in Holland, 84
Schiern, Professor, Copenhagen, 286
Schipper, Professor, Vienna, 168.
Schmid, P., Copenhagen, 286
School of Design in Edinburgh University, 219.
Scots College, Paris, 249 ; Douai, 250.
Scott, Alexander, poet, 59, 61, 153, 292.
—— James R. Hope, 280.
—— David D., Hawick, 272.
—— John, St. Andrews, 145.
—— Rev. Hew, D D , 272.
—— Sir Walter, Bart , 26, 28, 50, 57, 60, 67, 89, 90, 91, 92, 95, 118, 135, 155, 163, 165, 205, 221, 232, 250, 251, 257, 259, 261.
—— William, of Raeburn, 280.
—— —— minister of Cupar, 183.
Selkirk, Earl of, 205.
Sempills of Belltrees, 191.
Shakespeare Society, 54, 177, 195, 234.
Shairp, John Campbell, LL D., 222, 280.

Sharp, Archbishop, 184.
Sharpe, Charles Kirkpatrick, 29, 159, 219, 232.
Sheridan, Mrs. Joseph B., 303.
Shetland (or Zetland), 76, 181, 187, 199, 210, 283.
Sibbald, Sir Robert, 201, 246.
Signet Library, 63, 70, 78, 79, 80, 221.
Sigurdson, Jón, 287.
Simpson, Sir James Y., Bart., 280.
Sinclair, Alexander, Edinburgh, 280.
—— Sir John, of Ulbster, Bart., 280.
—— Sir David, of Sumburgh, 200.
—— John, Master of, 205.
Sion College, London, 268.
Skeat, W. W., Cambridge, 281.
Skelton, Sir John, 281.
Skene, W. F., LL.D., 281.
Skinner, William, W.S., 116.
Slezer, Captain John, 170.
Slidell, Mrs. Thomas, 272.
Sloane, Sir Hans, 135.
Small, John, LL.D., 156, 185, 230, 233.
Smellie, John, 212.
Smith, Adam (*Wealth of Nations*), 134.
—— John Alexander, M.D., 99, 115, 281.
—— R. A., musician, 281.
—— Rev. Sydney, 28, 281.
Smythe, William, advocate, 175.
Society for Propagating Christian Knowledge, 5.
Soltre [Soutra] Domus de, 208.
Sotheby, Wilkinson & Hodge, London, 138.
Southey, Robert, Poet Laureate, 66.
Spalding Club, 120, 212, 234.
Spelunca, 57.
Spenser, Edmund, poet, 146.
Spowart, of Broomhead, 228.
Sprott, Rev. Dr., 116.
Stamford, 94.
Stanley, Dean, 281.
Steell, Gourlay, R.S.A., 116.

Steenbock, Count, 286.
Stenhouse, William, 172, 194, 195.
Steven, Rev. William, Rotterdam, 73, 281.
Stevenson, Rev. Joseph, 281.
—— Robert Louis, 273.
—— Thomas, engineer, 273.
—— T. G., bookseller, 116, 152, 185, 191, 197.
—— W. D., sculptor, 93.
Stewart, Alexander B., 229.
—— David, Annan, 273.
—— Sir M. R. Shaw-, 281.
Stirling, William, of Keir, 281.
Stockholm, 25, 87.
Story, John, printer, 198.
—— Rev. R. H., D.D., 281.
Strathallan, Viscount of, 164.
Strathearn Stewartry, 190.
Struthers, Rev. Dr., 116, 273.
Stuart, John Sobieski, 273.
Stuarts, Royal Family of the, 188.
Studley Royal, 83, 243.
Sumburgh, in Shetland, 200.
Sutherland, Alexander, of Dunbeath, 199.
Swinburne, John, Capheaton, 273.
Symbister, Shetland, 187.
St. Andrews, 209, 218, 222.
—— Plan of the City, 200.
—— University of, 97, 170, 222, 243.
St. Anthony, preceptory of, 170.
St. Boswells, 107.
St. Clair, William, Earl of Orkney, 181.
St Columba's Abbey, Inchcolm, 219.
St. Duthac, Tain, 183.
St. Giles, Edinburgh, 110, 184, 206, 214, 236.
St. Kilda, 224, 227, [228].
St. Luke, Edinburgh, School of, 186.
St. Luke's Church, Young Street, Edinburgh, 123.
St. Margaret's Well, Edinburgh, 199, 207, 236.

INDEX

317

TAIN, shrine of St. Duthac at, 183.
Tassie, James, 135.
Thomson, Thomas, advocate, 80, 89, 167, 194, 197, 281.
Tingwall, in Shetland, 200.
Tintern Abbey, 82.
Todd, Dr. John H., Dublin, 281.
Torfaeus, Thormodeus, Danish historian, 199.
Townley, Charles, book sale, 23.
Traquair, Lord, 203.
Trevelyan, Sir W. C., Bart., 281.
Trinity College Church, Edinburgh, 180, 189, [203], 208, 211, 236.
Trotter, Henry, of Mortonhall, 281.
Trummer, Charles, LL.D., Hamburg, 287.
Tulloch, Rev. John, D.D., 97.
Turnbull, W. B. D. D., advocate, 172, 249, 265, 273.
Tynemouth, convent of, 162.
Tytler, James, of Woodhouselee, 63.
—— James S., W.S., 116.
—— Patrick Fraser, historian, 69, 274.

UNIVERSITY OF EDINBURGH, 10, 50, 62, 69, 94, 126, 127, 130, 152, 153, 205, 210, 219, 226, 239, 240, 243.
Upcott, William, London, 274.
Upsala, 87, 286.
Utrecht, 35, 86.
Urquhart, Adam, 172.
Utterson, Edward V., 282.

VALENCIENNES, 38.
Vallet, Auguste, Paris, 287.
Venice, 74, 75.
Vienna, 82, 168.
Volsenus [Wilson], Florentius, 162.

WADE, FIELD-MARSHAL, 135.
Walden, Lord, 200.
Walker, Sir Patrick, 282.
Wallace, Sir William, 146, 200, 202.
Walpole, Horace, 190.
Walsingham, Sir Francis, 161.
Warwick, 81.
Ward, Mrs., 303.
Ware, Dr. *See* Hibbert-Ware, Dr.
Waterloo, 37, 38, 43.
Watson, James, printer, 170.
Way, Albert, 282.
Welsh, John, minister of Ayr, 179.
Wemyss, Earl of, 5, 17.
—— Mrs., of Wemyss, 112, 113, 282.
Westreene de Tiellandt, Baron Van, 85, 287.
White, Rev. Robert, 135.
—— Mrs. Thomas J., 303.
Wiffen, J. H., librarian, 274.
Wilkie, Sir David, R.A., 110, 225, 259, 262.
Williamson, Charles, teacher, 18, 19.
—— Peter (Directory of Edinburgh), 1.
Willock, John, 178.
Wilson, Sir Daniel, 114, 121, 224, 274.
—— James (brother of 'Christopher North'), 24, 25, 28, 32, 35, 38, 39, 41.
Wintoun House, 191.
Winzet, Ninian, priest, 168, 169, 267.
Wishart, George, 178.
Wishaw, Laird of, 226.
Witches of Paisley, 226.
Witte, James de, painter, 201.
Wode (or Wood), Thomas, Vicar of St. Andrews, 218, 293.
Wodrow Society, 150, 176, 177, 182, 183, 189, 234.
Wood, J. P., Edinburgh, 275.
Worcester, 82.
Worsaae, J. J. A., Copenhagen, 287.

Writers to the Signet, 115. *See* Signet Library.
Wynram, John, 54.
Wyntoun, Andro of (*Orygynale Cronykil*), 10, 112, 114, 222, 231, 246.

York, 101.
York, James, Duke of [James VII.], 201.

Young, Sir Peter, of Seaton, 210.
—— Thomas, Vicar of Stowmarket, 220.

ZETLAND, 76, 181, 187, 199, 210, 283.
—— Bishop of, 181, 199.

Printed by T. and A. CONSTABLE, Printers to His Majesty
at the Edinburgh University Press

ERRATA

Page 255, line 11, *for* Frederick *read* Francis
,,   277,   ,,   17, *for* Dalzell *read* Dalyell